MW01107383

Rash Decisions and Growth Experiences

from the
BEST LITTLE WARTHOUSE IN KENTUCKY

by

Stuart Tobin, M.D.

BEARHEAD PUBLISHING LLC

- BhP -

Brandenburg, Kentucky
www.bearheadpublishing.com

Rash Decisions and Growth Experiences
from The Best Little Warthouse in Kentucky

By Stuart Tobin M.D.

Cover Concept:
Bearhead Publishing LLC

Cover Illustration:
Tom Dolin

Cover Caduceus:
Brooke Veith

First Printing - March 2013
ISBN: 978-1-937508-13-5
1 2 3 4 5 6 7 8 9 10

Proudly printed in the United States of America

Rash Decisions and Growth Experiences

from the
BEST LITTLE WARTHOUSE IN KENTUCKY

R̥

3/30/13

To Bob & Marcia

Read 2 chapters twice a day
for humorous health!

Refill x 5

A Message From The Author

While all the stories and incidents in this book are true, the names and any personal characteristics or features of the individuals depicted have been altered in order to protect their privacy. Any resulting resemblance to other persons, living or dead is completely coincidental and unintentional.

A NOTE OF APPRECIATION

This book would not be possible without the valuable assistance, suggestions and technical advice from family, friends, colleagues, and staff. A special thanks to my wife, Susan, who has had to suffer listening to countless rewrites and humorous events retold and then retold again. Many thanks to my publisher, Gary Drechsel and his wife Mary for their support and encouragement taking this work from manuscript into a publishable entity. An utmost sense of gratitude goes to Tom Dolan for his IT wizardry and Brooke Veith for her impressive aesthetic artistic talents in producing the dust cover jacket for this book. A special tribute goes to my assistant, Linda Combs, whose unbounded enthusiasm and technical and computer skills transformed a rough manuscript into a viable book and to Alison Emmons, L.L.B, whose wise legal counsel has assisted me in the editing and preparation of this work throughout all stages of development. Great appreciation goes also to my staff in private practice who besides having to tolerate me was exposed to each story as they evolved. I would like to extend a poorly articulated sense of deep gratitude to my patients who have been the inspiration and the most significant motivation for this volume. Without their own sense of humor, confidence and trust in me over a lifetime of professional practice this book would have to have been classified as a fictional work.

Table of Contents

Preface: This I Believe...1

Introduction..5

PATIENT STORIES

The Dressing Down of an Officer............................10

In the Limelight...12

Pickled Pink...14

Room Service - Is There a Doctor in the House?..............17

A Case of Weeping...22

Lost in Translation...25

Boop Boop a Doop...31

Raising the Dead...33

A Curbside Consult..35

The Carwash Consult..39

Butt Out...41

Breathing Easier...45

In the Beginning...52

The Songbird and the Squirrel..................................54

Her Blood Pressure Down and Mine Up.................................. 56

Don't Give Me any of Your Lip..58

Stereotypes..61

Beep, Beep, Beep.. 65

Rural Settings and Urban Prejudices..................................... 70

The Date with Fate...75

A House is Not a Home.. 80

World War II...82

Damn You Doctor...85

Thank You Doctor.. 88

Pen Pals...99

*Question: I'm From the Government and I'm Here to:
a) Help, b) Hurt, or c) Harass You?................................... 102

FAMILY AND FRIENDS

Goliath - Won; David - None.. 109

Train of Thought...112

My Mother's Final Journey... 116

The Short Version.. 122

Bawbie... 125

What Really Happened at Lexington and Concord.............. 128

What's in a Name... 133

Memory Lane..138

He Tried... 145

Publisher to Physician...149

Uncle Ben...155

It's About Time..158

Candy Goes Cuckoo?...164

The Red Glove Revue...171

SCHOOL DAYS

Bed, Breakfast and Beyond....................................... 174

Melted Chocolate and Big Cherries......................... 176

Who's Interviewing Whom?......................................183

VD and Me..188

All My Problems Are Behind Me.............................191

Old Lace...192

Crying Wolf..194

Dodging the Bullet... 196

The Penn College Reunion....................................... 198

YOU'RE IN THE ARMY NOW

A Major in the Army and a General Nuisance.......................208

Veteran Medicine..214

MEDICAL MENTORING AND MEANDERING

The Jock with the Itch.. 217

Digging in the Dermis and the Dirt......................... 219

Barbie, Beethoven, and Churchill (The BBC).......................224

The Ten Things They Don't Teach You in Medical School. 227

The Pimp, the Prostitute, and the John.................... 234

Ashes to Ashes...238

The Shoe on the Other Foot................................... 240

Good Judgment Comes from Experience, Experience
Comes fromBad Judgment...244

Anachronistic Misnomers in Medicine............................ 251

Life is Too Commercial... 256

Making the Left Turn in Life...................................260

WARTHOUSE WIT 262

Preface: This I Believe

A few years ago, National Public Radio, in an attempt to tap into the passions that exists in so many of their thoughtful, successful, and educated listeners, innovatively solicited essays from their audience as to their core beliefs. This produced an intriguing set of oral readings which aired weekly on local NPR radio stations. Integrated with the Edward R. Murrow original series, they eventually became the material for a collectible book of national prominence and, more importantly, worth reading. The name of this wonderful read was *This I Believe*.

I recalled visiting our Kentucky Book Fair one year with the editor of this special volume in attendance signing copies. I requested an autographed edition specifically made out to me and thanked him and left to visit with other authors. An hour or so later I returned to his table and complimented him on his book with the following interaction.

"I'm so glad you were able to make it to our small community in Frankfort, Kentucky, for this book signing. What a wonderful book you have edited. The choice of inspirational stories couldn't have been selected any better. I have been so anxious to read your book. I've been sitting in one of those chairs over there and so captivated by each of these individual stories I have read through them all. So now you can have your book back. I've finished reading it and don't see any reason to purchase it." The grin and smile of appreciation transformed into one of perplexity and quickly degenerated into apoplexy. The fellow author who shared his table, however, broke out into a bout of uncontained laughter. He got it, but the poor editor just seemed dumbfounded.

I turned to him and added, which now seemed necessary, the obligatory footnote explanation, "That was just an attempt at humor, and I would really like an autographed second copy to give to a friend as a Christmas present." He signed it in a perfunctory manner, but his body language remained unchanged and unconvinced.

Anyway, I walked away with two copies of a book, one author left laughing and another just confused. But what I walked away with most was this small vignette with the conviction that HUMOR is that which I truly believe.

While not the inspiration for this book of memoirs, this anecdote serves as an introduction as to the tenor and theme which plays throughout this modest volume. I believe in the power of humor to make us laugh and to defuse our anxiety and tension. I have woven humor into the fabric of direct patient care for over thirty-three years of private practice to become the sentinel stitch in the not so tightly knit healing process. I am always hoping that the patient will get that point.

Although not older than dirt, I am somewhere between sand and gravel. Over that span of time my sense of humor is the only sense that hasn't deserted me. However, if you're going to retain one, it's not a bad one to have left. It certainly makes, if not the loss, the diminution of the others much more tolerable.

The most important prescription any physician can dispense to his patients is reassurance, reassurance that everything will be all right or if not all right that we're working together for the best possible outcome. Humor empowers reassurance, builds confidence and credibility, reduces patient's anxiety, and engenders trust between practitioner and patient. It tells my patients that I recognize and care about your fears and anxiety and am making an attempt to diffuse them.

When an anxious patient lies on the operating table for removal of a skin cancer on their face, all the accompanying concerns and fears of having a surgical procedure, whether articulated or not, are there. After anaesthetizing the nose or cheek or forehead with a local I ask the anxious patient, "I want to be sure that you're good and numb. Do you feel anything in your right big toe?" They either laugh or answer incredulously, "My big toe?" I respond with, "Yes if it's numb, we'll call the 'toe' truck." The anxiety melts away and this inane vaudevillian one-liner which would produce the hook to drag you off any respectable comedian stage becomes the titanic ice breaker of surgical humor and thaws the tension in even the most anxious of patients.

When a child of eight or ten clings to their parent in a sense of desperation or dread when I enter the examination room, I introduce myself and turn to the anxious child and say, "Hello, Jimmy. I see on the history page under the marital status that you are single and still looking. You haven't found the right one yet?" The parent laughs, and the child reflexively does as well. When coupled with the additional question of "Jimmy, how old are you?" followed by the chronological age answer of eight or nine or ten. I'll ask, "Do you have a driver's license to prove your age?" This always produces more giggles.

That initially frightened child who couldn't have enough distance from me now allows me to approach him more easily. I know I'm well on the way of having a positive interaction with both child and parent. The tension evaporated not by virtue of me as the medical authority figure or because of my expertise and knowledge but rather because of humor. Laughter robs fear of its paralyzing power. Humor connects and binds, and laughter heals.

These following compilations of experiences in my life relate to my medical interaction with patients, colleagues, medical students, residents, friends, and family. Almost all have a humorous touch. Most of them are factual with an occasional embellishment to tweak their humorous outcome. The lion's share of these memoirs relate to my medical experiences as a dermatologist practicing in the small town of Richmond, Kentucky, which in turn has led me to title this volume *Rash Decisions and Growth Experiences from the Best Little Warthouse in Kentucky.* I feel comfortable with this header since the American Medical Association has permitted physicians to advertise or promote as long as done "tastefully."

For many years I have had a needlepoint banner displayed on my waiting room wall with the announcement proclaiming "The Best Little Warthouse in Kentucky" not as an advertisement to solicit but as an announcement to my patients of the humorous exposure that awaits the suspecting as well as the unsuspecting.

Rash Decisions and Growth Experiences
from the Best Little Warthouse in Kentucky

What happened after my patients passed from the wings of waiting to the main stage of the exam rooms or operating suite are among many of the scenes that play out in this book.

I hope that you too will want to venture through those portals and continue to read on with your eyes to the page, entertainment to your mind, and humor in your heart. For this is what I believe.

Oh, don't forget to turn to the next page!

Introduction

It was neither the best of times nor was it the worst of times. It was, however, the time of my birth, and I had no recollection of any time at that time. The year was 1945. The location was very close to my mother whom I had known from the inside out for the previous nine months. My parents had been living in New York City at the time of my not so grand entrance into this world and had not consulted me in that particular choice.

My father and mother had relocated from Lynn, Massachusetts to New York City, often referred to as the Big Apple or by the locals as "Da City" or by non-locals as "the City" because they had not yet affected the coveted accent, or as "the City" by certain locals who felt that "Da" was two socioeconomically levels beneath "the" in a similar manner that some Londoners disdain the east end cockney accent.

I was also sharing very close quarters with my identical twin brother in "the" aka "da" womb. Immediately after birth we had a parting of the ways, mostly due to the severing of the umbilical cord. He had the need to precede me by two minutes at that early first race down the tunnel of life. Those same results were to replay more than occasionally throughout our lives but without the negative consequences often interpreted by the genre of psychologists as competition/ resentment, which I never seemed to feel.

My father was just completing his residency in dermatology at Columbia University, and my mother had attended the Juilliard School of Music with a particularly gifted set of vocal chords that were professionally trained. I should have had the early insight that it was a mistake to get my mother angry since women in general possess an extraordinary ability to raise their untrained voices, intimidating every male within a thirty foot radius. Since my mother's voice was professionally honed her high decibel recriminations should have been licensed as a lethal weapon. Fortunately, she had a very sweet and permissive disposition and seldom broke the glass crystals in our home with high octave warnings.

Those first few years were in an apartment in the upper Manhattan Island in the area called Harlem. When my father completed his training we moved to Mt. Vernon, New York, the first suburb stop on the ancient New York/New Haven Railroad above the Bronx in Westchester County. It was in Mt. Vernon that I lived from the age of five till graduating from high school in 1963. It was in this small tree lined community of 70,000 that I grew up although the jury is still out as to if I ever did grow up and where the majority of my childhood memories reside. We first lived in an apartment on the fourth floor of 30 Cottage Avenue.

After a few years, my parents purchased an old Victorian mansion at 190 Archer Avenue, which became the scene of my father's private practice office on the first floor while the domestic acts of our private lives were played out on the two floors above where the family lived. The third floor had been an attic which was converted into bedrooms, un-air conditioned bedrooms, which became thermally apparent in July and August, especially at night when it felt like all the heat from middle earth was funneled directly into my small bedroom.

My dad finally installed an exhaust fan in my brother's window which produced a hot breeze, which although not changing the actual Fahrenheit sizzling temperature it did manage to produce a droning sound which I found hypnotic. It was during these summers in high school that I worked for the Liveright Publishing Company, without air conditioning, in Manhattan. I suspect that my "Uncle", the publisher, sometimes thought I was working against him rather than for him since after lunch I succumbed to a post prandial nap induced by an indigestible street vendor's hot dog wrapped in a bun of stifling heat.

After high school graduation, I and my twin left Mt. Vernon to attend college at the University of Pennsylvania in Philadelphia where my eleven month older brother was already ensconced as a sophomore. In reality, I should have received my undergraduate degree from the Van Pelt Library on campus rather from the college at the university, for that is where I spent "most" (that would be a subtle understatement) of my academic time. I was a nerd on Monday, Wednesday and Friday and a geek on Tuesday, Thursday and Sunday. Saturday I just rested from the weight of studying.

The next four-year rung on the education ladder was the University of Missouri Medical School in Columbia where I had the nucleus of my medical education. I then spent the year of 1971-1972 at the University of Kentucky in my internal medicine internship. This became the overture introduction to my lifetime concerto with the Commonwealth. Bouncing around the geographic as well as the American educational map found me coming full circle returning to "da" city of my birth for my specialty training at the Skin and Cancer Unit at New York University Medical Center.

During those years, from 1972 thru 1975, I wore another hat as well, that of a reserve officer in the U.S. Army. Immediately on completing my medical training I traded in my white coat for army khakis which were drenched in sweat for the next two years at Ft. Stewart, (no relation) in the swamps of southeastern Georgia. I probably heard the word "Sir" more times in those twenty-four months than King Arthur heard in a lifetime seated at the Round Table.

Out of service, out of training, and out of money, I finally had to work for a living. It was casual chance that led me to Richmond, Kentucky for the next third of a century. As I traveled to Lexington to investigate a job opportunity, I passed a sign on I-75 that read "Richmond - Home of Eastern Kentucky University." I suspect, as I look back, that I had spent so many years at this or that educational institutions that my body would have gone into withdrawal seizures, much like an addict, if I didn't relocate close to an institution of higher learning.

Reflexively I turned off the exit ramp and decided 'What the Hell, I'll give this unknown town a try for a while.' Careful, measured and thoughtful analysis for my future venue was replaced by an impulse du jour.

It was there, from 1977 to 2010, I satisfyingly plied my developing medical talents paired with increasing experience to a diverse and poles-apart population from my childhood. I became involved in community projects and activities, especially, as no surprise, libraries both on the local and state level. My medical background led me as well to serve on the Madison County Health Board as a member and chairman for 30 years.

In that year of 2010, young into the new century and millennium but much older in body, I made the transition to full time teaching at the University of Kentucky College of Medicine in nearby (40 minute commute) Lexington. I had convinced myself that I had a noble calling to mentor and pass on my dermatological knowledge to young, smart, and passionate student doctors. I further mused that this yearning had gone unsatisfied, and this was what I needed to do. In reality, I had become a standup comic, and I craved a varied and larger captivated audience. In between humorous stories and innuendoes I would add medical tidbits of knowledge and clinical experience as a filler, like in a Viennese sausage. Or maybe it was the other way around.

This is the bare bones skeleton of my chronological life. The book that follows is the meat, sinew, internal and external organs that adds shape and the DNA to this individual practitioner's life. Is it a memoir or is it a collection as a publisher asked me? Perhaps it's a collectoir or possibly a memoirlection. You can decide for yourself.

Getting back to Charlie Dickens who also had a wonderful sense of humor is this foolishness or is it wisdom? Are these vignettes and stories "the far, far better things I have done in my life?" Hard to say. What I can say is they are the things that I **have** done in my life. I think I will just leave the value judgment out and hopefully the humorous entertainment in.

PATIENT STORIES

The Dressing Down of an Officer

One of the great pleasures and rewards of practicing in a small community lies in the connection and friendships that a physician can develop with his patients. Colonel Punkett, retired from the U.S. Army, had served in World War II. Now in his eighties, he would visit my office for the past three decades periodically with his delightful wife of greater than a half century for skin cancer screenings and treatments.

On entering the examination room I would stand at attention and give him a military salute which he would return with an even more proper and crisper one. Reminiscing about our military service and well aware of my sense of humor, he told me of his own experience while stationed in London prior to D-Day as a military policeman. One Saturday evening he was called to a posh London hotel to detain a Major in the British Army for his out of character behavior. "The American military couldn't arrest an officer in the British Army but could detain him." He carefully began. "The officer in question was found running naked through the hotel lobby chasing a young woman who was also naked.

"British court martial proceedings were initiated against the Major on the grounds that his appearance and behavior were unbecoming of an officer in service of the King. If convicted he could have been sentenced to three years in prison as well as lose his commission."

The Major's military barrister, however, proposed the most unique and novel defense, "...that the Major was appropriately attired for the maneuvers in which he was engaged. Furthermore any other British officer in service of the King under the same circumstances would have adhered to a similar dress code perhaps more but certainly not less, and that was the indisputable naked truth."

The officer was acquitted. With the verdict barely in, the accused was heard confiding to his friends, "I told you they had nothing on me." As a footnote the Allies did go on to win the War. Whether the British officer's acquittal and subsequent service played a "major" role in that outcome can be best ad-"dressed" by the military historians.

It wasn't long after he shared this humorous anecdote with me that the consequences of age and lymphoma caught up with my patient and friend and he passed away. A few days after the funeral his widow came by the office and left an envelope that contained a perspective of his personal political views. He was planning to give it to me at our next scheduled visit. She also wanted me to know how much he enjoyed and cared for his dermatologist. I was very touched by his sense of closeness and fondness. All of which arose from a shared connection of humor and medicine.

I had told him at one of our many visits that my mother had been an opera singer and had attended the legendary Juilliard School of Music in New York City. He appeared one afternoon at the office and gave me a cap with "Juilliard" inscribed on the front. His nephew was now attending that outstanding school of the arts in NYC and he had obtained that cap from him.

Every time I venture out into the dreaded ultraviolet rays, I don it on my head. As the brim casts a shadow across the upper part of my face a not so veiled contented smile creeps across my lips and a warm gentle feeling wraps around my heart as I think of the closeness this physician had with his dear patient, friend, and superior officer.

In the Limelight

A young man of twenty-two arrived at my office with a constellation of small round dark brown dots on the back of his left hand. Not knowing what they were or if they were anything to be concerned about compelled him to make an appointment.

As I scanned the twenty or so small spots I first wondered if they could be the discoloration left from a rash that had resolved. It is quite common after some injury or breaking out on the skin for it to heal with increased color or what is referred to as post inflammatory hyper-pigmentation. He was quite adamant that he hadn't had any itching or red breaking out prior to dark spots onset. They just appeared as they were a few weeks ago. It seemed initially baffling to me. So I thought a little more history was needed and probed with more questions.

"Have you taken any new medicines that were either prescription or over the counter?" "Absolutely not, Doc. I don't take anything regularly or even occasionally." He answered very self-assured.

"What do you do? Are you going to school at Eastern Kentucky University?" I inquired. "Yes, I'm a student at Eastern." Realizing that most of the students also hold part time jobs to help pay for their education, I asked, "Are you working as well?"

"Oh yes, I tend bar at one of the local restaurants."

Then the connection hit me like a bolt out of the blue. He tended bar and made drinks. "Do you make mixed drinks?" I now anxiously as well as excitedly asked.

"Yes, all the time."

"Do you ever squeeze limes or work with mangoes or other tropical fruits?" I further inquired in a staccato manner.

"Of course, all the time," he replied.

I now noticed that he had a rich dark tan in the middle of winter. "Do you go to the tanning bed or ever drive with your hand out the window?"

"Yes, I do both."

"One final question. Are you right handed?"

"Yes, I'm right handed. What's wrong with me?" he then asked with a mixture of anxious curiosity and surprise.

I quickly jokingly quipped, "I don't have the slightest idea." Followed by, "Let me explain. You have an eruption we refer to as Berlock Dermatitis or Phytophotodermatitis. Certain plants, and in your case fruits like limes and lemons, contain a chemical called oil of bergamot or furocoumarin which in combination with certain wavelengths of light cause a darkening or pigmentation of the skin."

"You are right handed and while at work, you held the mixed drink glass in your left hand while you squeezed the lime with your right hand. The lime droplets squirted onto the back of your left hand depositing the bergamot/furocoumarin chemical onto your skin. Then by going to the tanning bed you activated the chemical with the long range ultraviolet rays which led to the pigmentation of the skin. The longer range light in the tanning bed is the exact one needed to produce this darkening reaction."

"We might be able to speed up the lightening of the dark color with the application of a strong prescription topical cortisone cream. However, they will eventually fade on their own. Of course stay away from the tanning beds. Limes don't mix as well with light as they do with alcohol," I added dryly.

"Hey, doc you're pretty smart to figure that out."

"Thanks, would you mind calling my wife and telling her that," I bantered.

I handed him his prescription and he smiled as he left the office. I was feeling pretty good as well having cracked this Sherlock Holmes skin mystery of being in the limelight.

Pickled Pink

Growing up in a medical family in whose father was an accomplished and respected physician and dermatologist in the 'shruburbs' of New York City, I would often listen intently at the dinner table to my dad's adventures and complaints of the day. As I matured and entered the medical field I became more attuned to his stories and encounters as to what was to become eventually my own specialty of medicine as well.

One evening after his long day of attending to patients in his office dressed in his starched white and pressed shirt with sleeves always carefully and neatly rolled up over his elbows accompanied with a variation of a drab gray or solid brown tie, he told me of a most bizarre and interesting case that one of his colleagues had encountered. Also a knowledgeable and experienced dermatologist in New York City this dermatologist friend of dad's was told by a peer about a patient that he had seen in his private practice.

A young woman came to this friend of a friend's office with a widespread itchy and alarming skin eruption that had appeared suddenly. The rash had the characteristic pattern of an allergic contact rash or dermatitis since it matched perfectly where her dress touched her skin. He became suspicious that she had a clothing allergy and consequently decided to do a series of patch tests to determine to which specific chemical she might be allergic.

The ensuing tests revealed a severe reaction to the ingredient formaldehyde or formalin. Armed with this medical evidence the suspicious physician probed further into her history. She then related how she had purchased a new dress from an expensive boutique but had received a considerable discount on the price. She had worn the dress but one time, the day prior to the onset of her rash. All the pieces of the pruritic puzzle fell together perfectly as to the dress being the culprit of her acute dermatological despair. She cleared nicely with appropriate steroid treatment.

On the surface that would have seemed to be the end of the story, but the patient became quite curious about that dress's history, especially since it had a strong odor about it. So she returned to the exclusive shop and questioned the owner who told her the reason she had sold it at such a discount was because it had been a returned item the week before. Still not quite satisfied she asked the owner who had purchased the dress so she might contact her.

With the name and phone of this other customer she located the original buyer and told her story and misadventure with the same dress that they both had bought. The original buyer then confided sheepishly to her that she had acquired that beautiful and expensive dress for her mother's funeral and how lovely the embalmed woman looked in the casket with it on.

Although she thought her beloved mother should be laid to rest in the ground for perpetuity she decided that the very expensive dress should not. So the pricey now formaldehyde soaked dress was removed and returned to the store for a generous refund. I listened enthralled at this story as a resident in dermatology at the time.

I stored that incredible anecdotal case of medical trivia into the recesses of my dermatology cerebrum. For the next thirty years I would wonder when evaluating my own patients with clothing dermatitis whether I would eventually see a repeat experience with one of them. Every time a patient presented with an identical eruption I would ask if their garment had a strong odor or if it were a returned item. While it has never occurred, I kept searching.

In the late 1990s I found myself one evening visiting one of my favorite haunts, the Jos. S Beth Bookstore in Lexington which has a wonderful assortment of all kinds of reading materials with comfortable lounge chairs and an eatery attached to the bookstore. Not looking for anything in particular I sat down in one of those cushioned chairs adjacent to a bookshelf and just casually reached over and picked out the first book I touched and flipped it open landing on page 196 serendipitously and there to my shock was the story of "The Poison Dress", the identical story that my father had told me twenty five years earlier. The name of the book? *Too Good to Be True - The Colossal Book of Urban Legends* by Jan Harold Brunvand. That book caught my attention as well as my pocketbook that evening.

Room Service –
Is There a Doctor in the House?

Both Mondays and Tuesdays are busy and pressured. Dermatologists and car mechanics are usually busy the first of the week with patients and clients whose weekend problems have escalated into an immediate emergency and crisis. An acutely appearing widespread rash can be a very frightening experience to a patient, just as a car engine that makes an unfamiliar clanking engine noise can be to a driver. Consequently I make every effort to work in patients the early part of the week when they just can't wait for a routine appointment. Jack was just such a person.

As I read Jack's information history I discovered that he lived in Richmond and was a businessman in his mid fifties and had an itchy rash that had been explosive on his skin for the past week. I entered the examination room with a medical student who was rotating with me to be greeted by a balding, over six foot tall, smiling, pleasant, well proportioned and well dressed professional man with a hint of anxiety in his voice.

"Hi, Jack. I'm Dr. Tobin and this is a medical student who is working with me for a month. However, I suspect sometimes he's working against me." A small grin crept over both the patient's and the medical student's face. "May I examine your rash?" I asked. "Sure, Doctor." he responded.

He was covered with a red and crimson inflamed eruption extending over his entire body from the neck on down. I explained to the medical student that this is what we call a morbilliform eruption. Morbilliform means measles like because it is basically flat and splotchy and the thousands of small macules or flat spots have merged together in a confluent way over all his skin. The most common cause for this type of eruption, in the absence of any systemic signs, is ingestion or exposure to a drug, although half the time a history of medication exposure cannot be found.

"Jack, had you been taking any new medications either prescription or over the counter?" I inquired. "No, doctor. The only medications I have taken were after the eruption began. Does that count?" "No, Jack that won't give us much information, as you already suspected," I answered.

I continued to explain that many medications don't come in the traditional pill form and consequently we aren't always aware of this type of exposure. Many of our processed foods contain preservatives, vitamins and chemicals that if we took in a tablet or pill form we would call a medication but because they are masked in food we don't recognize it as such. Even antibiotics that are used to fatten cattle can be found in trace amounts in our meat products and one could be allergic to one of them.

"Well, doctor," he interrupted, "I was in Houston when the rash began and I had eaten a lot of that good Mex/Tex food." "That certainly could be the source of exposure." I suggested.

He continued, "Let me tell you what happened. As I said, I was in Houston at a business meeting and I was staying at a pricey nice hotel downtown. I turned in early that evening and awoke the next morning with this rash. I wasn't sure what to do in a strange town by myself and very concerned about this eruption. I was scared that something serious was happening to me."

"I called down to the concierge and asked if the hotel had a house doctor that could see me. He said as a matter of fact that they did and that they could contact her and see me soon at the hotel. Inquiring as to the cost he said he wasn't absolutely sure what she would charge for a hotel visit but thought it would be about a hundred dollars."

"I told him to contact the physician and he said she could be there in about an hour or so. She knocked on my hotel door about eleven o'clock that morning and she introduced herself to me. After examining the rash she said she had just the thing to clear me up. Reaching into her medical bag she produced two syringes and told me she was going to give me a cortisone shot and an anti-itch shot."

I'm thinking to myself as I listen to this all too familiar scenario that I have heard too many times before. This doctor didn't have the slightest idea what was wrong with him. If a physician doesn't tell the patient the diagnosis it is usually because he or she doesn't know what it is.

If they pull out the 12 gauge shotgun treatment approach, that verifies it, twelve gauge shotgun because if you put enough different medications together you might hit the targeted disease process without ever knowing what you were aiming at. By using a short acting cortisone shot the patient might receive enough improvement for a day or so before it wears off, long enough until he leaves Texas but without the danger of it lasting longer in his system and having an undesirable side effect.

The itch shot was undoubtedly an antihistamine and probably a form of over the counter Benadryl. It wouldn't have done anything for the type of eruption that he had since his rash wasn't histamine mediated. I continued to listen as he continued to spin his itchy tale.

"So she gave me the two shots. She had been there about fifteen minutes and she told me that should do it and not to worry. She packed up her little black bag and then announced that she doesn't accept insurance for these type of visits and that her fee was eight hundred dollars. "EIGHT HUNDRED DOLLARS!!!???" I say in amazement thinking I have heard it wrong. "Yes, eight hundred dollars," she said again. 'Four hundred dollars for the office call, two hundred dollars for the one shot and two hundred dollars for the other shot."

"Well, doctor all of me is now red, not just the areas where the rash is. She then added that she takes cash or credit card but not a personal check."

"Well, what did you do?" I asked him hoping that he had the presence of mind not to pay her. "At this point I didn't know what to do but gave her my credit card for the payment," he lamented. I'm now thinking eight hundred dollars for no diagnosis and the wrong treatment. It reminded me of the old George Gershwin lyric, "Nice work if you can get it, and you can get it if you try."

Rash Decisions and Growth Experiences
from the Best Little Warthouse in Kentucky

He now turned to me and asked, "Do you think that was exorbitant?" I'm thinking to myself, he paid her eight hundred dollars and I might get forty dollars from his insurance company if I'm lucky and after they reject the claim three times on some minor technicality.

I quipped, "You know, Jack, I would love to answer your question but I really don't have the time. You see you're my last patient since I have decided to give up my private practice to become the house physician for the Hyatt Regency and Radisson Hotels in Lexington." My medical student now exploded in laughter.

"Look, Jack, that was an awful lot of money for the services rendered and I usually won't comment on another physician's fees. But since you asked, you certainly are no stranger to the medical world and must realize that level of fee scale certainly sounds exorbitant."

He then added, "And doctor I was the third person she had seen that morning! What should I do?" "Look, Jack, you could complain to the credit card company and they will tell you that it's not their concern and it's a dispute between you and the vendor.

"You could complain to the physician, I doubt that would be very productive since she felt her fee was quite appropriate." I'm thinking to myself that the second most common psychiatric disorder that physicians suffer from after obsessive compulsive disorder is narcissism. The narcissistic personality by definition entitles the physician to do anything he or she wants to do by virtue of the fact that they are they.

I continued, "You could complain to the administrator of the hospital to which she is affiliated and nothing will happen either since administrators are more adept in hiding than exposing uncomfortable and embarrassing issues. You could even complain to the Houston Medical Society but I doubt any substantive action would follow.

"The only recourse that would trigger a thorough investigation and response would be a thoughtful non-angry letter to the State Board of Medical Licensure whose duty is to address these questions and complaints. I'm sure you can get their address off the internet.

"Anyway, getting back to your medication reaction, let me put you on a tapering course of oral prednisone for the next fourteen days which should clear you up in about a week." I proceeded to alert him to the possible side effects of the medicine and why it was important to continue for the full dosage even if he cleared quickly. I suggested to him to come back in a couple of weeks if he weren't improved and I would do a biopsy to investigate why he didn't improve as we both expected.

"Oh, by the way Jack, we take your insurance here and there is only your co-pay of fifteen dollars that you are responsible for, but if you feel that I did an exceptional job there is a tip jar at the checkout station. If you want to leave me a seven hundred and eighty five dollar tip you could." He now laughed.

Jack didn't come back as a patient but as fate would have it I saw him two weeks later at a local discount store and he greeted me with an expansive smile and a firm handshake. He told me that his rash had cleared completely as we had both hoped it would.

A Case of Weeping

Having finally retired after a third of a century from private practice, I accepted a faculty teaching professorship in dermatology at the University of Kentucky Medical Center in Lexington. My motivation for such a dramatic change was rooted in two personal reasons: first, to engage my passion to teach young and aspiring medical students and physicians and secondly, to achieve my life-long professional ambition and goal to become a state employee.

The vetting process was incredibly and unexpectedly involved, from background checks, drug testing, supporting credentials, letters of recommendation, and even having to present my passport to prove my citizenship. Displaying the soft back blue paper official U.S. document with the simulated textured cover, I quipped to the authority figure behind the imposing desk, "Here's my passport as requested. The last time I used it was when I went to Ohio." Dead silence followed. Hmm, I wondered, could she have worked previously for the TSA? After what seemed like a never ending process I finally began my new position.

It wasn't long afterwards that my little beeper started to chirp with that piercing very audible sound announcing that someone was looking for me. The scrolled text was a phone number to call. The Emergency Room had a very seriously ill patient and needed an immediate consult. A man in his forties had been seen by his primary care physician about a week ago with a blistering eruption on the left side of his forehead. Diagnosing the condition as shingles (Herpes Zoster) he started the patient on the appropriate antiviral medication acyclovir.

However, instead of improving he became dramatically worse with his whole face blowing up like a red balloon and his eyes swollen shut and with red and blistering lesions on his arms and scattered on his torso. The emergency physician had already consulted the Infectious Disease specialists who in turn had called me. "Dr. Tobin, we believe this patient has disseminated herpes zoster (shingles). We have already had a consult with ophthalmology who has assured us that he doesn't have eye involvement. We would like you to see the patient," confided the ID specialist with a touch of anxious concern and a sense of urgency in his voice.

My nurse practitioner and I dropped everything and hurried to the new sophisticated Emergency Room to see this very rare complication and possibly life threatening case. We dressed in the protective isolationist blue disposable gowns and donned surgical protective masks and gloves as is customarily done in infectious disease cases. In the secluded bay, the patient lay with eyes swollen shut and his whole face bright strawberry red and inflamed with weeping wet sticky exudates. The blisters were numerous and covering his arms and clustered in a linear fashion with many weeping and forming the consequent crusting. Sounding like an off key duet my nurse practitioner and I simultaneously blurted out the same diagnosis. "It's Poison Ivy!"

Questioning the patient who was very cooperative and alert, I probed, "Had you been outside a day or two or three before breaking out and exposed to any brush or plants?" "No," he shot back. His significant other sitting in a chair immediately looked up and corrected him with, "Honey, don't you remember the day before the rash began you were in the yard trimming bushes and around a lot of plants?" "Oh, that's right," he corrected himself. "Well, you have an extensive but not dangerous case of poison ivy, and we can fix you right up with a short course of oral steroids and some cortisone cream and home applied milk compresses," I suggested reassuringly.

As luck would have it the admitting attending internal medicine professor had also rushed to the ER to see his new patient. I explained to him the new and significant history along with the classical clinical findings of poison ivy which included the typical linear blisters, the wet exudative eczema (which comes from the Greek meaning to weep) and the red swelling and distribution, all of which fit with an allergic contact dermatitis, poison ivy diagnosis.

Rash Decisions and Growth Experiences
from the Best Little Warthouse in Kentucky

"Instead of admitting him why don't you place him on a tapering dose of oral prednisone and topical steroids and some compresses and he should clear up nicely in about a week," I suggested. He agreed. The internist was relieved. I was relieved, and most importantly the patient was relieved with the changed diagnosis. He did clear quickly.

This case brought to mind an old adage that I had learned in medical school. When you hear hoof beats think of horses and not zebras. However, I have since learned that in a large referral tertiary university medical center there are plenty of black and white striped four legged animals galloping around the hospital corridors as well.

Lost in Translation

This particular day in practice was no more usual or unusual than any other with patients arriving to have skin cancers removed, pre cancer checks, acne treated, warts frozen, and poison ivy cleared. All of which grants me the unique distinction of being the only person in the county who gets paid for making rash decisions. However, no matter how serious or inconsequential any of my patients' problems were, every single one of them has disrupted their normal and busy routines and schedules to come to my office to address what is on their mind.

That act in itself reveals the importance and significance as well as concern to which they attach to their individual skin problem. I make every attempt with each patient never to minimize their level of concern prompting their visit, while at the same time hoping that I will be able to minimize their anxiety about their skin condition if possible. Fortunately the worst case scenario often is not their scenario and I end up dispensing reassurance as the best and most common form of medication.

This is in stark and vivid contrast with the philosophy that I learned as a medical student and later as a resident in my academic learning programs. Subliminally or not the young physician leaves medical school and residency training with the ingrained philosophy that you in some way have failed the patient and yourself if you haven't diagnosed a recognizable and established medical disease entity and the more exotic the better. Anyway, I was half way through the morning working at my usual pace attending to my patients concerns and questions finishing with one patient and ready to see a new one.

My mid morning appointment found me confronting a new patient who was a slender young man with neatly combed sandy brown hair and fair skin in his early twenties. He was polite and anxious as many patients are who present for the first time to my office. I asked him why he had come to see me. He answered, "I have some moles I want you to look at them, doctor." I quickly responded with, "Are they on your skin or in your yard?" This attempt at humor broke the medical ice and warmed the professional atmosphere. He responded with a chuckle and a grin, "They're on my skin, doc." "Good," I continued, "you probably couldn't have afforded me to make a house call."

He seemed now more relaxed and comfortable. I prepared to do the necessary skin examination. Often as I prepare to evaluate a patient's nevi or moles I am reminded of a learning experience I had while chief resident in dermatology in the Big Apple at The Skin and Cancer of New York University Medical Center.

During my residency at NYU I had the unique opportunity to apprentice with the Chairman of the Department in his private office. Dr. Baer who had studied under some of the great legends of our profession and now would be considered one in his own right, was born in Europe and spoke with a distinct Austrian or German or Swiss accent. They all sounded the same to me but I'm sure there are subtle differences just as there are in the American dialects.

I always wondered in those black and white World War II movies that I watched as a kid how those Americans who escaped from POW camps and in civilian clothes just happened to speak not only prefect German but also with a perfect regional dialect as well, fooling every native German that they encountered. Wouldn't that be the equivalent of a New Englander with his Yankee accent attempting to pass as a Southerner from Mississippi?

Anyway, Dr. Baer's patients were among the wealthiest and most prominent gentry of New York City. Sensing the need for the appropriate demeanor and attitude, I suppressed my more egalitarian and humorous core for a more acceptable proper Fifth Avenue veneer. One day Dr. Baer confided to me after we had examined a patient who also presented with a set of moles about his technique for examining patients.

"Stuaert you know vhat is the difference between me and other dermatologists vhin examining moles?" Recognizing that as a rhetorical question I knew how to play the straight man and answered with the expected, "No, Dr. Baer, what is the difference?" "Vell, Stuaert, other dermatologists vill glance at the patient's moles and vithout hesshitation vill render an opinion, 'they're all vright.' I, on the other hand, vill get the patient on the exammening table and get out my magnifying glass and shine the exammenation light onto the mole and thein staand back and strooke my chin followed by a moments hesshitation and then pronounce, they're all vright."

While this experience didn't add to my diagnostic skills it certainly gave me pause to reflect on the theater of medicine. I now proceeded with my own skin examination of my new patient carefully scrutinizing each mole with a hand held magnifying lens under the enhanced illumination of the overhead operating light, followed by the thoughtful pause, then pronouncing that they all had the landmarks and features of normal moles.

Dr. Baer had neglected to inform me that experienced physicians who are greater than fifty need assistance and extensions of their senses. That the magnifying glass and extra light are not props but are essential tools to see and diagnose accurately. I then explained to this young man how I came to my opinion by showing him pictures of those clinical changes that we associate with abnormal moles, the A (asymmetry), B (border irregularities), C (color variance), D (diameter changes) and E (evolving) that give rise to suspicion. None of which he had.

After explaining all this in detail as well as the limitations of clinical visual evaluation, I offered him the option of a biopsy on any if he wished or just to follow them for any change. He felt as comfortable with his moles as I did and opted for observation. We then spent some time discussing sun protection and prevention of skin injury.

Since I always like to make a personal connection with every patient, I noticed that on his information form that he was a student at the local state regional college, Eastern Kentucky University. So I inquired, "What are you studying at EKU?" He proudly proclaimed, "Law enforcement, doctor."

Rash Decisions and Growth Experiences
from the Best Little Warthouse in Kentucky

Eastern has outstanding and in-depth programs in the College of Criminal Justice and Law Enforcement, attracting students not only nationwide but internationally as well. He told me about his studies and aspirations to become a criminal sleuth and investigator. He seemed genuinely enthusiastic about his career choice. Having touched on all his concerns I was getting ready to end our visit together and asked him if he had any additional questions. "Yes," as he turned to me and asked in a puzzled manner, "Doctor, why did you go to medical school in Mexico?" "Mexico!" I exploded in surprise followed by "Mexico?" with a hint of pondering curiosity. I'm now thinking to myself is this guy delusional or is he hallucinating?

I did take Spanish in high school for three years instead of French. My decision was prompted by the academic intelligence from my older brother that the French teacher was hard, rigid and demanding, and that my chances for a higher grade in a foreign language seemed to lie better south of the border than across the Atlantic pond.

"Why do you think I studied in Mexico?" I asked nonplussed. He now responded confidently and proudly utilizing all the deductive detective skills and logic that he had acquired in his studies, "Your diploma hanging on the wall in the hall is in Spanish," he answered proudly.

Unable to contain myself, the medical professional dam holding back my swelling reservoir of humor cracked into a turbulent smile and then the whole wall broke, followed by a crashing wave of laughter that registered 4.3 on the Richter tsunami humor scale.

"What are you laughing at?" he asked. "Son," I continued, "we need to look at that diploma a little more carefully." I escorted him into the hall where the "Mexican" diploma in question was hanging on the wall. "You have just told me something about your foreign language skills. You never studied Spanish, did you?" I asked. "No," he replied. "You also have never studied Latin either?" I continued. "No," he replied. "Well, the diploma is in Latin." "Oh," he said bashfully.

Of course if he had recognized Latin as a language I guess he would have deduced that I had attended medical school at the Vatican, which doesn't have a medical school, or perhaps Latin America, which would have brought us back to Spanish. I also wondered why he would think the only Spanish speaking country with a medical school would be in Mexico when it could have been any one of a dozen or so other South American countries or even Spain for that matter.

I never delved into that mystery, and it has remained unanswered along with those other unanswered eternal questions that have intrigued mankind since the dawn of intelligent thought. How was the universe created? What happens to you after you die? What is the nature of God? And the most elusive one of them all, did my car really need the repairs that the auto mechanic said it did?

"Don't feel embarrassed," I added. "Let me tell you the story about this diploma. It's not my medical diploma but my college one. When I graduated from the University of Pennsylvania in Philadelphia, I felt very intelligent, smart and educated. Then at graduation the dean, or more accurately his secretary, handed me my diploma commemorating this 1.67 kilometer-stone aka milestone event in my life and I couldn't read it. After four years of post high school education, multiple in-depth specialty and esoteric course work at Penn, I couldn't read my own diploma!"

I've never been quite sure if a) dear old U of P was preserving some antiquated tradition by using the mother romance stem language in this document or b) they were having their little joke on all those bright, confident and knowledgeable graduates, or c) was this the unrecognized final test of an Ivy League institution to see if the new capable graduate could research if not the meaning of life at least the meaning of the sheepskin? If not a, b, or c perhaps all of the above were the correct answers.

"So what would you do if someone handed you a diploma you couldn't read?" I asked my young aspiring investigator. He thought for a moment and replied, "Have it translated?" "Exactly!" I enthusiastically answered. "You know, I never did that either. I had spent the next thirty years remarking to my office staff that I couldn't read my own college diploma. I always did this with a sense of pseudo ignorant smug pride, the same kind of pride that the illiterate farmer with a keen common sense likes to visit on the over-educated professor who doesn't know how to hammer a nail.

"However, my staff didn't seem to derive the same satisfaction from the retelling as I did, especially after hearing this same story hundreds of times. For my birthday a few years ago, my employees reaped their revenge by presenting me with a translation in English, a language which I am fluent in to some degree. In turn it granted them a reprieve from hearing the oft repeated anecdote. That translation which apparently missed your keen observational skills lies framed under the original. By the way I discovered something that I had suspected for all those years. I did graduate from college."

As way of a footnote, every one of my alumni friends from Penn with whom I share this anecdote about the diploma has asked me to fax or email them a copy of the English translation. Hmmm?!?! I wonder?

Boop Boop a Doop

As part of my long term exit strategy from a private dermatological practice spanning 33 years, I hired a physician extender to assist me in the care of my patients. I spent more time searching for the right nurse practitioner than most men spend time in seeking out a spouse.

After six months of interviewing many applicants I hired Ragan, an experienced RN recently relocated to the Bluegrass area of Kentucky. Her husband, an accomplished pilot, had been recently hired to fly a private jet for a wealthy successful entrepreneur.

Despite her excellent background and broad experience her specialty training in dermatology was a bit anemic. So she shadowed me for a year until I felt comfortable that she was adequately trained to undertake care of my patients. My wife as a gag gift had bought me a Betty Boop tie which I had worn to the office one day. Ragan, being a very independent and self-assured mature woman of the new millennium, took great offense to my tie. She felt that Betty Boop was a relic of a bygone male chauvinistic pig exploitative era in which women were looked upon as mere sex objects. She expressed her feelings strongly and without reluctance and repetitively, which wasn't a bad idea considering my dwindling attention span and memory.

My defense that Betty looked pretty damn good for a woman of at least 80 years of age fell on, if not deaf ears, at least diminished hearing ones. I exacerbated her negative feelings by insisting that we could claim that Betty was our patient and that her amazing youthful appearance resulted from our great dermatological interventions. "It could be a good PR ploy," I pleaded. She remained unimpressed and unmoved.

31

Rash Decisions and Growth Experiences
from the Best Little Warthouse in Kentucky

I found myself falling into the Damon Runyonesque scenario of, "When you're guilty don't squirm it only makes you look guiltier." I was squirming and only looked guiltier. No defense seemed acceptable or possible.

A week later in collusion with my office staff I secretly purchased Betty Boop nurse's tops for all my employees as well as a Betty Boop calendar and clock which I surreptitiously hung in her office one morning. With their assistance we surprised her before office hours with everyone dressed in Betty Boop attire. So she wouldn't feel ostracized I placed with great ceremony on her white lab coat a pin of the dreaded lady icon. She relented and laughed along with everyone else.

It was so well received by my patients and even grudgingly by Ragan that we adopted every Tuesday as Betty Boop day. She never took down the wall clock and she has used the calendar daily to track her appointments. I haven't had the courage to confess that I really find Betty Boop two dimensional and rather shallow.

Raising the Dead

As a medical intern in the years 1971-72 at the Albert Chandler Medical Center in Lexington, Ky., I rotated one month working at St. Joseph Hospital with one of my fellow interns. One weekend I was called by one of the nurses to examine an elderly terminal patient from whom she was unable to obtain any vital signs.

Sunday in Kentucky often becomes family day in which people gather with their loved ones. It only follows that tradition would be extended to hospital visits as well. I entered the crowded hospital room in which a dozen or more relatives spanning three generations had gathered on this particular Sunday afternoon to visit their very ill relative. My presence was hardly noticed as a half dozen conversations were ongoing and small children had converted the hospital room into a play area with the smaller ones whose amusement of racing around the room and jumping on the bed was spawned out of boredom encased in a shell of hyperactivity .

After taking his vital signs of which there were none as the nurse had told me, I hooked the patient up to an EKG machine for an electrocardiogram. All the while multiple conversations and relentless activity continued unabated around me. The tracing was flat. No activity.

I now turned to the family and sensitively interrupted with a muted and solemn, "Excuse me." But the conversations and activity continued unabated. It wasn't until the third "Excuse me," with three times the decibel level, that I could capture everyone's attention and I could announce, "I regret to inform you that your loved one has passed away." I wanted to add "unnoticed …….and an hour ago" but decided to delete it from my pronouncement, fearing it would impact on the piety of the moment.

Rash Decisions and Growth Experiences
from the Best Little Warthouse in Kentucky

I left the room with the EKG machine in tow and marveled at the surreal thought of children jumping on the dead man's bed with his rigor mortis movements simulating a live person from their bouncing for the past hour. All the while everyone else in the room remained so involved in their personal conversations they were totally oblivious to his demise. It was macabre, bizarre, yet so Monty Python noir humoristic. I wondered what types of conversations transpired after their loved one expired.

A Curbside Consult

My home is tucked away in the rear of our small subdivision five miles from town. My house, situated at the end of a cul-de-sac, offers considerable privacy and every home in the subdivision is located on approximately an acre of land to accommodate the septic tanks which allow the picture perfect homes to be habitable. These lots afford each neighbor enough distance from each other to insure our privacy but at the same time allow us to be close enough to develop a friendly relationship. As in love, neighbor friendships often follow the same rules. Sometimes "distance makes the heart grow fonder" or "out of sight, out of mind," which in this case is a good thing.

My next door neighbor Sam and his wife moved into their rambling dark brick ranch style home a few years ago. Sam, a giant of a man standing 6'4" and weighing about 270 pounds of well proportioned muscles, appears more like a linebacker than the successful realtor, businessman, and entrepreneur that he has become. With a booming auctioneer voice and an assertive attitude he makes his presence known whether beckoned or not. As with any relationship there have been bumps in the road, but I'm glad he lives next door for it has given me an opportunity to learn more about him. I have become genuinely fond of him. With a generous heart that matches his size, he contributes to many local causes and constantly volunteers to help out with the Rotary Club, civic functions, and church activities.

He loves his home and constantly tinkers with all his cars, including a brilliant crimson Model T-like vehicle in mint condition complete with a rumble seat which he often pilots in local parades when he's not riding his 1930s black and brown pickup truck, also in immaculate mint condition. His driveway also sports a non-vintage Mustang as well as a large white pickup truck of more recent, as well as utilitarian use.

I also find myself fluctuating between amusement and amazement to see this giant of a man huddled behind the steering wheel of his shrunken white vehicle of a son of a Hummer blazoned with huge blue lettering on the side and rear of the vehicle announcing his real estate and auction company. Sam is definitely a man of contrasts and everyone in town knows him and he knows everyone. His wife, May, at 5'2" petite in size adds another contrast, as does the vehicles she drives, a little green Volkswagen beetle. One might think that with all those automobiles located next door that my street, Bittersweet, might have become more bitter than sweet. However, not so. Sam has gone to great expense and care to house his treasured collection of vehicles in a tastefully and exquisite matching bricked garage at the end of his driveway.

In the summer of 2005, Sam developed some urinary tract symptoms and problems and after much investigation, including a colonoscopy, biopsies, and a thorough evaluation by his physicians, a benign non-cancerous mass was found in his lower colon to be pressing on his bladder. Surgery became imminent for him. Since he expected some down time for recovery after his colon resection, he and May decided to spend a week at their summer home in Gulfport, Mississippi. Returning a few days prior to the surgical date, I encountered him in his driveway, and he informed me of his impending medical adventure.

"Doc, you know how I like to be active and there were a number of fallen trees on our Gulfport property because of hurricane Katrina and since there wasn't a lot else to do I decided to get out the old chain saw and pruning saw and clear the debris." He not so casually mentioned. Continuing, he added, "Well, after a couple of days I got this tremendous itching and breaking out around my tummy and groin. I'm worried that it might keep the surgeon from doing the surgery. Do you know anyone I can see before Wednesday to clear it up?" he asked.

I'm thinking to myself, has Sam forgotten that his next door neighbor is the proprietor of the Best Little Warthouse in Kentucky and that I'm the only guy in the county who gets paid for making rash decisions. If this wasn't up my alley or at least down his driveway, nothing would be. Before I have time to vocalize these thoughts he continued.

"Doc, I must have lost my mind. You're a skin doctor! Should I call your office? What should I do?" he asked plaintively. "Sam, the waiting list to get an office appointment with me is weeks to months long depending on the problem. Personally, I don't think I'm worth the wait. And once I see you I can't wave a magic wand and make you better instantly. Every treatment takes time to work and you don't have that much to spare.

"Most surgeons when they see any kind of skin rash will want to delay cutting through the skin to prevent infection or to prevent delay of healing." I added. "Neighbor, if we're going to keep you on your surgical time line, let me look at you now and see what I can do for you," I said, offering him a curbstone consultation.

Before I had a chance to add anything else, Sam unbuttoned his pants and dropped them revealing a perfectly symmetrical poison ivy-like eruption following the distribution of the elastic of his underwear. The afternoon light is good and I'm able to determine quickly that he had developed an allergic reaction to one of the chemicals in the elastic of his shorts that was leached out by all the perspiration of his outdoor physical exercise in the summer heat of Mississippi.

I crouched down to examine him more carefully in his driveway just as a car came around the bend and almost crashed into a tree across the street as this unknown driver arrived on this unexpected scene in our cul-de-sac street infrequently visited by any motor vehicles of me bent over in my neighbor's driveway with his pants down and my face on the same line of vision as his underwear. The thought occurred to me that the driver may also not be aware that I'm a dermatologist consulting with a patient. Embarrassed, Sam quickly pulled up his pants. "Let's go into the garage to finish the examination," I suggested.

Sam had no objections. I explained to him the cause of his

skin plight and concluded by adding, "Sam, I'll phone the pharmacy in town for a prescription for a very strong topical steroid which should clear you up before Wednesday. Apply it to the affected areas four times a day. If your surgeon has any questions or reluctance in performing your surgery have him give me a call in the office tomorrow or the next day," I added.

"Thanks, doc," he replied as he climbed into his big white pickup to retrieve his prescription as I turned to enter my home to call the pharmacy. The rash cleared. Sam had his successful surgery without complications. And the unknown driver had his story that he had witnessed with his own eyes, whatever that means. All's well that *ends* well.

The Carwash Consult

After a discontented winter in which we were pummeled with an ice storm leaving us without electricity, heat, and humor for 6 days and with temperatures dipping to 3 degrees Fahrenheit at night, Spring finally arrived, more like Summer, in April. I removed the protective tarp from my wife's Solara convertible and volunteered to clean it up. I had purchased it for her a year before and she allowed me to drive it on occasion if I left a copy of my driver's license and a $100 deposit.

I navigated the sleek vehicle with ragtop down to the local carwash on Keeneland Drive close to our home. After vacuuming the interior and cleaning the sleek body with a soapy foam brush followed by a high pressure water rinse, I carefully dried it with a soft towel to remove any water spots. As I stood admiring the shiny silver vehicle as it glistened in the bright sunlight I heard a voice behind me shouting, "Hey Doc, that's a beautiful convertible. Is that the car I helped pay for?" as I spun around to see one of my patient's and friend calling out.

"No," I shouted back. "You helped pay for the Beemer. This is my wife's car. Come to think about it, another payment is due soon on the BMW. Why don't you give the office a call tomorrow and make an appointment for next week. I could use a few more bucks. I'm sure I can find something wrong with you."

"Hey, Doc, I'm just a poor track coach and can only afford a clunker to drive. My elderly mother gave it to me since I couldn't buy one for myself." He playfully bantered back as I perused the 10 year old drab brown Toyota with a dent here and paint missing there.

"Don't worry about a thing. We'll take the clunker as half your co-pay and you'll only have to pay the other $5 as an out of pocket expense." I added unsympathetically and with more than a touch of sarcasm.

We now exchanged stories of a winter past and promised to meet for lunch some day as I cruised back home and as he limped along in his ancient chariot. However, if the running shoe had been on the other foot, he would have run circles around me in a cross country or any kind of race. We both knew it.

Butt Out

Occasionally, I receive a request from another physician to consult on one of their hospitalized patients. Since the Pattie A. Clay Hospital lies only yards from my office building, which is located on the hospital's campus, the journey becomes a short one accomplished on my lunch hour or in between appointments with my own patients. These requested consults usually revolve around a drug reaction or some unrelated skin disease that remains a mystery to a non-dermatologist specialist. The particular physician making this request for a consultation was our pulmonary specialist, an immigrant from India, whose diagnostic and therapeutic acumen, coupled with his profound commitment to his patients' medical needs, have earned him the respect of the entire medical staff, his patients, and the community as well.

Our medical staff is populated with many talented foreign trained physicians with different religions and from exotic cultures, which has led to occasional amusing experiences. Around the Holiday Season it is customary to send a small gift or Christmas card to express one's well wishes and feelings of the season. Many of our Hindu and Pakistani doctors have adopted this cultural practice. I often receive a delightful fruit basket or card from them as expressions of warmth and good tidings. Where else but in America can a Muslim or a Hindu send a Jew a Christmas card or present and everyone accepts it as natural and normal? I crossed the driveway of the Emergency Room with the intent of External Medicine assisting my colleague and friend in Internal Medicine with his patient.

I rode one of the two elevators of the one hundred bed hospital to the third floor where the medical patients are housed and wandered over to the nursing station to retrieve and review this particular patient's medical history. The woman, 65 years of age, suffered from advanced, severe, and probably terminal respiratory disease after having spent all of her adult life, and most of her adolescence as well smoking many, many packs of cigarettes. Now she was dependent on supplemental oxygen to function and to survive.

Cigarette addiction is always difficult for a non smoker, especially a medical non smoker, to understand why people would engage in such known self destructive behavior. After years of practice I have come to the conclusion that in order for people to alter any destructive medical behavior, whether it's smoking cigarettes, overeating leading to obesity, not exercising, or what I see most often as a dermatologist - abusive sunlight exposure leading to skin cancer, two separate factors must come into play. First, patients must have the knowledge that their behavior is injurious, i.e., smoking *causes* lung and heart disease, obesity stresses your cardiovascular system, and sunlight causes skin cancer and accelerates the aging process.

That particular insight will carry you about 2 to 5 percent down the road on the journey to change. The other 95 to 98 percent of the road less traveled requires personalizing and internalizing that information to one's self. All my patients who smoke tell me that they understand and know why smoking is risky behavior and dangerous and then go on to give multiple assorted rationalizations which allows them to continue their behavior, e.g. "you got to die of something," "my father smoked his whole life and lived to 90," etc., etc. Until they personalize that information to themselves and make the statement that smoking is truly going to injure me, there is no hope for any positive change in destructive behavior. The impediment or illogic that most people use to prevent internalization is sailing the Egyptian River of D-E-N-I-A-L. Overcoming denial means confronting your fear and accepting it as a motivator for change. Fear is the best motivator and often the only motivator that works. As I read through this patient's history it became apparent that my consult had successfully navigated the Egyptian River for many years.

I made my way down the hallway to her semi-private room and found an elderly wizened woman lying in bed with the head of the bed elevated and a green life line pumping oxygen from the wall to her nose thru a nasal cannula at the rate of six liters per minute.

Crowning her mane was a shock of gray, lusterless hair, unkempt from days of hospitalization, and her breathing was labored with every heave of her chest. She was receiving antibiotics through her vein to treat the pneumonia that had compromised what little pulmonary function remained. Her skin had what we dermatologists refer to as "cigarette skin", the marked excessive wrinkling and furrowing that comes only from nicotine and other tobacco toxins' exposure, a form of severe wrinkling that far exceeds that of sun damage. Overlying her cigarette skin was a black coat of film and charring of her entire face. She took one look at me and rifled the following question, "Who the hell are you and what do you want?"

After this not so gentle prompt I felt a proper formal introduction was indicated. "I'm Dr. Tobin, the dermatologist, and your primary care physician asked me to come by and visit with you about your skin," I responded.

"Well, I didn't ask you to come up here to see me." She growled.

"Sorry your vote doesn't count. Only your doctor's does." I countered. Continuing, I asked her, "Tell me Mrs. Smith, what happened to you?" "They won't let you smoke in here," she sneered. The prohibition against smoking in the hospital did not come as news to me, and I sensed that she was not trying to increase my fund of general knowledge. Her response reflected more a condemnation of the hospital's insensitivity to her habitual needs.

I repeated, "What happened to you?" Again she complained, "They won't let you smoke in here, and they took away my cigarettes and I needed a smoke!" "And?" I prompted. She continued defiantly, "I needed a smoke real bad, and I found a butt out there on the floor and I lit it up." The twenty watt light bulb now went off in my head and all seemed illuminated. No further medical history was needed at this point, and the answer to the reason for the hastily requested consult was written across her face. In her haste to light up she had neglected to remove the oxygen life line to her nose, and she had ignited her face, resulting in the black burn eschar along with the melted green tubing over her face.

As she glared at me I asked her, "Mrs. Smith, whose fault is it that all this happened to you?" Without a moment's hesitation she rebutted, "It's the hospital's fault, they won't let you smoke in here." Also without hesitation, and more from reflex than from reflected thought, I made the sound of a buzzer as heard on the old TV program *Family Feud*, and replied, "Eeehhhh, wrong answer survey says. Let's try again, whose fault is it that this happened to you?" This time she resignedly admitted, "Well, I guess it was my fault, but they should allow you to smoke in here!" I sensed that a discussion on navigating the Egyptian River with Mrs. Smith would only jeopardize my own hull from receiving a severe injury to my stern side.

So I ended our visit with, "Well, Mrs. Smith, I'll make some suggestions to your doctor about how we might treat your burn and prevent any permanent scarring." So I sailed out of her room into the less turbulent waters of the nursing station, wondering to myself if any of her favorite songs or musical lyrics could be "I don't have to set the world on fire, I just want to start a flame in your...." or "You Light Up My Life" or "When You're Hot You're Hot" or "Smoke Gets In Your Eyes," or "Come On Baby Light My Fire"?

Arriving back at a small work station I gathered up her chart, extracted my fountain pen from my shirt pocket, and wrote my consultation note suggesting that the skin be cleansed and debrided to prevent traumatic tattooing, silvadene burn cream be applied to speed the healing process and prevent infection, and a tetanus toxoid vaccination be administered to prevent "lock jaw" and consequently preserve her freedom of speech. I mentioned to the nurses that it might also be prudent to remove any incendiary devices from her bed stand as well.

Breathing Easier

Johnny had been my patient for many years. So many Kentuckians who trace their ancestry to the Scots and the Irish can also trace their fair skin complexions to that heritage as well. Skin that has little natural protection from the sun serves people well or at least adequately in northern Europe where the latitude parallels that of Alaska in our own hemisphere. The injury from the sun matters considerably more when those same skin types find themselves on the same latitude as Athens, Greece which is roughly the same as Athens, Kentucky, thirty miles down the road from Richmond where I live and practice.

Consequently, the incidence of skin cancer escalates dramatically in the Sunbelt, especially in an American culture that values the outdoors and encourages people to have a "good tan". That term has always bothered me while at the same time it reveals considerably about our own cultural values. I have always doubted that the medical profession, and the dermatology specialty in particular, would ever make a significant dent in the incidence of skin cancer in the United States as long as people coupled the words "good" and "tan" together in the same sentence.

When we begin to think of tans as bad then Americans will be changing their attitudes which in turn would lead to an alteration in the destructive behavior of abusive sunlight exposure. However, let me return to the story.

Johnny, at over 6'2" tall and with his Celtic skin and love of golf, as well as a farming heritage and frequent sunlight exposure, inevitably came to see me as a patient for those "funny things" growing on his skin. Most of which were skin cancers known as basal cell carcinomas. Fortunately, the basal cell carcinoma has a low mortality rate associated with it since it doesn't spread or metastasize but unfortunately is very locally destructive. Patients can lose an eye or a nose and this form of cancer many times can present quite a challenge to cure. So Johnny would visit me periodically for skin screening examinations and surgical removal of his basal cells.

Honest, straightforward and loyal, he didn't care for anyone who didn't share those values as well. He also had a wry country sense of humor and would share funny stories and country witticisms with me. He would ply his country humor on this city doctor, who in turn would expose him to my own form of cavernous urban humor. The bond took and we developed more than just a sterile patient/physician relationship.

One day, on a routine six-month skin exam, I noticed an unusual mole that I hadn't seen before on his back. "Johnny, I don't like the looks of that mole on your back. I think we should biopsy it. How about if I take a small sample of it today?" I asked him as I had so many times before. "Sure, doc, if you think it needs to be done." He lackadaisically responded with a sense of confidence and trust that arose from our longstanding professional and evolving personal relationship.

I prepped and prepared the area and made a conservative excision to remove the lesion and placed a few well placed mattress sutures to close the defect. When he returned ten days later I explained to him that the biopsy came back as another skin cancer, but it was different from the ones we had excised previously.

This time it was the early stages of mole cancer, a melanoma. However, I went into great detail to explain that since the lesion was so early in development that if we performed a second excision with larger margins that it was unlikely that he would ever have another problem with it. No other treatments would be indicated or necessary. I scheduled him to return on a Friday morning when I would have more time to perform the larger re-excision.

He returned in another ten days or so for the second procedure. Since we had a very comfortable relationship with each other I decided while exposing his skin tissue to my surgical skills I would also expose him to my brand of cutting humor as well - I as the standup comedian and he as the captured audience. It's questionable which would be more painful, the surgery or the banter. "Johnny,

46

before we get started on the procedure, let me ask you an important question. Do you have good insurance?" "I've got great health insurance and it has paid you well in the past," he answered abruptly. "No, no, not health insurance, life insurance. I'm your doctor after all!" I shot back. He started to laugh which only encouraged me more.

"Johnny, I know you have good health insurance and I want to thank you for making a number of car payments on my luxury car. Today's procedure should cover another month's lease payment. Two more skin cancers and you will qualify for a free ride." I continued. "Anything a poor country farmer can do to help out a rich doctor." He added with a sly grin.

As my medical assistant prepped and cleansed the area, I gowned up, placed a surgical mask over my face, and quickly slipped into a pair of size 7 1/2 sterile surgical gloves. My assistant adjusted the surgical lamp. "Johnny, now I'm going to outline with a gentian violet pen the area I will be removing today." I carefully drew a purple elliptical line around the melanoma.

"You know, Johnny, I learned this surgical principle to cut along the dotted line when I was in kindergarten. You never know what you learn in life that you can utilize later," I added. "Doc, I hope you continued your education after kindergarten for the rest of the procedure," he pointedly quipped back. I anesthetized the area on his upper back with a local anesthetic of xylocaine with epinephrine to control the bleeding.

"Johnny, I want to be sure you're numbed up really well before we get started. Can you feel anything in your left big toe?" I asked seriously. "My big toe?" he asked incredulously. "Yes, I can feel my big toe!" "That's good, we can cancel the call to the 'toe' truck," I answered hardly able to contain myself as he starts to laugh as well.

Over the years I have been amazed at how many of my patients laugh either controllably or uncontrollably to this inane archaic and vaudevillian pun while facing a surgical procedure. It 'cuts' through the ice of anxiety and tension and relaxes them more than any other comment in my humorous repertoire. It strangely remains the "Xanax" of operating humor. On stage or on the written page it lacks the impact and humor that it carries in these particularly stressful moments in the operating room suite, proving once again that humor is often situational.

"Johnny, if you get any phone calls in the next few minutes we'll tell them you're all tied up." I quipped, as I continued to incise into the subcutaneous fat tissue to ensure adequate margins. Encountering a few small bleeders which were easily dispatched with cautery, I began the closure with subcutaneous absorbable sutures. The wound was now coming together well as I performed the last part of the surgery to close the skin being careful to avert the incision line to yield a better scar line result.

We banter back and forth during the entire procedure as I attempted to keep him involved in the conversation on the lighter side. Patients who actively engage and talk during a procedure will diffuse their own anxiety. Accomplishing this sometimes becomes a formidable challenge among some of my country and mountain folk male patients whose cultures don't emphasize verbal communication as a valuable resource and linguistic tool.

"Well, Johnny, the procedure has gone just the way I hoped it would and it looks very good." My medical assistant now pipes in, "It really does look good, Johnny." "Don't listen to her. I pay her to say that no matter how it looks," I added. "I learned that in PR school," as I snapped a medical photo for documentation to add to his chart.

"We're going to cover the area with a surgical dressing now. What's your favorite dressing?" I asked. Before he has a chance to reply I added rhetorically, "Say house. It's the only dressing we have." Followed by another chuckle from him.

As my assistant applied a three layered surgical covering over the wound site, I counseled him on the postoperative care instructions. "Now, Johnny, I know you're reluctant to take anything for pain and you don't need to if it doesn't hurt. However, let me write you a prescription for a small number of mild pain pills just in case you need it. If you're not having any pain you can just throw the prescription away."

He's receptive to this suggestion and as he reached for the prescription which I extended towards his open hand. I then turned to his spouse who was seated next to him and added. " I almost forgot to tell you the most important part of his post-operative care. Mrs. Levy, if he gets to be a pain you take the pain pill."

"You know, doc, I might need two," she responded with a grin on her face. Johnny wasn't laughing and just sat there shaking his head in false disbelief.

As he started to leave, I turned to him again and added seriously, "You know, Johnny," as I paused to stroke my chin slowly and professionally as if in deep surgical thought, "I don't know if we can say this," as I again pondered, "but I guess I can, (followed by an anticipatory pause) I couldn't have done the procedure without you." He just smiled, shaking his head again as he left to schedule a follow-up appointment in ten days.

He returned a week and a half later and the wound looked well cared for and was healing as I had hoped. I removed the sutures and discussed with him the results of the second biopsy report which showed adequate margins for his melanoma. "Let me see you back in three months for a routine follow-up," after which we engaged in some small talk and humorous pleasantries.

Twelve weeks passed quickly and he returned for his scheduled follow-up visit. But this is a different Johnny than the one I had known for so long and on whom I had just operated on a short time previously. He lacked the spontaneity and easy going and relaxed demeanor that I had come to associate with him on so many of our previous visits.

He seemed ill at ease and concerned about something and his body language spoke of anxiety. "What's the matter Johnny?" I asked. "Well, doc, a few days after I left your office last time my left chest started to hurt and I got really short of breath. I mean really short of breath. I couldn't walk up the stairs without resting half way and when I lay down I began to smother and had to sit up to sleep."

"So I went to my doctor back home and he took an x-ray and told me that my lung had collapsed. They took me to Lexington to the medical center and operated on me and took out the whole lung. I recovered okay, but it's just not the same. I can't do all the things that I used to do. Had to give up the golf and you know how much I love that, especially beating my brother."

I'm totally absorbed in this surprising and shocking disclosure. My mind began to wander between medical explanations for this untold series of events that were unfolding in front of me and wondered if any of them could relate to my surgery. As he continued his story he removed his shirt to reveal an enormous surgical scar that extended from the chest plate and curved around his thorax almost to the spine, a scar that dwarfed mine and was a mere inch or so away from my recent one.

First I wondered could I have inadvertently entered the thoracic cavity while performing the melanoma surgery. Oh, my God, could this be the result of some unintended error on my part? Oh, my God, could I've performed some form of malpractice on him? Oh, my God, could this result in a malpractice claim? Oh, my God, have I paid my malpractice insurance? All these thoughts raced through my mind almost simultaneously.

"Doc, do you think this could have happened because of your surgery?" he now asked. Trying to remain calm, "Johnny, I don't think so. I can't think of any reason why the two could be connected." I answered with a deliberate air of measured and controlled speech trying to retain a detached clinical composure in my response. "You know, Johnny, coincidences do occur in life," I answered, attempting not to sound too defensive.

"Well, it's a hell of a coincidence that it happened right after your surgery," as his eyes locked on mine just as a laser guided missile would on its target. He continued, "I asked them at the medical center what they thought caused it. They said that they weren't really sure. That's what their mouths said, but you know they had a look on their faces that said they weren't telling you everything they knew. You know that look, doc." I didn't respond.

My heart was beginning to race and I'm feeling very uncomfortable at the events that were unfolding. "Well, this has really been bothering me and it's made me pretty upset. I just can't get any straight answers from anyone. My friends tell me that I should talk to someone about it," he concluded. "Talk to someone else? Like who?" I ask very tentatively, already anticipating the answer "You know, a lawyer." I'm thinking a lawyer, the words that strike utter fear in every physician's myocardium. What three words will send absolute terror into any man's life, "some assembly required," and the four words for a woman, "I broke a nail," and for a physician it's "I'm getting a lawyer." Anxiety and fear were my intimate companions at that moment.

He now turned to me and observed, "Doc, you don't look too good. Your face is all flushed." "It seems kind of warm in here. The air conditioning may not be working well," I managed to utter. "No, it doesn't seem warm to me," he countered. "Well, it seems warm to me!" I protested. "Do you think I should get a lawyer?" he repeated.

Before I had a chance to respond he broke out into a huge smile and started to laugh as he said, "Got you! Yes, my lung did collapse and it did happen just after your surgery but it had nothing to do with what you did. The reason was not only did I have melanoma that you took care of beautifully but as luck would have it they also discovered lung cancer in me and the surgery saved my life again."

I didn't know if I should hug him or strangle him and I decided to do neither and just joined him in laughter. "Oh, by the way, I can still play golf and I can still beat my brother," he added. I'm thinking, yes, he always tells me how he beats his brother on the golf course, and when his brother comes to the office for a visit he tells me how he handily beats Johnny.

In the Beginning

Many of my patients exposed to my humor at the office wish to share their own funny stories and jokes with me. One afternoon one of my female country patients in her seventies arrived for her yearly skin cancer check up. Dressed in a plain solid black full length dress, long gray hair cuffed as a bun, no makeup or jewelry except for her wedding band, an embarrassing smile began to emerge on her face.

"Doctor, I know a funny story and want to tell it to you but don't know if I should. You know my son is a preacher." Sensing she was right at the threshold of telling me I decided to see if I could gently coax her over the line. "You know I love a good joke or story and if you have one you would like to tell me, I'd love to hear it."

"Okay," she relented. "Adam is moping around in the Garden of Eden by himself. God says 'Adam, I'm going to make you a partner and call her woman. She's going to be beautiful, intelligent, sensitive, caring, nurturing, the mother to your children and a wonderful companion. She's going to meet every one of your needs and be the perfect mate.'"

"God, that's exactly what I need," Adam replied. "Here I am in this wonderful place but don't have any one to share it with. I'm lonely." God answers. "Adam, even I can't make her from nothing. I'll need something from you."

"What will you need, God?"

"An arm and two legs."

Adam ponders for a moment and asks, "So what can I get for a spare rib?"

After laughing for a considerable time, my patient then offered up the following sequel.

52

"Adam and Eve were wandering about the Garden of Eden and Adam seems unusually happy and more jovial than normal. Eve turns to Adam and accusingly demands, "Adam, do you have a girlfriend?"

No honey. You're the only woman in the world for me. Come to think of it, you're the only woman in the world. No, I don't have a girlfriend."

"Okay," she relented.

Well that night they're sleeping under the tree of knowledge and Adam wakes up feeling something on his chest and there is Eve leaning over him. 'What are you doing?' he asked."

"Counting your ribs!" she indignantly answered.

The Songbird and the Squirrel

In the fall of 2007 I relocated my office to a larger facility to accommodate my newly hired Nurse Practitioner. All the problems associated with a new office after having been in my previous one for eighteen years occurred. The monumental chore of physically moving equipment, furniture, computers, exam tables, medical instruments and every other assorted item occupied the greater part of nine days of work for me and my exhausted office staff.

We also decided this would be an apt time to convert our medical records from paper to electronic format. So I invested a ton of money into new software and laptops as well. Fortunately, we found an office that had been used by a group of oral surgeons and required just some minor structural changes. After a couple coats of coordinating earth tone paint, new matching tiles for the exam and procedure rooms, as well as new commercial carpet and updating the electrical fluorescent lights, we were ready to move in.

After a few weeks life was beginning to return to a normal pattern. A new patient of mine had presented with a rather large skin cancer called a basal cell carcinoma in front of his right ear. After confirming the diagnosis with a small biopsy I scheduled him to return for a complete excision of the area and a flap reconstruction repair in the office. After infiltrating the area with a local lidocaine anesthetic I sent the specimen to the hospital to be examined for margins before attempting the reconstruction closure.

Relaxed and feeling no pain, Mr. "Songbird", who was in his late fifties and who was employed in a local retail warehouse, acted as if I had given him truth serum. He began to relate, not necessarily in chronological order, his sexual exploits or at least the highlights. The trigger was when I told him that we would keep his wife who had accompanied him for the surgery informed of our progress.

"No, doc. That's not my wife." he protested. "While she is the mother of our children and we live together, we aren't married. Although sometimes she claims to be my wife, we ain't married, doc." You know I'm getting older and I'm not the Romeo I used to be but I still want to see if women want me. So at work a lot of those young women like me and I come on to them just to see if they respond. A lot of them do and boy, they get upset when I don't follow through. You know what I mean doc, don't you?" he asked in a rhetorical way. Not sure that he meant it to be rhetorical I lied. "Sure, I do. I have read a lot of romance novels and watch reality TV." He continued to inform us of women he had known intimately, but not well, in Alabama and other states. It was a long two-hour operation and he was certainly entertaining us with his horizontal endeavor adventures.

Unbeknownst to us a squirrel had climbed into a transformer box of the electric company and caused a short circuit, which in turn caused a power outage in our building. All the lights went out instantly. The florescent and overhead surgical beam sputtered and darkened. I was well into the procedure. I had his entire cheek exposed and was preparing to rotate the undermined and exposed skin into the large defect in front of his ear which would require considerable meticulous suturing when we were bathed in a sea of darkness.

Our patient, sensing that he hadn't gone blind from relating stories of sexual endeavors, just as a teenager had been told that masturbation would cause blindness, now piped in, "Gee doc, it's gotten awfully dark in here all of a sudden. The lights have gone out. What are you going to do now?" he both jokingly and seriously asked at the same time. I confidently answered. "Don't worry, James, I do my best work in the dark." I felt he could relate to that kind of answer. Meanwhile I sent one of my medical assistants to my car to retrieve a flashlight and we opened the window shades to allow in the sunlight and I finished the surgery without missing a stitch. He returned a week later and the area had healed well.

Her Blood Pressure Down
and Mine Up

My internship year in 1971 was a grueling one. Every third night on call with 4-5 hours of sleep and an 80-hour work week left my mind stretched and agitated to its limits and my body constantly physically exhausted in search of the one commodity that always eluded me, adequate sleep. Coupled with caring for the most severely ill patients who suffered from multiple complicated medical problems, I and my fellow house officers were rewarded with the compensation of 13 cents an hour.

One of my most complicated patients that I cared for that year was Maudie Sue who appeared out of nowhere from the mountains of eastern Kentucky one night late and dreary. She presented with an inflamed gall bladder that she had self-diagnosed as indigestion and promptly ignored for weeks. As the pain escalated she finally relented to seek medical attention. By the time she arrived in my care, the gall bladder had ruptured, spewing its toxic chemicals and bacteria into her blood stream. Her body reacted to the infection by going into a state of septic shock which threatened to shut down her kidneys and end her life.

The race was on to connect the dots and save her from dying. As I scrambled to stabilize her blood pressure, treat her shock with a mass infusion of antibiotics, and arrange for the diseased gall bladder to be removed by the surgeons, every minute ticked away and I wondered are we going to win this race or not?

She had a rocky road to recovery with multiple complications and setbacks. After weeks in the intensive care unit, followed by the slow recovery of drains, IVs, and ventilators, all accompanied by sleepless nights, she was about to be discharged.

As I entered her hospital room, I informed her that we needed just one more set of lab tests and if they turned out all right she could go home tomorrow. Maudie Sue turned to me and said in her provocative and unique inimical way, "I've had about as much as I can stand of you and you ain't taking another drop of blood from me. So just get out of here, sonny."

It's hard to say which trigger set me off. Was it the sleep deprivation or the hostility of her remark or my sense of rejection or the "sonny" remark or a combination of them? In any event, instead of just walking away I personalized her comment and turned to her and blurted out. "You know Maudie Sue, you won't understand what I'm going to say but I'm going to say it anyway, not for you but for me."

"Your sense of gratitude and appreciation for the care we've rendered you this past month is only exceeded by your natural external beauty and charm." I walked out of the room and prepared her discharge papers feeling at least better that I had ventilated my feelings.

Don't Give Me Any of Your Lip

A number of years ago I became involved in a leadership role with the movement to establish a public library in our county. Madison County was the largest and most prosperous county in Kentucky without public library services. This became a very divisive and controversial issue which polarized the entire community. On the surface the focus was the library but the heat and passion aroused centered over control within the community as well as an additional property tax. The feelings and passions spilled over into my private practice with a number of patients refusing to see me and my patient volume waned during this episode as our community struggled to define itself.

One morning, a farmer whom I had seen the year before re-presented to the office for the same wart I had diagnosed the year before on his upper lip. He had decided not to have it removed then and wanted me to re-examine the lesion again. "Doc, it's still there and hasn't gone away," he announced. As I examined him it still had all the characteristics of a harmless wart and told him so. After explaining his options to him of either continued observation versus freezing it with liquid nitrogen or surgical removal he decided to have it cut off.

I sent the removed specimen to a world respected university specialty dermatological laboratory for a biopsy. Much to my surprise the lab diagnosed it as a squamous cell carcinoma skin cancer. When he returned for his follow up visit I explained to him about the unexpected diagnosis and what his options were now given this new information. I further explained that it wasn't that serious. It could be easily cured and would only require a second in office small procedure performed under local anesthesia in a similar manner as the biopsy was done.

Stuart Tobin M.D.

He interrupted me in mid sentence and exploded with all the anger that had been welling up inside of him. "Doc, you don't know what the hell you are talking about. You told me last year that it was just a wart and two weeks ago you told me again that it was just a wart and now you tell me I have a skin cancer. One, you don't know what you are talking about. Two you don't know what you are doing and three you were one of those damn people fighting to get a library and raised my taxes. Why don't you go back to New York where you came from?" He stammered as he stormed out of the office.

It's been my deduced experience that when people list three reasons in life for doing or not doing something reason number three is usually reason number one. When a wife asks her husband to accompany her to the mall to do some shopping, her spouse will often respond with something like, "Honey, I'd love to go but I'm so tired from doing the yard and besides Jim asked me to help him move some stuff and I promised him I'd be around this afternoon if he called and the ballgame starts on TV in half an hour." Reason number three is reason number one. And so it was with my patient I imagined.

The rest of the evening I kept thinking about this incident and the more I thought the more confused I became. Surely, after all my years of practice and experience I could distinguish the clinical difference between a wart and a skin cancer, I thought. However, the most experienced clinicians do make errors and miss diagnoses. I resolved that the next morning I would call the laboratory to discuss the case.

I related my confusion about the diagnosis discrepancy to the secretary of the laboratory on the phone without going into any of the details about the interaction with my patient and asked her to have the pathologist recheck the slide and give me a call back. Later that morning my medical assistant interrupted me with the anticipated returned telephone call. I recognized the voice of my friend and colleague who was not only an experienced clinician but an acknowledged expert in the field of dermatopathology.

"Stu, an error was made. We have just installed a new automated system that prints out the diagnosis and description with a push of the button. As it happened the wart button is number 22 and the squamous cell cancer button is number 23 and I inadvertently pressed number 23 instead of the intended number 22 and it really was a wart," he explained.

"I'll send you a corrected and updated revision of the diagnosis." "Thanks that would be very helpful in this particular case," I added without going into detail. I then sent the patient a certified letter explaining that it had been a wart all along and that the lab had made an error which now had been corrected. I sensed that it didn't make any difference what I sent him and that our professional relationship had ended regardless because one I was a lousy doctor and two I didn't know what I was doing and three I was one of those damn library supporters who had raised his taxes.

Stereotypes

Living in Richmond, Kentucky, a town that borders on rural Appalachia yet lies only twenty-five miles from urban Lexington, provides me with a very mixed patient population base. The residents run the gamut from mountain and country folk, as well as farmers, to middle class businessmen and women, as well as university employees and professors.

One morning I found myself examining a rural farmer who lived out in the county and who because of his fair Celtic Scots/Irish heritage and considerable sunlight exposure became concerned about developing skin cancer. A man in his seventies with a very disarming and gentle manner, he also possessed a very modest education and hadn't graduated from high school. Wearing his bib overalls and well worn denim shirt, I examined him thoroughly and while I didn't find any skin cancers he did have those textural and wrinkling changes so common in people who spend great periods of time outdoors as well as a few actinic keratoses which were precancerous lesions. I dispatched them quickly by freezing them with liquid nitrogen.

After discussing the importance of sun protection and use of an effective sunscreen, I asked him if he had any additional questions. "No, doctor," he answered but commenting on our musical stereo system that played classical music as a background distraction he asked, "Doctor, do you like classical music?"

"Yes, I personally enjoy it. However, the reason I play it in my office is it's the only radio station that my sophisticated and expensive stereo receiver will pick up. I attribute that unique reception to the fact that you can see the radio station and it's antennae from my office. It lies a mere few hundred yards on the University's campus away from where we are sitting while all the other stations are not in visible range," I responded.

"Do you like Mahler?" he now asked. "I guess he's ok, but I prefer the eighteenth and early nineteenth century more traditional classical composers such as Mozart, Beethoven and Schubert," I answered curiously. "Well, doc, my favorite composer is Mahler," he continued. "Why Mahler?" I asked, wondering that my stereotype impression of this delightful and pleasant lifelong resident farmer didn't include an interest in classical music, much less that of Mahler.

"Doc, a few years back my wife and I went to a yard sale. Oh, how the little woman loves yard sales, and she always drags me along. Well, on one of those Saturday mornings someone was selling some classical records of Mahler, and I bought them for a few bucks and started listening to them. I really like Mahler and his music. I have since bought every piece of music that he ever wrote and I have read all about him too. I listen to them all the time and over and over again. I just love Mahler." He concluded triumphantly.

Stereotypes which are born out of either prejudice or experience or both had just been altered at least temporarily in my mind about rural farmers and classical long hair composers. A mix that I neither expected to encounter or hear made me wonder how secure I should be in other stereotypical thoughts I have about other people.

It wasn't long after that encounter that a biker entered my office for evaluation for a jock itch he had acquired from spending many hours riding his Harley on the back roads of Kentucky. A man of forty with a pronounced beer belly and who sported multiple blue tattoos of daggers and women on both arms as well as his chest and who had his hair pulled back into a pony tail of stringy oily hair created a stereotypical impression in my mind of Hell's Angels, The Peacemakers, or some other motorcycle gang.

His face had many ice pick scars and crater like depressions, the remnants of severe acne as a teenager. His black leather wallet dangled from a large silver metal chain attached to his thick black leather belt. All of which accompanied his black leather riding jacket embossed with the name of his motorcycle club.

Stuart Tobin M.D.

He remained genuinely pleasant, polite and attentive during our visit together. I discussed how the long hours on his chopper had created the heat and environment that let the jock itch or fungus grow and that our treatment would incorporate the dual approach of killing the fungus with a prescription anti-fungal medication and secondly, changing the environment to keep the fungus from reestablishing itself.

I wrote a prescription for treatment of his condition and checked off multiple refills for his convenience. He seemed well satisfied with our office visit and thanked me for my time and explanation. As he was about to exit the examining room he turned to me and confided, "Doc, I really like your music and I listen to classical music all the time at home and when I'm on my bike." As he wandered down the hall with the sound of thick leather rubbing and metal chain clanging from his belt I am left speechless as another stereotype is altered as the strains of Schumann's piano concerto wafted in the background.

Not all bikers present with such visible cues announcing their love for the two-wheel culture of the open road. Andy, who owned a jewelry store in town, also was a dedicated motorcycle enthusiast and his shop displays photos of his cycle and an assortment of Harley-Davidson memorabilia. Andy, who has a cherub like countenance with a receding hair line and an advancing waist line, always seemed to have a jewelers magnifying glass either around his neck or close at hand for fine examination of precious stones. I found myself one day in his store looking for a present for my wife and at the time the whole state was embroiled in a controversy about pending legislation of whether motorcyclists should be compelled to wear a protective helmet.

The visual and print media had numerous articles about the pros and cons. The pros centered about the safety and health hazards while the cons revolved about individual rights. It had become the hot topic of conversation and since I love to engage people in conversation, I asked Andy what he thought about the controversial subject.

"Well, doc, I'll tell you a little story that happened to me a few years back. It was a gorgeous day and I had a little free time,

Rash Decisions and Growth Experiences
from the Best Little Warthouse in Kentucky

and I took my Harley out for a spin on some of our county back roads. I hit some gravel and the motorcycle flipped from under me and I was thrown to the ground and if I hadn't been wearing my helmet I would have had a severe head injury and may have been killed," he added emphatically.

From his personal experience I made the inaccurate, although logical leap that he would oppose the legislation granting bike riders the choice of wearing helmets or not. For as Paul Harvey would say, 'for the rest of the story'...... Andy then added, "But you know, doc, I never wear my helmet around town when riding my cycle because nothing is going to happen here," he concluded with a sense of emphatic insight and deliberation.

I thought to myself, if experience is the best teacher in our lives Andy must have been asleep at the handle bars during this most important road lesson of life. Shocked, the only thing I could think to say was, "Andy, what earrings do you have for my wife as a present?" Although I wasn't sure how much I should trust his judgment on this particular subject as well. Anyway, she liked them, so I guess his judgment wasn't too far off base.

Beep, Beep, Beep

Sunday morning, the one morning of the week that the unwanted alarm clock doesn't pierce my sleep cycle and I don't have to rise to an early pre ordained work schedule. Except this Sunday morning. I was in that pleasant twilight sleep that the psychologists call Stage I in which one half of your senses are aware and respond to the environment around you while the other half remain in a drowsy peaceful hypnotic state. Suddenly and unexpectedly a piercing and sharp beeping sound awoke one-half of those senses. One can guess which.

Startled, my cognitive brain kicked in trying to decipher from where the noise was coming and what did it mean. Having heard that sound before, I realized it must be the smoke alarm and the battery must be in need of replacement. Well, since my home has three levels and each has a smoke detector and since there is always the remote possibility that it wasn't a false alarm and that there could really be smoke and consequently fire (having been brought up by parents whose favorite metaphor was "Where's there smoke there's fire") was now ringing in my head.

To be sure I decided to investigate. So I dragged myself out of bed and checked each alarm on each floor, and feeling confident that the house was not ablaze, returned to my warm and comfy bed (which was no longer warm) in an attempt to recapture that drowsy Stage I sleep. Stage I sleep became a higher priority than battery replacement.

As I nestled back into bed with the comforter around me, I again heard an intermittent sharp singular piercing beeping noise every sixty seconds. Suddenly it occurred to me that the noise that I thought was the smoke alarm in reality was my beeper. Being a dermatologist and having performed surgeries on Friday two days before, the beeper almost invariably was announcing that one of my post operative patients was having a serious problem.

So I reached for that little black rectangular box which is more like an electronic leash that lay on my bed stand and depressed the large red button. Immediately an LED display of a telephone number with that familiar greeting of a new message flashed across the screen. So I fumbled for the phone and punched in those identical numbers. Well, I thought they were the identical numbers and got a busy signal. I tried again and still got a busy response. I couldn't locate my glasses and discovered after the third attempt that I had transposed two numbers.

Since I couldn't remember where I had left my eyeglasses I fumbled for a magnifying glass which was lying on my bed stand and would serve just as well. This time after punching in the correct number I got my third favorite Bell South recording. "The number you dialed is no longer a working number, if you'd like to try again....." For those who are interested, my second favorite recording is "We will keep trying this number for you for the next half hour for an additional charge of 30 cents" and survey says the all time winner for the favorite message is "If you'd like to make a call," followed by a piercing sharp unrelenting beeping noise for those of you like me who suffer from obsessive compulsive disorder lasts exactly 90 seconds. Needless to say, by this time I have had my limits tested to shrill beeping noises on what had been a peaceful Sunday morning.

Also, by this time I'm quite alert and have convinced myself that someone out there needed my assistance and that this failure of modern technology wouldn't keep this medical knight from locating a frantic patient with a post operative emergency and coming to their rescue. Reasoning that since I tell all my patients to call the hospital if they need me after regular office hours, I decided to call the local hospital.

So I dialed the Pattie A. Clay hospital, casually wondering how many times it would take the average person to press telephone keys to get a callous on their index finger. This thought was interrupted by a pre-recorded message announcing that "If you have an emergency you can dial "0" now or any time to interrupt this message." By this time I knew it was an emergency so I punched in with great force "0" and the prerecorded message continued unabated and unimpressed by the strength of my index finger against the "0" key. I was inadvertently testing my own hypothesis of index callous formation. The message continued to list all my options from contacting patient rooms to billing inquires. Again and again I punched in "0" with greater force each time to no avail. Did I mention that by this time I had revised my list of favorite recorded messages and that the hospitals prerecord was climbing the charts and rivaling that of the phone company?

Finally, I got a live voice connected to a live person who sounded bored and or annoyed that someone was calling the hospital with an emergency on a Sunday morning. I told her who I was and patiently inquired if anyone was attempting to get a hold of me. My greatest fear at this time was now realized. "Yes, doctor one of your surgery patients needed to talk to you." I briefly asked why the wrong number came up on my LED beeper display. I knew better than to ask having had similar encounters with many individuals over the years in similar circumstances only to discover how clever is the human species in inventing plausible fictional explanations, all of which have the same theme, "It's not my fault, it's your fault because....."

Given the order of priorities that now were on my mind, I felt locating the patient was of greater urgency and importance than locating the truth from the hospital operator. So I asked for the patient's phone number, which had no resemblance to the original phone number displayed on my beeper but which became indelibly displayed in my mind even more than my own phone number.

So with great speed and anticipation I now dialed the correct number, and this time no busy signal, no prerecorded message and an actual non-piercing, non-irritating familiar ringing sound greeted my ear. A male teenager's voice answered and I announced to him that, "This is Dr. Tobin." Anticipating that the whole family had been anxiously awaiting this return phone call, he said, "Wait a moment, I'll get my dad." After a moment another voice asked, "What do I want?" Again I repeated that, "This is Dr. Tobin" and he said, "Hold on a moment while I get him." Figuring that there can't be many more family members performing triage, certainly the next person that I talk with will be the dad, aka my patient.

Finally, I recognized my patient's voice from whom I had removed a large skin cancer from his cheek. Has the area become infected or has be had unusual bleeding or has the pain become unbearable and unresponsive to the pain medication that I had prescribed? He then informed me what the early Sunday morning emergency was. "Doc, I had been working out yesterday and had sweated profusely and the bandage had come off. I had gone to Walmart and couldn't find the ouch-less Band-Aids that you had recommended to purchase in the event that the dressing accidentally came off." He seemed more upset that he couldn't find this particular type of Band-Aids than the dressing had come off and that I should have warned him that Walmart that has everything didn't stock ouch-less Band-Aids.

All the time the following thoughts are racing through my mind, "profusely sweating?" I spent two hours outside yesterday, cleaning out my gutters, digging holes for plants and bushes and then an additional three hours at a picnic flipping hamburgers and cooking hot dogs in front of a hot grill blowing smoke in my face on a beautiful spring cool 70 degree day and I didn't sweat. What the hell was this guy doing? Why the hell didn't he just get another band-aid that wasn't "ouch-less"? And of course why didn't he read the post-op information sheet that explained how to handle such a "crisis", that same instruction sheet that cautioned against any excessive activity that would unloosen or remove the Ban-Aid dressing because of "profuse sweating." To be sure that there wouldn't be any confusion I had also verbally instructed him on what was written down. All these thoughts flashed through my mind as I was now "profusely sweating."

I asked him if he had remembered us discussing these scenarios and how to handle them. I knew intuitively that would be an exercise in frustration. He must have been related to the hospital operator since his answer came off as a variation similar to hers, "It's not my fault," it's yours with more than the hint of suggestion that I had failed my charge by not instructing him adequately. All of which I ignored and just suggested that he return to Walmart and purchase a non ouch-less Ban-Aid to cover the area. Was that the end of this medical odyssey? Not quite.

My wife was annoyed at me, not for waking her up on a Sunday morning because of a patient's perceived surgical non-emergency but for waking her up while I was working at my computer attempting to capture the mood and essence of this little misadventure on my word processor. To which I responded "It wasn't my fault!" I can't help it if I responded to my emotions in a constructive therapeutic way by putting them down on paper articulating them verbally as I typed.

Rural Settings and Urban Prejudices

Regardless of how much education, experiences, or insight we have in life, some of our prejudices are so deeply rooted that they just cannot be dug out of our psyche. They lie in our inner core and define us as unique human beings. Under my own veneer lies one of those prejudices burrowed into the deepest rings of my own mind and which has grown into the pulp of my soul. That firmly planted bias is: NEVER TRUST THE JUDGMENT OF ANYONE WHO HAS BEEN NAMED AFTER A POPULATION CENTER OF GREATER THAN A MILLION.

It was Monday morning and I was facing a deluge of patients and work-ins. It's difficult enough to start the week with a rush of enthusiasm after a weekend of hobbies and family. That may be why the Carpenters hit song of the early seventies *Rainy Days and Mondays Make Me Sad* resonates with so many of us. My first patient of this particular rainy Monday morning was Dallas, a part time barley tobacco farmer, whose occupation had enhanced his six feet tall and muscular frame. I hadn't seen Dallas for about a year and now found him in my office. I walked into the exam room with my hand outstretched and my customary smile, which was more forced than usual, followed by my standard overture greeting of, "How are you doing today, Dallas?"

I noticed a different Dallas than I had seen before. He seemed ill at ease, avoiding direct eye contact as well as shifting his bulky portly frame uncomfortably in the exam chair. Small beads of perspiration settled on his crown in the air conditioned exam room. He appeared easily distracted as if engaged in some deep impenetrable

70

thought. We always use the term deep thought when we really mean deep feelings of emotion. In our modern, technologically oriented western culture it is always less threatening to mask our emotions as thoughts. Dallas's body language betrayed a sense of heightened anxiety. Dallas was definitely having a rainy Monday. Dotting the "I's" and crossing the "T's" needed to be done. So I decided to probe a little.

"Dallas," I asked somewhat casually but with an air of professional concern, "You seem as if something is bothering you?" I remembered from my psychiatry rotation in medical school that the leading question followed by the interminable pause while your eyes remain fixed on the patient is one of the more effective techniques to elicit the desired response. While this may work well and convincingly in a professional office setting, I would advise against attempting it at home with your spouse, unless you wish to escalate mild annoyance into the full spectrum of rage and anger. Since we weren't at home and since Dallas wasn't my spouse, he opened up and recounted the following dominoes of events that had tumbled his world earlier that morning. "Doc, I have this old favorite pick-up truck that I let me ten year old son start every morning. He can't really reach the accelerator pedal so I tied a brick on the pedal so he could reach it."

All the time he's ventilating, I'm thinking there probably isn't a large demand in the pick-up truck market even in rural Appalachia to accommodate ten-year-old children's leg distance, followed in rapid succession with the incredulous emotional response, you let your ten-year-old son start a dangerous vehicle every morning unsupervised!

He rambles on, "Well, doc, this morning his arm slipped, hitting the gear and putting the truck into reverse. The car started to go backwards and he knew something was wrong. He reached with his foot to hit the brake but hit the brick instead." Of course this could happen to any ten-year-old starting a pick-up truck, especially since both brick and brake start with "br".

He anxiously continued, "Well that mother took off like a rocket, down the driveway and across the street, knocking over the mailbox, crashing through a bunch of neighbor's bushes and finally coming to rest in a small gully after hitting a tree. I ran across the street just as the boy jumped off the truck. He was crying and all he wanted to do was run to his mother. The boy wasn't hurt, but damn if he didn't ruin my truck. There's my favorite old truck with tires bent off the rim and the hood crushed beyond repair. Damn! The wife was kind of upset though."

I'm wondering was his wife upset because of the possible injury to her son that he had miraculously avoided or because the truck was destroyed? If it's because of the truck damage what large population center is she named after? Since I'm more interested in how this adventure unfolds, I suppress the urge to glance in his medical chart to see if her name is Paris or Savannah.

He continued and concluded with, "Well the boy was ok, shaken up some but I made him go off to school. Damn, my truck was ruined!" He again repeated. "And that's what happened this morning, doc." He finished his tale and slumped back into his chair with a sigh, relieved having gotten all this off his chest.

After listening to this catharsis of incredible events, I decided to explore a little further. I said in my most professional non-judgmental understanding voice, "You know, Dallas, sometimes God or the universe is trying to talk to us to teach us something from things that happen to us." I could have gone on with other analogies such as what doesn't kill us makes us strong or good judgment comes from experience and experience comes from bad judgment, or out of our greatest failures comes our greatest opportunities, or even quoted from Shakespeare's *As You Like It*, "Sweet are the uses of adversity…." Quoting the great bard to Dallas seemed a bit of a stretch anyway. But I think I had penetrated enough and continued with, "What do you think you learned from this experience?" followed by the customary interminable pause and the non-judgmental expectant and penetrating fixed stare.

Again Dallas picked up on the cue and without hesitation piqued up, "You know doc, I've been thinking about that all morning and I figure next time if I use a block of wood instead of a brick it'll be ok." I wondered if only his head could spare the knotty pine. Feeling that he had missed the point entirely I decided to phrase my point in another way and come at it from a different direction. So I related to him a story I had just read the previous day in the newspaper.

"You know, Dallas, it's odd that you should have just had this unfortunate experience, but just yesterday I was reading *The Lexington Herald Leader* (which is our local newspaper), and buried in the city section was an article about a woman who was returning a video to the Blockbuster's Video in Louisville. She too had, what a coincidence, her ten-year-old son, the same age as yours, with her. She left her van idling and ran into the video rental for just a 'second' to return a movie and the son also accidentally placed the car into gear. This time it was drive and the vehicle crashed through the front window of Blockbuster and killed a college student standing in line."

Dallas's body language now changed from wandering all over the anxiety map to a fixed latitude of certainty and a longitude of conviction. He leaned over and looked me in the eye to be sure he had my undivided attention. With great assurance and with the conviction that only comes from knowing a GPS eternal truth, he punctured the air with a rising volume in his voice. With his index finger piercing from the true north of his personal epiphany insight, he pronounced the Dallas Doctrine, "Doc, let me tell you, it's like riding a horse. If you fall off and don't get right back up again you ain't never going to ride again!"

Visions of a ten-year-old boy back in the saddle of a 200 horsepower engine guided by his father's horse nonsense raced across my mind. I realized that Dallas and Doc were riding on two very different tracks, two tracks that were unlikely ever to meet. His logic lay in the valley and mine on the crest, or so I believed.

The anxious and depressed Dallas that had entered my office a short time before now exited as an angry and self-assured patient. So it is that the source of all anger is pain and if internalized manifests as depression but externalized translates to anger. As he stomps from the exam room slamming the door I pondered rhetorically, so who protects the children of the world from the Dallas parenting of the world? Never to be seen again by this physician, Dallas left the office that morning to farm and continue his wayward parenting with the unshakable conviction that he was right and doc was wrong. Although Dallas didn't seem to gain a lot of insight from our patient physician interaction, what wisdom did I acquire? This experience just further entrenched my long standing deep seated prejudice: NEVER TRUST THE JUDGMENT OF ANYONE WHO IS NAMED AFTER A POPULATION CENTER OF GREATER THAN A MILLION.

As I left the exam room shaking my head in disbelief but not without surprise, I surveyed my appointment schedule for the rest of the day. I couldn't help but notice that my two thirty afternoon patient later in the day would be Houston. Yes, middle aged with a maximum midriff, good old boy Houston who is a local plumber and who had "fixed" my leaky faucet at home every other week last summer until I had it repaired by another plumber not named after a large population center, and the water never dripped again. Yes, Mondays and rainy days can make you sad or ....smile.

The Date with Fate

My single status led me to seek out company from the opposite gender. While living in Richmond I had met an attractive woman who had originally migrated from Scotland to the Bluegrass and was living in rural Appalachian Powell County where she had built a home. "Annie's" slender and petite delicate female frame, however, housed a will of iron. She weighed a scant 100 lbs with a narrow waist and porcelain Celtic skin.

Her eyes were her most engaging feature. Those huge blue eyes just sparkled. If the eyes are the window to the soul, hers were a bay window vista with an endless enticing panoramic view to the human horizon and beyond. They radiated a striking intelligence but warned of a woman of independence and hinted at a sense of timeless mystery and hidden vulnerability. Yet at the same time they beckoned.

When I say she built a home she literally built her own home. A trained nurse practitioner and an untrained carpenter, she was actively constructing her house from lumber and nails with hammer and saw from a mental blueprint. Eschewing power tools, she labored on the A framed house that would eventually be completed as her home.

At the time we briefly dated she was actively digging a trench with a shovel to capture run off rainwater from the side of the mountain to funnel into a cistern to become her only source of fresh drinking water. She didn't have electricity either and heated the house and loft with a potbelly firewood stove.

I have always found it fascinating how some women express their independence in different ways. That physical shelter from nature's harsh elements in one of Kentucky's most rural Appalachian communities became for her the symbol of independence that guarded her from the pain of vulnerability and dependence on others.

She had expressed to me an eager interest in seeing the Alvin Bailey Dance Troupe which was touring central Kentucky at the time. I told her I would arrange for a couple of tickets for its one and only performance in the Bluegrass. She was difficult to reach in her modest and primitive home that lacked almost all of those conveniences including reliable phone service. Communication with her remained challenging and infrequent. All my homing pigeons had flown their coop. Even if they hadn't she probably wouldn't have been able to read my medical handwriting attached to their banded legs. So we had prearranged to meet in Lexington for dinner before the concert.

Not anticipating that many other Kentuckians shared her interest in modern dance, I delayed calling for reservations until the day before. When I finally made the phone call I was informed that "the performance was completely sold out." That expression has always confused me, as if a performance could be incompletely sold out.

Anyway, we had agreed to meet at an upscale French restaurant for dinner a couple of hours beforehand. When I called the restaurant also for reservations the maitre-de informed me that they too had no tables available that evening. Since I couldn't reach her I decided just to meet as we had previously agreed and confess to her of our plight and hoped that she had left her shovel at home and wouldn't "ditch" me on the spot.

Arriving at the restaurant that evening shortly before 7:00, I found to my pleasant surprise every table empty. The maitre de greeted me with the expected and usual, "Can I help you, sir?" "Yes," nonplussed and casually I responded, "I would like a table for two for dinner." "Of course, sir," Upon leading me to a table which shared a generous view of the parking lot, I demanded, "This just won't do. The cozy one by the fire would be much better?" "Of course, sir." He answered contritely.

Annie arrived shortly afterwards. After updating me on the ditch, the dirt, and the cistern's progress and welcoming her from the trenches, I told her of my mishaps of planning. I quickly and enthusiastically added, "You, know Annie, I really think this is going to be our lucky night. First, they told me that the restaurant had no tables and we got one so easily. I just sense that if we venture to the theater that we'll serendipitously get some tickets. So let's give it a try." I don't know if it was my Horatio Alger gregarious outlook or the fine French capons that convinced her but she relented and agreed.

Off to the box office we raced arriving just in time in hopes of seeing the much heralded dance performance. Standing in line in front of us were two other couples also without tickets, both of whom were immediately informed that the performance was "completely (and not incompletely) sold out."

Realizing that I wouldn't have any more success than they, I casually shifted to the next line which was "will call." Confidently, I engaged the young girl guarding those preciously reserved tickets in those neat little white vellum envelopes and I addressed her with a casual monotone voice, "Tobin, two tickets called in advance."

She thumbed through all those envelopes that contained tickets reserved in advance. Unable to locate mine, she answered apologetically, "Sir, I can't find them." Struggling to think of my next move, I rejoined with a hint of irritation peppered with desperation. "Look again, they must be there."

A dignified man in his forties with a finely trimmed black moustache and his hair fashionably combed back and dressed in a neatly pressed black tuxedo apparently witnessing our interaction turned to me and asked, "Sir, I'm the manager. What seems to be the problem?"

Not wanting to share with him that the problem was that I had procrastinated in obtaining a couple of tickets, I diverged. "They seem unable to locate my tickets." "Could they be under your first name?" he now questioned. "Possibly so," I answered, knowing well unless there was some hapless fool also named Tobin Stuart who just out of coincidence decided to stay at home to watch a football game on TV instead of attending the dance performance and consequently relinquished his two seats and seventy five dollars I would be out of luck.

"No, sir, they're not there," came his answer after reviewing all those little envelopes again. To buy more time I countered, "I just don't understand what happened. I told my secretary to call and reserve two seats for tonight's only performance. She is so efficient and I'm sure she did so. And we have traveled from out of town to see this once in a life time event. We would be so disappointed if unable to do so." I now pleaded.

"I think I know what the problem is," the tuxedoed manager announced with the confidence that comes from a man in charge who provides impeccable service to the arts oriented public and has deduced the solution to the disappearing dance ticket mystery dilemma. Of course it was no mystery to me. I'm also thinking if he really knows what the problems is he's also a mind reader in which case I'd better find a quick exit strategy.

"Are you with the phone company?" he now unexpectedly asked. Now I'm thinking, "Am I with the phone company?" Yeah, I have been with Bell South as my phone company's local carrier service provider for years. Not having the slightest idea where any of this was going, I answered with a hint of surprise and self assurance, "As a matter of fact I am!" "Well that solves the mystery of the missing tickets." I confidently nodded in agreement not having a clue why.

"The phone company has reserved a block of tickets for tonight's performance and somehow your name must have been misplaced." "Of course!" I echoed in agreement with a sigh of relief. "Unfortunately, we don't have two tickets together in that block and I regret that you two will be separated," he lamented. Not wanting to push the little white vellum envelope, I answered with a hint of resignation and relief, "That's perfectly all right considering the circumstances. That will be a small but necessary inconvenience."

He gave us the two tickets and we arrived at our seats just as the curtain rose. During the intermission of the performance, he noticed us standing in the hallway of the theatre chatting about the elegance of the performance and the talent of the dancers. He approached us with an expansive smile over his face and said, "I have located two seats together so you can enjoy the performance together."

I responded with, "You have been very kind. Not only have you extended yourself for two people that you don't even know, but you also have made this a very special evening for us with your generosity, thoughtfulness, and charm. Thank you very much." I concluded as I reached out and shook his hand in genuine appreciation.

"We are having a special reception after the performance for select patrons and the dance group. Would you like to attend?" He now offered. "Of course, that sounds surprisingly delightful as well as irresistible," I answered not wanting him to suffer a sense of rejection or ingratitude on my part.

As we settled into our new seats in the middle of the orchestra section, Annie, who had been quiet throughout this successful charade, turned to me and announced, "We are not going to that reception!" "Why not? It'll be fun and who knows what further mischief and adventure we might encounter?" I added. "I am NOT going to that reception and that's final!" I have seen that determination in those independent ice blue eyes before and knew that if I went it would be a solo appearance.

That ended our night of fate and fun. I enjoyed the quest of getting there more than the actual dance performance or as the Greyhound Bus TV commercials used to say, half the fun was getting there. Although Annie's and my dating relationship didn't last, the memories of that untold eventful and uncertain evening of events did. Did I feel any slight pangs of remorse from my deception of that night? Let me just dance around that question.

Postscript: I did send a generous donation in a small white vellum envelope to the university a few weeks later which more than made up for cost of the tickets.

A House is Not a Home

Early in my developing medical practice career, I, like so many young physicians attempting to establish a practice, found that I had more time than patients. In an attempt to reverse that ratio I contacted one of the more established dermatologists in neighboring Lexington to inquire if he could utilize my services. Consequently, I found myself commuting a day or two a week to his practice doing locum tenens.

My professional colleague who was to become a lifelong peer was very conscious and proud of his English heritage and had located throughout his office memorabilia and photographs of the United Kingdom which apparently isn't as united or as much as a kingdom as in days past. One morning as I was attending to his patients, I being my chatty self was behind schedule as usual.

I walked into one of his examining rooms to be greeted by a pleasant and casually, but smartly dressed and apparently educated and well traveled Lexingtonian wearing khaki pants and a racing green golf pullover with loafers and who was in his early forties. After the customary introductions and pleasantries were exchanged, he turned to me and asked. "Doctor, I have been in this room for about fifteen minutes and there aren't any magazines to scan and I didn't bring a book or a newspaper to read. The only thing to look at is that wonderful and spectacular photograph of an English castle on the wall."

For the first time in my friend's office I noticed this beautiful black and white photo of a medieval stone castle complete with an aging stone turret. All of which spoke of history, cultural heritage, and connection to a British past. The ancient and weather-worn castle sat surrounded by lush vegetation in a bucolic setting of rolling

80

hills in the English countryside. It certainly was a striking and scenic picture, and I could understand why he was drawn to it.

He continued, "You, know doctor, as I stared at this impressive castle, I began to wonder if this is just a photograph you hung in your office for decoration, or could it have some personal meaning that resonates with you?" Without afore or after thought and without hesitation I blurted out. "Yes, it indeed does have a personal connection. The photo is a picture of my ancestral home. But less you become confused it's not the castle but the tree next to it that my ancestors descended from."

My whole life has been in service of humor and this was an opportunity I just couldn't resist. He wasn't quite sure how to react and seemed more bewildered than amused. Perhaps he was disappointed to discover that I was more related to comedy off Broadway than Counts from Britain. I guess he was about to count me out. In any event, I thought it best just to shift the focus back to his skin problem and treat him.

World War II

For many years I have had an interest in the Second World War and have read a number of books to learn about that terrible catastrophe that engulfed and consumed my parents generation. When a patient would mention that they had served in that conflagration my interest would peak and I would frequently ask them if they would mind telling me about their own personal experiences. Most marvel that someone of my generation had even heard about Saipan, the Battle of Leyte Gulf or Tinian Island. These overtures have been generously rewarded with personal historical vignettes reminiscences by many of my fellow Kentuckians.

Darrell was one such patient who had served in the U.S. Army during World War II. Because of his fair Celtic skin combined with his sunlight exposure on the sub-continent of what is now India and Pakistan as well as having served on Tinian inevitably led him to my office for removal of multiple skin cancers and pre cancer treatments.

He was a man modest in circumstances with a short cropped white hair crew cut and he always looked to be in need of a shave. While serious of demeanor he had a sly smile and keen sense of humor. I would be rapt in attention as he told of how the "natives" could throw one of their home made knives a distance of fifty or sixty feet and the knife would land on its intended target and exit the other side of the person at which it was directed.

One day he returned for a follow-up visit and he had brought two gifts for me. "Doc, I don't know many people who would appreciate these items and I really don't have anyone to leave them to and I thought you would like them. So I brought them for you."he said.

"Well, thank you so much," I responded with amazement on my face and pleasure in my voice. "This is the Gurka knife I was telling you about, Doc," as he held in his hand a 13-inch long steel knife shaped like a boomerang with a 2-inch wide razor sharp blade that would rival any of my surgical scalpels.

As the blade tapered to the wooden ringed handle there were two small "U" shaped notches resembling a can opener which apparently could be used for some unknown purpose. The handle had eight circular rings in its native wood polished grip. The most intriguing part was the hand etched and engraved dotted and whorled intricate lace like design with a letter "A" and what appeared to be a floral pattern on one side of the blade. All of which remains a mystery to me as to its meaning.

As time has passed I have resisted the temptation to decipher it's meaning and rather hold onto a cacophony of imaginations as to what stories this knife could tell if it could.

The second gift related to his second tour of duty on the tiny but immensely strategically important island of Tinian in the South Pacific Ocean. The capture of Tinian during World War II had great importance in the air war against the empire of Japan. The island's geography allowed the new B-29 super fortress bombers to strike at the heartland of Japan and return without refueling.

Darrell was stationed there in 1944 and 1945. On the island was a special detachment of B-29s that were kept isolated from all the other planes. These were the planes that were training for the first and only dropping of the atomic bombs in 1945.

Darrell now showed me a stainless steel sixteen ounce coffee mug with a flip top that would keep the coffee inside from spilling all over the cockpit while these planes were airborne on their long and difficult missions. The only markings on the mug were the number "2" and directly under it the letter "B." What that meant has also eluded me over the years.

"Doc," he continued, "I was also stationed on Tinian. After the Japanese surrendered we gathered up all these mugs from that special detachment of planes and I took this one home as a souvenir.

"I can't tell you for sure that it came from the Enola Gay (the B-29 that dropped the first atomic bomb on Hiroshima) but there's a damn good chance that it did." "Wow!" I said. He with his sly smile said, "Doc, say that backward." "Wow!" I repeated with a smile added to my shock and amazement. As he left we shook hands, not the handshake of patient and physician parting after an office visit but a longer and firmer handshake of friendship and gratitude.

It wasn't too long after this exchange that I read in *The Richmond Register* obituaries of his passing and felt more of a personal loss than I had previously. The Gurka knife lies in a display case in my library at home and the coffee mug sits on a shelf of prominence in that same room next to a photograph of the Enola Gay. Anyone who is foolish enough to wander into that room is subjected to the story of each.

The photo of the Enola Gay was taken a week after that B-29 delivered its devastating payload beginning the Nuclear Age, the consequence of which my generation has had to deal with. I don't know what it is about the island of Tinian and Kentuckians with skin diseases but another patient who was attached to the photographic unit at the same time Darell was brought to the office a number of original photos of the Enola Gay.

He presented me a small 2x2 inch original black and white print as a gift. I thanked him profusely and then asked him if he would let me borrow the larger fading 8x10 inch print for a few days so that I could download it onto my computer and store it on Photoshop. He readily agreed and I returned it to him along with a few extra enhanced 8x10 inch glossies as a means of saying thank you. He seemed well pleased with that gift.

I was telling these story vignettes to another patient and friend of mine who was a retired one star army brigadier general. I joked with him that he was an Army General, a Kentucky Colonel and that his wife and friends found him a Major nuisance. He listened intently to my World War II stories with my other patients. It wasn't very long until he brought me a copy of the top secret orders issued that fateful day to Captain Paul Tibbets, the pilot of the Enola Gay. Now if that wasn't a fascinating and exciting read.

Damn You Doctor

Kroger supermarket has the greatest selection and freshest produce in our town. I found myself doing the weekly shopping on a free afternoon. As I passed from aisle to aisle pushing and filling my bascart with fruits, vegetables, meats and canned and dry goods checking compulsively the cholesterol and fat content of each package, I noticed a rather large and unkempt seventyish man who was dressed somewhere between a street person and a tenant farmer.

He had on dirty Bibb overalls and was wearing a layer of three flannel shirts. The first was a burnt orange plaid, the second a dark green and the last a faded red striped. Two of the three shirt tails hung out from his britches. A bulky and tattered kerlix white gauze dressing protruded from the frayed denim cuff of his right leg. The dressing must have extended down the entire foot since you could see it unraveling from his large big toe which was quite visible through the hole he had not so carefully cut from the top of his tattered and well worn shoe. The shoe laces were gone and the bulk of his foot and dressing kept him from losing them.

His thinning white matted hair had the appearance that comes from assiduously avoiding shampoo for extended periods of time. The most curious thing about him was that every time I would wander down an aisle there he was twenty feet behind me. As I traversed from canned vegetables to frozen foods to house hold items he kept reappearing.

Having watched a few detective mystery movies I decided to double back to an aisle that I already visited to determine whether I was truly being followed. So I pushed my cart of half full groceries back to the detergent aisle to pick up the fabric softener that I had forgotten to get anyway. As I placed it into my cart I casually looked over my shoulder and again there he stood.

Rash Decisions and Growth Experiences
from the Best Little Warthouse in Kentucky

I now was convinced that I was being followed. Why am I being stalked? While the thought of confronting him fleeting passed through my mind, my instincts said ignore the situation and just finish your shopping. I decided to go with my instincts. After a couple more passes down aisles ten, eleven and twelve to pick up a few last minute items I proceeded to the check out counter. After paying for my groceries I pushed the cart out of the store and as I not so casually turned around behind me. A sigh of relief, he wasn't there.

As I proceeded into the parking lot, however, there he stood waiting for me and approached me and without even the courtesy of an introduction angrily stammered, "My leg ain't no better!" Of course it flashed through my mind he must be one of my patients and I just didn't recognize him.

Usually and often as I encounter patients in public that I don't remember I'll remark, "I'm sorry I didn't recognize you with your clothing on." This works well especially with the opposite gender to disarm and cover my embarrassment and elicit a smile. I sensed that in this particular instance my wit would not carry the day. So I put on my most professional demeanor.

"You, know sir I don't have your medical record with me and it would be inappropriate to examine you in the parking lot. If you're not any better, why don't you call the office tomorrow and I'll reevaluate your problem and see if we could move in a more positive direction to help you," I replied.

My instincts are now telling me that I need to move in a more positive direction myself which would mean away from him. He snapped back. "You, just want my money. You just want me to come back to your office so you can charge me more money." While his skin and limb may be impaired his vocal chords were not as he raised the decibel level and volume of his voice. Attempting to regain control of this escalating deteriorating situation I reacted.

"I'm sorry you feel that way, but I would like to help you, but here is not the place nor is it the time and if cost is an issue I'll make allowances to assist you." "No, no, all you want is my money," he shot back even louder and angrier. Am I detecting a recurrent theme in his one track thought I muse. People are now walking by and beginning to notice this interaction. So I made an important and crucial decision.

I gauged his infirmity and decided that I could resolve this confrontation easily. I decided not to answer him which I felt would undoubtedly just lead to that same old familiar chorus of, "All you want is my money" and what funds he had certainly didn't make it to his wardrobe. Following my instincts I decided to initiate an exit strategy. Off I took running pushing my groceries ahead of me as fast as one can go pushing ten sacks of produce in a shopping cart in a paved parking lot. He in limping pursuit all the time shouting at the top of his lungs and waving his cane menacingly at me, "All you want is my money! All you want is my money!!"

I made it to my car and threw the plastic bags onto the backseat in a non obsessive compulsive manner. I sped off with him shrinking in my rear view window waving his hand at me and not with the friendliest gesture of good-bye I hope to see you soon. The chorus of, "All you want is my money," trailed off into the background like a song's medley. In this particular case distance did make the heart grow fonder, at least for me. That was the end of the story, and the end of the parking lot consult, and also the end of our physician patient relationship. Thankfully he never showed up again in my life.

Thank you Doctor

It was the middle of the week in the middle of the month of mid-Summer and I was half way through the morning attending to my patients. Practicing as long as I have in a small tight knit community has all the benefits of small town life which is everyone knows everyone else, but also suffers from the disadvantages of small town living which is everyone knows everyone else. As I reviewed the chart sitting in the small bin in front of the exam room a smile came over my face as I recognized my next patient.

Smoot was recently new to my practice but his wife had been a patient of mine for a number of years and I had become quite fond of both of them. Ruth had a winning smile and the most brilliant long natural wavy red hair I had ever seen. Every time she visited the office the same thought crossed my mind. How long does it take her to dry those long auburn locks and how difficult and painful it must be to drag a brush through such a forest of long entangled strands? Such thoughts always remained where they originated and never made the leap from my mind to my mouth.

Many women from the country will wear their hair long because of religious reasons. Others do so out of cultural habit and Ruth was one of the latter. She had that easy open confiding manner that many mountain and Appalachian women exude and you never have to guess what they're thinking. They articulate their feelings candidly and without hesitation. If they like you, you know it if they don't you know it.

She had encouraged her husband to see me for some non-healing sores on his leg and arm which had been present for a number of months. He had returned for follow-up on those sores. Patient referrals are always so much easier to deal with than physician referrals. I know when a peer has sent me a patient to evaluate or consult on I have to prove myself to them. However, when a new patient is referred by a spouse, friend or relative I have a lot less to prove. One would think it would be the other way around. However, when a friend refers you to a physician they can and will ask all the questions that they can't ask their physician. What's he like? Does he know what's he's talking about? Do I have to wait forever in the waiting room? What does he charge? Is he personable? Did he help you with your problem? When was the last time a patient asked their referring physician those same questions? And even if the referring doctor had been asked in all likelihood he couldn't answer any of them anyway.

Smoot succumbed to his wife's persistent request and presented with two large crusted ulcer like sores with a thick ring like edge, one on his ankle and the other or his upper shoulder. They had all the features of a deep and serious fungus infection called North American Blastomycoses which usually invades the lungs and makes its way to the skin as the presenting symptom. Most commonly it occurs in farmers.

I had biopsied the lesion and confirmed the diagnosis and he was now entering his fifth month of treatment for this potentially dangerous infection and had responded well to the oral ketoconazole medication with both the skin and lung lesions clearing. Both he and I were very pleased with his improving and uncomplicated course.

Clutching his chart in one hand and opening the door with the other I entered the room with a large and hopefully contagious smile and they both responded with the same. "So, Smoot how are you doing?" I asked. "I'm doing just great, Doc. All the spots have healed," he happily related.

"Doc," he continued, "I know a man back at home who had the same thing I had but they didn't figure it out like you did and he got sores all over his body and he died. He looked just awful the last days of his life. I'm so really lucky that I came to see you," he said with a genuine sigh of relief.

"Smoot, I don't know what your friend had and sometimes different conditions can look similar and can be challenging to diagnose even in the most experienced hands. If we are going to thank anyone let's not forget the pathologist who interpreted your biopsy for me. Of course the person you should be most grateful to is Ruth who made you come here," I added embarrassed by this sudden rush of adoration.

"No, Doc, he had Blastomycoses, I know it for a fact," He explained emphatically. "Well, Smoot I don't know about your friend and I'm sorry that he had died, but I am glad that you are doing so well." "So am I, Doc."

My eye now spied a large brown cardboard crate sitting next to him. It was the type of crate that college students used to move items from their home to their dorm or apartment; large enough to hold a lot of stuff yet can be carried by an average adult.

He noticed my gaze which was now fixed in curiosity at the cardboard box at his feet. "My wife and I just finished harvesting the garden and thought you would like some vegetables," he confided. Do you garden, Doc?" "No, I do all my gardening at Kroger supermarket," I sheepishly and jokingly answered.

"Well, we thought you'd like some fresh vegetables." The box was now open and there crammed from top to bottom was a cornucopia of summer squash, cucumbers of all sizes, and types of tomatoes from small delicate miniatures to robust splitting at their seams beefsteaks as well as large ripened green tomatoes.

"Thank you so much, I never expected anything like this. My wife and I love fresh vegetables and we'll certainly put them to good use." Although they didn't respond verbally, the broad smile of satisfaction that the gift was well received radiated across both their faces. Accepting gifts has always been challenging for me and many times in the past I have tried to return them because of a certain level of embarrassment I have felt. It has taken me quite a long time to become a gracious gift receiver. As they left the office I felt their genuine gratitude and generosity and knew that they had received more than I did in that act of giving and thanks.

The rest of the morning progressed uneventfully as I would think between patients how excited, surprised and pleased my wife would be with all the fresh produce. After returning from lunch I started attending to the afternoon schedule of patients, screening for skin cancers, following up on small surgical procedures and treating acne and warts. About mid-afternoon, Sharon came in to see me for some growths she wanted evaluated.

Sharon had been my patient for the past few years and she was a grandmother who was now placed in the role as guardian and parent to her grandchild. She would always proudly update me on how he was growing. She also had a lifetime passion for hunting Indian artifacts and had scoured many areas of the county in search of arrowheads, and other Native American tools.

Kentucky for many centuries had served as a hunting ground for the Adena Indians but never had a permanent Native American presence despite the location of numerous burial mounds that pepper the countryside and now are protected by state law.

On her previous visit she had brought to the office a gray stone pipe with fine delicate symbols very intricately etched onto the surface and painstakingly hollowed out with rudimentary tools that she had found. In her twenty five years of digging the ploughed fields and farmlands of our county she had never found anything quite like it. She estimated it to be over five thousand years old. I was so impressed by the find that I had photographed it and contacted a friend anthropologist/archaeologist at Eastern Kentucky University about this most unusual artifact. The two did meet to talk about the find.

As she updated me on her grandchild and as I answered her questions on her moles, the conversation inevitably shifted to her long time hobby and passion. I asked her if she had found anything new of interest lately. "Nothing unusual," she said, "but I did bring you a present," as she removed a small rumpled brown paper bag from her purse. "What is it?" I asked curiously. "I brought you some arrowheads and Indian tools." She then produced the most exquisite stone arrowheads some with barbs and others without. She then explained to me how to tell the difference between an arrow head and a spear head. Then she showed me how our nation's first residents would use a sharpening stone to make these and other implements.

I sat fascinated listening to her explain one item from another. Listening to her talk and seeing these stones turned into prehistoric tools of a lost long ago culture I began to understand the archaeological "bug" that affects those who search for clues to civilizations that no longer exist. I began to realize the vicarious exhilaration that one experiences on making an original discovery after a long and exhaustive search in the field.

My mind fleeting turned to Richard Leakey of east Africa and the thrill of discovery he must have felt in finding Turkana Boy in Kenya. Certainly his joy could not have been any greater than that of Sharon's in her own sense of search, exploration and discovery.

I told Sharon how honored and appreciative I was and that I would proudly place these artifacts in a display case in my library at home. She seemed well pleased with that decision.

As the day progressed I continued to see patients and I then finished the afternoon by completing all the paper work, retuning phone calls and reviewing lab results. After leaving the office as is my habit I decided to go to the gym for one of my usual three day a week workouts as I have done habitually and compulsively for years.

Leaving my newly acquired treasures in my car I entered the gym and proceeded to the locker room to change passing the beauty salon that is also located on the premises. I went directly to my locker and turned the combination lock right 16, left 7, and right 32 opening it with ease and started to change from my work clothes into my exercise gray cotton shorts, green T-shirt with the stenciled message on it that said "Cut along the dotted line" with a series of dots under the phrase.

I mused how the T-shirt also had been a humorous gift from my office staff for one of my birthdays. I operate on patients for skin cancers in my surgical suite. I always explain to the patients as I outline the area of excision with a gentian violet pen, "I learned to cut along the dotted line in kindergarten at the age of five. I didn't know back then I planned to be a skin surgeon but you never know what talents you pick up in life that you can utilize later on in life." I'm sure this perspirational thought came to me after reading the delightful and wise inspirational book *All I Really Needed To Know I Learned in Kindergarten by* Robert Fulghum.

As I started to undress, in entered Levi who owned and operated the beauty salon. I'm in the midst of changing into my gym clothes and to use the colloquial expression that I was half dressed would be a half-truth since in reality I was 95% naked. "Hi Levi, how are you doing?" I inquired. In our culture that translates to hello. And he responded back by saying hello. "Doing fine, doc."

As I continued to change, he asked me, "Doc, I really should call your office for an appointment and I apologize for asking you this but would you look at this bump on my cheek that came up a few months ago and hasn't gone away?" he asked with a measure of concern in his voice. "Sure," I casually responded.

I searched for my eye glasses that were in the bottom of my gym bag and opened the case and placed them over my nose. Now I was only 94% undressed. I positioned him under one of the florescent lights to examine the benign mole like structure which had elicited so much concern. "It looks just fine, Levi. It has all the hallmarks of a benign or harmless growth and none that I would associate with a skin cancer, but rather a barnacle on the ship of life that attaches to our skin hull as we age. If you ever want to come to dermatology dry dock I'll be happy to remove it for you or you can just leave it alone," I reassuringly added.

"Thanks so much, doc. That's a big load off my mind, I'm sure relieved," he confided. "Glad to do it," I responded as I removed my glasses and replaced them in my bag attempting to continue changing thinking that was the end of this informal gym side consult.

"What do I owe you?" he now asked. "Levi, you don't owe me anything. You asked me as a favor if I would look at you and I answered 'Yes' as a favor and that's the end of it." "No, no doc I want to pay you for your services," he insisted. "Levi, I don't want any money from you, I'm glad that I was able to save you an unnecessary visit to my office." "No, no doc, let me give you a free haircut?" "I don't want a free haircut," I again responded. "Well, let me give one to your wife," he persisted. "No, that's not at all necessary," I shot back. "Well, when you finish your exercise, come by the salon, I'll have something for you," I relented. "Okay."

I finished changing and walked out into the main exercise area to do my usual exhausting elliptical glide of three miles in twenty six minutes converting my dry T-shirt inspirational workout into a perspiration soaked cut along the dotted line T-shirt. While many of the young men are bench pressing, lifting weights and pumping iron I have preferred to do my muscle toning routine of pumping aluminum foil on non-free weights.

Most of those who work out regularly have personal goals they're striving to achieve. I know quite a few young men who were training for a marathon, competitive weight lifting events or to reach a specific anatomical girth and appearance. My goal on the other hand has been much more modest, and has been to be able to wake up the next morning and tie my shoes. So far I have been successful in achieving it.

Occasionally, the gym is crowded and I have to work in with some of the younger and much more buffed weight lifters. They are always polite and let my 5' 10", 160 pound aging frame share the use of the crowded equipment. After they have completed their ten lifts they ask me at what weights I want mine set. I always answer with my pre-prepared canned retort, "Either geriatric or pediatric, it's all the same for me."

Knowing many of the die-hard committed and very muscular weight lifters and some since their childhood days in grade school I joked to a group that day that I used to look like them before I started working out. Having completed my regimen for the day I went back to the locker room and quickly changed so I could arrive home in time for supper.

As I started to rush out the door passing the beauty parlor, I remembered about Levi and stuck my head into his salon. He quickly nodded for me to enter and handed me a huge container of Biolage Shampoo and accompanying jar of conditioner which he had set aside. I thanked him for his unnecessary but generous gift of appreciation and off I hurried to the parking lot to retrieve my car and head home. As I opened the front door and greeted my wife a quizzical look came over her face which quickly translated into the question, "What is all that stuff you're carrying?" "Oh, just a typical day at the office, with payments of an assortment of fruits and vegetables, arrowheads and shampoo and conditioner from my patients," I answered dryly.

All my interactions at the gym don't always have a positive and humorous outcome. One evening I sat on my perch of the elliptical glider walking the miles away. Even with the diversion of a musical swing tape affixed to my ears the repetition and monotony of aerobic exercise still translates into a high level of boredom punctuated with pain. People watching becomes an important distraction to aid me in completing my workout.

On this particular Friday afternoon I had a panoramic view of the entire gym. A man in his late thirties or early forties who always seemed very isolated and solitary in his workouts was engaged in his weight lifting. My eyes settled on him. Usually, he would wear a T-shirt but today for whatever reason he had on cut-offs. My eyes fixed on his right shoulder where I noticed a dark looking lesion on his deltoid muscle.

Curious I wandered over to his workout station to scrutinize it more carefully in a casual and non-intrusive manner. I was appalled to notice that it had all the features that I would associate with a melanoma mole cancer and an advanced one at that. The lesion had the asymmetry and border changes appearing more like an island with indentions and pseudopoding as well as varying colors from light shades of brown to a dark black foreboding color as well as being a very large lesion. Clinically, it was very worrisome.

After debating in my mind whether I should approach him with my concern or just keep it to myself, I decided I would be doing him and myself an injustice to just walk away. So I walked over to him and said, "Hi, my name is Stu Tobin and I have noticed you working out here from time to time for the past couple of years." He just stared at me without any reaction. I continued, "I apologize for interrupting you during your work out time but I couldn't help but notice that mole on your shoulder. I'm also a physician and a dermatologist. Your mole looks very suspicious."

He interrupted me with, "Oh, I had it checked by my doctor last year and he said it was all right." "I'm glad to hear that." However, what a patient hears or remembers is not always what the physician said. His physician could have said I think it's okay but I would check it out further. And "last year" could have been five years ago and it could have changed considerably in the interim. In any event I continued with, "That was last year and now it looks quite suspicious and needs further evaluation and definitely a biopsy. I'm not attempting to solicit business; I'm very busy and don't need more patients. If you would like to see someone else for a biopsy and removal, that would be great. But it needs to come off and be tested." I found myself now imploring him.

I explained the rationale in detail for my on the spot diagnosis and why melanoma is such a dangerous disease. "If you call my office ask for an appointment I would be happy to see you. We can skip the consultation and do the removal then. It will save one step," I added.

All the time I felt his body language response was more rooted in a desire to get rid of me than from a sense of justifiable and needed concern. He never did call the office and when I've seen him occasionally since, the mole remained quite visible and scarily present. Soon afterwards I changed gyms and haven't seen him since.

So why do patients go to the doctor to seek medical consultation? Because they're scared to death that something is wrong with them. Why do others not go to the doctor to seek help? Because they are scared to death that something is wrong with them. Navigating the Egyptian river, Denial, keeps so many people from seeking timely and critical help. Fear, the great motivator for change, can also be the stubborn impediment and barrier to timely medical care and intervention.

Over the years I have received many other gifts from patients. Little Mrs. B would show up to the office with an assortment of minor skin issues. She was the most delightful retired school teacher with gray hair coiffed into a tight bun and a slender aging figure but still exhibiting an assertive personae, determination and control of an experienced and wise secondary school educator. Sometimes when she was in my examining room I felt like if I didn't behave she might send me to the principal. So I stayed on my best behavior.

At the time I was very involved in the movement to establish a public library in our county. Out of over 110 counties in Kentucky, we were the largest of three that didn't have public library services. This undertaking developed into a ten year crusade and finally came into fruition. However, at the time the outcome was uncertain and the last chapter of library evolution hadn't been written yet.

Stuart Tobin M.D.

One day Mrs. B, who was in her eighties, came to the office for a routine exam and was carrying a very ancient looking book. She announced, "Dr. Tobin I taught school for more than 40 years and when I was a very young school teacher a wonderful old teacher and mentor gave me this book as a present. She had it for over fifty years and I have had it for about the same time and I would like you to be the third owner of it."

I was absolutely dumbfounded by this singular act of generosity and touched by her having tapped me for this responsibility to protect and care for a book that obviously meant so much to her. I didn't know what to say, which is very unusual for a man who fell in love with his own voice at the age of four and who has had an ongoing love affair with it ever since. I fumbled for a few words and thanked her so much.

I surveyed the cover, a thick well-worn and aged brown cover with the title embossed in exaggerated Victorian flowing script, *Pearls of Thought in Poem and Song.* The binding had become separated from the main volume and the fragile non-acid paper seemed on the verge of crumbling. Every page, while still legible, had a dull fading antique brown color and texture. As I carefully opened the cover as carefully as I would perform a surgical operation, I was greeted with a beautifully inscribed note penned by Mrs. B.

"To Dr. Tobin,

When I started to give away some books you were the first one I thought about, Dr. Tobin I know that you must like books by the way you worked to get the Madison County Library. I know that it will be a great Blessing to the people of Richmond and Madison. This book is full of childhood poems, lectures, pictures and songs and I hope you enjoy them as much as I enjoy giving this book to you. It is a hundred years old and since you are such a kind, sympathetic and capable doctor, you may doctor this book and keep it many more years.

Wishing you much success and happiness in whatever you undertake.

God Bless, Mrs. B.

The book indeed needed some doctoring. I phoned a friend in the Library Science Department at Eastern Kentucky University and asked if the binding could be repaired and what could be done to slow the aging process of the pages. She was able to get the binding fixed and also had an acid free cover case made to protect and house this precious book.

Many times I have carefully and gently lifted this treasure from its protective case in my home library to read poems by Shelley, Byron, Carlyle, Longfellow and Tennyson and others and to marvel at the wonderful 1892 black and white illustrations of those aquiline porcelain women in their Victorian dresses with perfect skin and idyllic feminine features. They appeared so fragile, delicate yet so strong and endearing which created an image of that era and culture just as Norman Rockwell did for a much later generation.

However, of all the great poets and authors whose thoughts are preserved between those impressive covers the one that touches me the most is the one by Mrs. B in her unsteady but delicate script in blue ink on the first blank page of this treasured anthology of the English language. It has resided in an honored place in my home in my own library and always will until it can be passed onto someone in a new generation who can act as the next guardian and custodian for it for a while as she did and I am now doing.

Pen Pals

In this world of laptops, palm pilots, personal PCs and the ubiquitous cell phone-camera nuisance, I use an ancient writing device called a fountain pen. This has amazed my older patients. Upon seeing me uncap it many have reminisced about their own school days of being compelled to write with one. This contrasts vividly with the quizzical look I get from anyone under twenty-five who will always ask what is that? That antiquarian device the fountain pen is like marriage. It's a lot of trouble but if you have the right one it's worth all the effort.

A fountain pen will leak ink onto your shirt and it becomes thirsty every two days. Filling it requires the concentration and expertise of performing a surgical procedure. No matter how careful you are I have always managed to get little ink drops on my fingers that despite a surgical operating room scrub it still takes two days to wear off. Then it's time to refill the thirsty empty bladder again.

Like a spouse the pen and ink have a will of their own. If you spill the ink on your clothing it will never come out despite the application of five lemons. However, if a drop of water spills onto the ink written page the entire page runs becoming smeared and unintelligible.

While I love my PC and enjoy working with my photographs to tweak them with Adobe Photoshop software and use my Microsoft Works and Word software to compose, nothing compares with the flow of wet jet black ink onto the plain white page as an experience in writing. The fountain pen is much less forgiving and in a many ways much more demanding than a word processor. There is no going back to erase and edit as on a computer. I have often wondered if the type of writing device we use molds and defines our culture.

Rash Decisions and Growth Experiences
from the Best Little Warthouse in Kentucky

In the age of the fountain pen one would have to be very deliberate and think out your thoughts before committing them to the printed page. I have often wondered if just that act made a previous generation more thoughtful in their actions and deeds before committing themselves to any endeavor? I'll let the sociologists ponder that concept. Hardly a day or two passes without someone while visiting my office comments on the use of that sleek green tapered plastic instrument of pleasure and utility, the fountain pen.

Mrs. S, an octogenarian returned one day for freezing of some pre cancers on her face. She had in the past remarked on my use of my pen and reminded me how it brought back fond memories of having used one herself. As a child she remembered how her mother had used one as well. This time, however, she reached into her plain black pocketbook and retrieved a small and exquisite petite fountain pen and presented it to me as a gift.

"Doctor," she began, "I don't have any one to leave this pen to and certainly no one who would understand and appreciate it. It has been sitting in a coffee cup in my home for years and it belonged to my mother. When I saw how you use and care for your own fountain pen I knew I could find it a good home."

The charcoal gray bakelite surface with its S-shaped whorl pattern of this 4-inch slender writing tool was certainly designed for a woman's delicate hand. There was no snap on the cap as found in so many later pens to carry in a shirt pocket. No this pen was designed to stay where it was going to be used on the writing desk in a lady's home.

Conklin Pen Co. of Toledo, Ohio delicately engraved on the barrel of the pen announced the proud manufacturer with a date of "Dec 1902" etched next to it. The gold nib while plain and delicate also had engraved Conklin on it. Instead of the metal snap filling mechanism that would deflate when lifted perpendicularly as seen on so many old fountain pens, it had a circular gold arch that could be depressed when turning the bakelite guard to fill the pen's ancient ink bladder. It was certainly a unique filling mechanism that I hadn't seen before. I carefully placed this rare gem into my pocket and took it home with me. I proceeded to my library and lifted the glass top to the cherry wood pen display case which sat on a larger display cabinet that kept the medical memorabilia of my fathers and carefully removed one of my own pens to display this wonderful gift and symbol of gratitude and trust from a dear and special patient with a kind and generous heart.

*Question: I'm From the Government and I'm Here to: a) Help, b) Hurt, or c) Harass You?

After thirty years of dermatology practice in Richmond, I decided to plan for, if not retirement, at least slowing down the pace of practice. While I had often humorously quoted a famous American writer I really didn't literally believe in his longevity philosophy, "I knew that everyone was eventually going to die but I thought in my particular case God would make an exception."

Consequently the tapering work strategy evolved along these lines. Since I couldn't maintain my overhead and cut back to half time I would enlist the help of a physician extender, a nurse practitioner. So the search, which seemed more like a quest, lasted over six months till I could find the right one. I spent more time and effort searching for a nurse practitioner than most men spend time looking for a spouse.

Despite her excellent qualifications and background she lacked the specialty training needed in dermatology. She shadowed me for a year learning the nuances of practice before I felt comfortable enough to allow her to undertake care of my patients. Since my present office of seventeen years was designed for a solo practitioner we needed more space. Locating an available office near my old one which suited our needs in terms of space, location and convenience, we undertook the move, investment of new equipment, the renovation, the new floor coverings, and repainting and repartitioning of walls to suit our new expanding needs.

Anticipating that all the insurance companies that we participated with would need our new address, weeks before the actual relocation we notified them as to our new location. Over 75% of my practice is Medicare patients. Consequently Medicare was the first insurance company we notified by phone.

After 2-3 weeks in our new office, my office manager came to me worried. "Doctor, we haven't received any Medicare reimbursements." "Well, call them on the phone, again." I responded. After hours of trying to get through, she was informed that we couldn't make a change of address over the phone. It didn't do any good to remind them that is 180 degrees from the compass of misdirection that we were given a few weeks ago.

The forms, yes the forms, many pages of them, arrived for the change of address. We quickly filled them out and returned them by fax to expedite the process. Two to three more weeks went by again and still no reimbursements. After numerous phone calls we were now informed that our request was incomplete.

Incomplete?!?! We filled out every space, dotted every "I" and crossed every "T". "We need a copy of your original business license," we were now told by the official 'don't dare challenge me' voice of the government. My office manager then complained to me, "We don't have a copy of your original business license from the City of Richmond. I called the city and they told me that they don't keep records that far back from thirty years ago. They don't know where it could be found."

After many phone calls and days later the independent monarchy of the Kingdom of Medicare reluctantly agreed to accept a current business license which the city provided us. Now thinking that every hurdle had been overcome we faxed them the business license.

Two more weeks go by and still nothing. Again the multitude of phone calls. We're now informed that it would take 4 to 6 weeks to process a change of address provided that all the forms are properly filled out. "My God," I frustratingly responded to the official government employee on the other end of the phone. "I have moved into a new office, doubling my space, which has also doubled my rent, and I have hired 3 new employees and spent a small fortune on renovating this new facility and purchasing new medical equipment, and we have had no income coming in for over the past 3 months, a quarter of a year. We have used up all our financial reserves. After thirty years of practice I'm about to be forced out of business and go bankrupt because Medicare can't process a change of address!" I exasperatedly explained.

Her response was, "Would you like to speak to a supervisor?" "Of course!" was mine. "We can put you on the list." "List, what list?" "It takes 7 to 10 working days to speak to a supervisor." "Yes. Put me on the list." I resignedly answered. Of course speaking to someone up the next rung of the Tower of Babel ladder of government gave me little comfort that my fiscal crisis would be finally resolved.

No sooner than I had hung up on her, I now called my attorney. After going through the litany of complaints and lists of repeated frustrations peppered with the imminent danger of my practice folding because of a mere change of address, he sympathetically counseled, "Stu, you're dealing with the government. You're using the wrong approach. You're starting from the bottom up. With the government you have to start with the top and work down. Contact your Senator and Congressman."

My next sets of phone calls were to Congressman Ben Chandler's and Senator Mitch McConnell's offices. I was surprised that each office immediately placed me into the hands of a case worker. I'm thinking is that what our convoluted labyrinth of government has become? No individual citizen can navigate the official channels of government without a guide, a Congressional case worker?

Secondly, I must not be the only person with a justified frustrated encounter with our own government since the social case worker network system was already well entrenched in the legislative branch of government.

To reinforce the immediacy and crisis nature of my individual case I authored an urgent letter to each case worker outlining the journey of frustrations and why it needed ASAP status to be resolved.

Stuart Tobin M.D.

One week later, Senator McConnell's case worker phoned me to inform me that he had resolved the impasse and that Medicare was about to release our long overdue reimbursements. Whew, went my heart. I'm still waiting for the Medicare supervisor to call me back.

Just when I thought my problems with my Uncle were behind me, a new preposterous and even more absurd problem arose in my office. A few years previously we converted our retirement plan to a more updated 401K matching retirement plan and a profit sharing plan for all my employees. This required the annual submission of a Form 5500 to the government.

Somehow, the form for '05-'06 was submitted late and was incompletely filled out. When called to our attention by the Dept. of Labor, my agent immediately responded and we worked with Ms. L in St. Louis who kept assuring us it was just a formality and not to be concerned and that we would get it processed eventually and properly. After months of back and forth she concluded that all was settled and satisfactory.

A few weeks later I received a notice from the government informing me that since the form had been filed late there was a $25 per day penalty and that I was assessed a $15,000 penalty fee which was due immediately and I would incur outrageous interest charges if not paid immediately. In a panic I called my lawyer who referred me onto a tax attorney specialist in Lexington to handle the case.

No taxes or money were involved in the original filing. It wasn't like I had failed to pay my fair share of taxes to the government. It was just a form that wasn't processed on time. How is it possible for someone to charge you $15,000 for a form that wasn't filled out on time or correctly, especially when the representative for that entity kept telling us that it was just a mere formality and not to worry about it.

Is there any private entity or business that could perpetrate such an outrageous, egregious act? Could your credit card company or bank or any large retail business get away with charging you $15,000 because you failed to fill out your application form correctly? Could Macy's Department Store charge you $25 a day for a penalty of $15,000 because you forgot to dot one "I" or cross a "T" in a timely manner?

What court in America would honor that claim by a private corporation as legitimate? Would any reasonable jury of your peers agree with that claim? I doubt it.

Once again I found myself unable to navigate the channels of the U.S. Government without another guide, a tax attorney. After weeks of letters and pleas the government graciously reduced its penalty to a fine of only $2250. Of course that didn't include the $4000 in legal fees for my navigator.

As I pondered these episodes by the government of the people, by the people, and for the people, but against the person, I wondered could I be the only one in America who has had these or similar types of injustices visited upon them? Surely not. There must be thousands of citizens who have had similar experiences. Of course the news media has an inexhaustible supply of government waste and abuse which they share with us in the print as well as the visual media if not on a daily at least a weekly basis. This is not good public relations for the largest industry in the country.

As I pondered this more and since I'm given to an analytical mind, I stretched the corners of my cerebrum to see if there was any possible solution for all those victimized by a government that governs by rules and not a sense of fairness and for which there is no recourse by the individual other than an attempt to stay under the radar.

The epiphany came upon me during lunch at a time when I guess my hunger for nourishment stimulated my hunger for an answer to so many people's dilemma. Why not create a Cabinet of Common Sense. We have a Department of Defense, a Department of Homeland Security, a Department of Interior as well as Health, Education and Welfare, etc, etc. This new Department should easily reach the status of Cabinet level with all the issues it would have to deal with. I can envision it becoming the largest in the President's cabinet, dwarfing even the Pentagon in size and manpower.

However, think of how well it would be received by the people. Actually the government is finally policing itself. It may be the first time that both parties would agree that by making a bigger bureaucracy they would be creating a smaller and fairer government. I'm sure that's some kind of oxymoron. The cabinet's motto would be something of the order. "That's stupid! You're fired." Or perhaps, "You're kidding me, you did what to the little guy? And you're fired." Of course the downside would be it would deprive the media of its entertainment to mock the government.

All this provides just a little food for thought. However, I suspect that if ingested by the government rather than being digested and absorbed where it will do some good, it probably will be excreted instead as waste.

*Answer: b and c

P.S. If you got the wrong answer you either work for the government or if you don't you should.

FAMILY AND FRIENDS

Goliath - Won; David - None

As a junior in high school I was successfully developing into a nerd. Although my metamorphosis wasn't complete, I was well on the way towards geek academic stardom. The ever present pocket protector assured that my peers wouldn't confuse me with the "All American boy".

I didn't shun sports and played a fair game of tennis. I even took a few lessons in judo for self defense. However, I never managed to master the concept that I was supposed to subdue and injure my opponent, and inevitably I would always return home with more self-inflicted injuries than those incurred on my opponent. Consequently, as a teenager I gave up the martial arts until later in life when it was replaced with the more challenging adversarial and dangerous marital arts.

I was also a member of the Marshals, the student monitors who regulated student traffic flow in the overcrowded hallways before and after class. Matriculation to this quasi student pseudo police force depended more on academic endowment than physical prowess.

One morning as I made the half-mile journey from my home on Archer Ave, Mt. Vernon, New York, to the local high school, named after A. B. Davis, whoever he was, I was cornered by two very large football players. I sensed that they weren't interested in becoming my new bosom buddies. "Hey, you," they baited, followed by "Dirty Jew, we don't want your kind here!"

Inexplicably, I felt the need to defend my entire religious nation and reflexively responded with the ill thought out response, "Take it back." They didn't stop to ponder or craft a diplomatic reply to my suggestion. The next thing I knew the biggest one was all over me and the fight was on.

Rash Decisions and Growth Experiences
from the Best Little Warthouse in Kentucky

The first thing I did to "protect" myself was to hurl my groin into his knee as hard as I could. Then I followed that initial defensive gesture by throwing my jaw into his clenched high school ringed fist at a "dizzying" speed. I now found myself on the ground on my back writhing in pain. As I looked up from my new horizontal perspective, the football player seemed not only more gigantic than I had initially perceived but also he had cloned himself and there were now two of him.

I thought if I altered my perspective he wouldn't seem as big and as imposing. So I got up again. We now repeated the scene all over again with the same results. I tried it once more and received an additional painful pummeling. I finally figured out that the third time was more of a harm than a charm.

I now decided to follow the advice and counsel of someone in the crowd that had gathered around us. "Don't get up again, he's going to kill you," my unknown advisor shouted. Half dazed, out of breath, and all in pain, I lay there and the fight was now over. The crowd dispersed and the bully football players left with one of those twisted smiles of smug satisfaction etched on their face.

I gathered up my books that had been strewn over the massacre site and headed to class. Later that morning I was called to the principal's office. I had deduced that the invitation was related to the early morning, one-sided conflagration. The principal informed me that my twice my size adversary and his companion had already been to his office and registered a complaint that I had provoked him into a fight that he had wanted to avoid by me calling him a derogatory slur.

I'm thinking to myself, does this idiot of a principal really believe that I would precipitate a suicidal physical altercation with two large football players each twice my size? Me, a member of the academic student establishment whose only other known confrontation at the A. B. Davis High School was at the gaming board in the chess club with the non-provocative remark, "checkmate"?

I was so surprised and confused that I said nothing in defense or offense. Well, at least I wasn't suspended or expelled. Life went on and my body repaired itself, and I did learn a few valuable lessons about myself and how adversaries may exploit lies to their advantage. I don't know what ever happened to my assailant but suspect that he may have gone on to have a very successful career working in the spin of politics and election campaigns.

Train of Thought

My dad as a young man in the midst of the Great Depression still clung to his cherished dream of becoming a physician. My immigrant grandfather had morphed himself from an illiterate teenager from the Ukraine who could not read, speak or understand English to a successful entrepreneur businessman in the soft drink industry in the early years of the twentieth century. Eventually he sold his liquid profits to Canada Dry Ginger Ale. Prior to the stock market crash of 1929 which ushered in the Great Depression, he had easily financially underwritten his other children's academic college dreams. Despite the economic crisis of the era he still managed to gather enough resources to help pay for dad's tuition and partial room and board.

Growing up in Lynn, Massachusetts, dad had a need to defend himself from local bullies and had taken up boxing as a sport and became a fairly proficient pugilist in high school. This translated into a partial bantam weight scholarship at the University of Pittsburgh to defer some of his expenses.

As a young man of eighteen in the fall of 1931, Louis Tobin boarded the train from Boston, Massachusetts bound for the industrial town that the steel magnates had revolutionized in western Pennsylvania to attend Pitt for his undergraduate degree. Stuffed in his pockets was enough money to see him through his first semester if he carefully counted every George Washington.

The click clack of the railroad over the ancient tracks and the boredom of such a long and lonely trip made him seek out some form of diversion. He stumbled onto two older men engaged in a friendly card game. Invited to join them he found the hours going by much more quickly. As the local stations passed they suggested that to make the game more interesting why not play for some penny ante amounts. Since dad had been winning and at the age of eighteen convinced of his own invincibility to any form of failure, he didn't need a lot of persuasion.

As the hours and the local stations whizzed by he started to lose. Anxious to recoup his losses he bet even more heavily. As the stakes grew larger his bankroll shrunk smaller. By the time he reached Pittsburgh, his money was gone as well as his two new "friends". A journey that had begun full of hope ended with empty pockets and a sense of personal despair that rivaled America's own mood of severe depression.

His father, a very devoted and loving man, came from a culture in which the patriarch acted more like a rigid paternal authoritarian than an understanding fatherly counselor. Confiding in him of his misadventure was not even a remote option. The shame and disappointment his father would feel surpassed any of his own aspiring dreams. So instead he wired by Western Union his brother, Nate, the attorney, about his financial crisis. His other older brothers clandestinely joined in. Each made a sacrificial monetary contribution to keep my dad financially afloat for that first semester until his father would send him more money for the next academic half year.

The disaster was averted and the education continued, and my dad eventually did achieve his goal of becoming a physician and dermatologist. However, that is not quite the end of the story.

As a child growing up in Mt. Vernon, New York, I remember my dad would meet monthly with a group of his friends and play poker. The stakes were always small and whether he won or lost remained a mystery to me then and until this very day. I really never gave it much thought and was glad that my father, the tireless worker and unselfish provider for his family, had a diversion that he occasionally indulged and enjoyed.

I also remember as a child watching dad sitting in his favorite chair in the evening laboring and studying the Value Line, a stock investment service which aided him in his decisions of investing his money in the New York Stock Exchange for retirement and our college funds.

He would sit in his favorite well worn easy chair in his starched white long sleeve shirt with the sleeves always carefully rolled up over his elbows revealing his strong and well developed arm muscles which still remained from his boxing youth. My brothers and I affectionately nicknamed him Popeye because of those impressive forearms.

How excited he would become on discovering a potentially new star on the stock exchange horizon that was predicted to become a soaring good investment. Sometimes they did as predicted and some did not. I always marveled at his determination and thoroughness before investing. While never becoming rich, he was able to save enough to educate his children and provide for my mother in her later and last years.

My own personal reaction to his investment strategy was one of incredulous yet detached observation. Studying the stock market held as much enthusiasm for me as going shopping at the mall with my wife now does in the later years of my married life. I promised myself I would not waste my evenings studying and expending time and energy on the market in an attempt to improve my personal investments. I would rather read about history and the principles of our political founding fathers than the accumulation of principal by the fledgling tycoon barons of Wall Street.

My dad's other passion in life was the horse races. On Friday afternoons after work he would drive to the Big A (Aqueduct Race Track) in New York City and place his two dollar bets and watch the ponies run. It gave him great pleasure. As an adolescent far too young to place a wager legally, I remember him underwriting my first two dollar bet on my first race. I hadn't been that excited since the first time as a five year old I wrote my name and received my first library card. However, that initial exhilaration soon passed and horse racing never captured my interest or my pocketbook.

On Friday, April 19, 1974, my dad didn't attend the races which he loved so much because he just didn't feel well. He died of a massive heart attack in the middle of the night at the age of sixty one.

It took me years to decipher the gambling code that was in front of my eyes my entire life and that I just couldn't see. My dad loved the thrill of the gamble. He may have won or lost at the races, the poker table or the stock market, but it remained the exhilaration of the chance of winning or losing that he enjoyed the most.

However, he had learned many years ago on that train ride to Pittsburgh of the dangers when the impulse controls you rather than when you control it. For him it became a safe diversion and contained passion that never interfered with providing for his beloved family. The devastating loss of all his money on that one youthful railroad trip in the fall of 1931 had changed his entire train of thought, derailing his runaway gambling impulses.

My Mother's Final Journey

My wonderful, theatrical, and vibrant mother lost her battle to dementia in the summer of 2005 at the age of 87. For the last four years of her life she remained unaware and oblivious to all that transpired around her. An independent and accomplished woman with a great deal of natural vocal talent, she lay in bed unable to communicate, much less sing, which was her greatest passion in life. Unable to walk or control any of her bodily functions, finally the only remaining quality of life was taken away when a feeding tube was placed the last six months of her life to prevent the recurrent aspiration pneumonia which threatened her survival.

The decaying mind robbed her body and spirit of all that made her that unique woman I called mother. Watching her decline so slowly made those frequent visits more and more painful for me as the days turned into weeks and the weeks became months and the months mounted into years.

My good friend and dentist asked me one day as we were discussing the deteriorating mental conditions of our parents how do you make the decision on when to end the inevitable? As in most questions like that he wasn't really asking me about my mom but his. I responded, "You know Jim, that's an issue that works so differently for many people, and I can't give you a universal general truth. The only thing I can tell you is that despite the hopelessness and lack of quality of life she has, I cannot euthanize my mother. So I will continue to give her adequate and good non-heroic medical support and care as long as she needs it and as long she is not suffering any pain." It wasn't long after that conversation that she succumbed to a rapid sequence of medical emergencies. The simple urinary infection became generalized sepsis or infection which led to shock and triggered off the heart attack that caused the pneumonia and resulted in her ensuing death.

Living in Richmond, Kentucky, and wanting to honor her request to be buried next to my dad who had been waiting for her for thirty-four years in New York, I made arrangements with the local funeral home. The funeral director, who had been a friend offered to help, and I certainly needed and welcomed his assistance. As we discussed all the arrangements for a visitation locally and a small service in Richmond, he reminded me of how he had visited me on several occasions in my office and how I had suggested to him on renaming his funeral parlor, Cobb, Oldham, Roberts and Powell. In a never ending search for the true meaning of humor (some of which is noir), I had suggested that he combine the first initials of each name to CORP. And with a little imagination he could alter the name to the Corpse CORP or even CORP Corpse Corp. All of which he thankfully ignored.

My mother died on Wednesday and the visitation in Kentucky was scheduled for Friday and the burial in New York on Sunday. He made all the plane reservations through Delta for my mom while my secretary made travel arrangements for me and my wife through Northwest Airlines. Our flight scheduled to depart Blue Grass Airport on Saturday at 9:50 am was cancelled. We had arrived over an hour early to pass thru security since my wife was always being wanded because of her knee replacement. So we waited for the next flight scheduled at 11:25 for Detroit to connect to LaGuardia in New York. This flight did leave on time or relatively close, only twenty-five minutes late. The plane quickly left the gate, traveled one hundred yards, and stopped. It then proceeded to sit on the tarmac for forty-five minutes until the weather cleared in Detroit.

As we neared Detroit the flight attendant announced that almost all the departing and connecting flights out of Detroit were also delayed because of the inclement weather and we should make our connections without difficulty. Well, Northwest had decided to have one connecting flight on time, ours. We found ourselves running to the gate and were the last two people on the plane. The heavy concave metallic door was slammed shut just as we boarded.

Rash Decisions and Growth Experiences
from the Best Little Warthouse in Kentucky

As we breathlessly fastened our seat belts the plane easily glided away from the terminal on time and stopped one hundred yards from the gate and sat on the tarmac for one hour while the weather cleared in New York.

Always attempting to discover the laws that govern the universe I came to a conclusion which maybe doesn't rival Einstein's $E=MC^2$ but which seems always to work when traveling by air. The service received from an airline carrier is inversely proportional to the cost of air travel. While I'm not sure I could translate this into a numerical equivalent, I have found most people agree with this concept which I'm calling Tobin's Law of Flight. We finally landed at LaGuardia.

We wandered over to baggage claim to discover that although we had made the flight, our luggage had not. We went to the baggage claim office and told the agent that our luggage had been lost. He immediately corrected me that our luggage wasn't lost, only delayed. Luggage is not lost until twenty-four hours have elapsed. Somehow I didn't find that thought particularly comforting. His explanation did, however, remind me of similar logic I had encountered while in the Army.

After patient chart after patient chart failed to show up at my clinic I inquired why so many charts were lost. I was informed that the military never loses charts, they are just temporarily relocated. The military also does not have the word "retreat" in their vocabulary or lexicon. The nearest equivalent would be "retrograde maneuvers". The baggage claim agent then assured us that our bags would be on the next connecting flight - an assurance that by this time didn't seem so comforting. He promised that our luggage would be brought to our hotel by 7:00 or 8:00 that evening.

Off to the Hertz rental car we went. I remarked to my wife Susan how much easier it is to travel through an airport without toting luggage and maybe in the future when traveling we should just forget about packing anything from home and just buy what we needed when we arrived.

We waited and waited for the ground transport service bus to the Hertz car rental. After seeing five Avis, six Alamo, and four

Stuart Tobin M.D.

Budget minibuses pass and not one yellow Hertz bus, my wife decided she had to go to the bathroom. As soon as she left the Hertz van arrived. I told the driver that my wife had just gone to the bathroom and would be back in just a moment. He said, "I'm running late and off schedule and can't wait." The fact that he was running late didn't come as news to me.

I said, "Listen, we've been waiting here for you for almost a half hour and after we have waited this long for you, you can wait two damn minutes till my wife gets back!!" I engaged him in direct eye contact to impress on him my resolve. He waited. We climbed into the van and he asked, "Where's your luggage?" Not wanting to revisit our previous frustration in the midst of our present frustration I answered, "We're traveling light."

We arrived at the rental car location and the courteous woman behind the counter told us to retrieve our Taurus from slot number 153. We exited the building easily since we weren't hampered with the inconvenience of any luggage and wandered around this huge lot in the 90 degree heat and finally found slot number 153. There was no car. I joked to Susan and said, "Oh, my God, there's no car, and they are going to claim that it's been stolen and that we are responsible for it because it's in our name."

I went back to the counter and told the woman that there was no car. She apologized and said, "Someone had mis-programmed your reservation and that your car would be in slot 28." Lo and behold there was a car in slot 28. Of course we hadn't had anything to eat since breakfast at 6:30 that morning with the exception (if you refer back to Tobin's Law of Flight) while flying to New York we were able to PURCHASE a bag of trail mix from an angry passive aggressive flight attendant at thirty thousand feet.

I have decided the reason that they keep the fasten seat belt sign on during the entire time you're in the air is to keep some irate passenger from justifiably reaching up and strangling a provocative flight attendant.

We finally arrived at the hotel starving and were met with the rest of the family. We ate out and came back to the hotel. After dinner I checked with the front desk to see if our luggage had arrived. "No," he answered. I asked him to be on the lookout for it and to send it to our room as soon as it came in. Before retiring for the evening I asked again and again came the answer, "No."

We went to sleep in the condition that we arrived. I awoke at 12:30 a.m. and had dreamed that the luggage had arrived. Looking around the room I realized that it was just that, a dream. I called the front desk again to receive the third "No" of the night. I hadn't received so many no's since I was dating in high school. I thought, well, I should call the luggage agent at the airport. I retrieved the delayed and not lost yet slip given me. The fine print said that the office wouldn't open till 5:30 a.m. I tried to fall back to sleep and tossed and turned till finally finding some rest about 2:00 a.m. I awoke at 5:30 and jumped out of bed and made the phone call.

The new agent said, "Your luggage was picked up by the courier last night and should have been delivered late the previous evening. But don't worry Mr. Tobin, it should arrive sometime today." I responded with my best 5:30 in the morning two hours of sleep response, "Listen, Miss, let me explain to you the situation and why I don't find your promises reassuring. My mother died two days ago and the funeral is in four and half hours, and I can't go to my mother's funeral in shorts. I need my luggage!" She promised that she would check on it and get right back to me. The phone rang fifteen minutes later. "Mr. Tobin, I have located your luggage and the courier, and you will have it by 7:00 this morning." At 6:30 the doorman banged on the door and there was the luggage. I didn't give him a tip.

Shortly later there was another knock on the door. It was my brother. "I've been trying to get a hold of you since last night, but every time I asked the operator to connect me, she says you're not registered at the hotel, and that there is no one in this room."

Let's not forget that is only one half of the travel adventure. My mother was being flown by Delta. Her flight should have landed in New York via Atlanta connection by 4:00 p.m. the previous evening. She arrived at 12:00 midnight. There's an old joke that I have heard bantered around for years. When you die, whether you're going to heaven or hell, you still have to change planes in Atlanta. Well, my mother not only had to change planes in Atlanta but was delayed there as well.

Fortunately, the rest of the day I can't say went well, but at least the funeral and burial proceeded as we had hoped, and it gave me some sense of closure and comfort to know that my mother was finally where she needed and wanted to be, next to my dad.

The Short Version

My twin brother, Morris, also a physician, practiced in Paris, Texas as a nephrologist (kidney specialist) almost as long as I practiced in Richmond. Purchasing old maps and vintage books as well as famous autographs has been his collective hobby and passion for years. Apparently my autograph is not highly desirable and his only request for it has been on a blank check which I have avoided giving to him despite his occasional request.

My favorite twin has also complained over the years that I have forgotten to acknowledge his birthday. He has refused to accept my simplistic defensive/offensive explanation, "Hey, Morris, you can't expect me to remember everybody's birthday."

This past year I decided to make amends and not only remember to acknowledge the day of our mutual birth but also to give him an appropriate present as well. On that auspicious day, September 22, I presented him with three autographed books. However, they were autographed by me. The first was Herman Melville's *Moby Dick* with the following dedication:

To Mo,
  The whale did it.
          Herman "Shorty" Melville

P.S. A lot of people don't know that my nickname is "Shorty"

The second book was Jack London's *Call of the Wild and White Fang* with the inscription:

To Mo,
  The dogs and wolves are a giant metaphor for people.
          Jack "Shorty" London

Stuart Tobin M.D.

P.S. A lot of people don't know that my nickname is "Shorty"

The third and final of the trilogy was *The Complete Works of Shakespeare* with the dedication:

> To Mo,
> Roses are reddish
> Violets are bluish
> I hope you enjoyeth
> The stuff I wrote from start to finish
>   William "Shorty" Shakespeare

P.S. Aloteth people don't knoweth that my nicknameth is "Shorty"

Before presenting these cherished and most rare books to my brother I dragged them to my office and showed them to my staff. My office manager asked incredulously? "How could you possibly explain to anyone that you obtained an autograph from an author who has been dead for almost 400 years?" I confidently explained, "That's what makes it such a rare find. Anyone can get an autograph from someone who is still alive, but it's a real challenge to get an autograph from someone who is dead especially for that long a period of time."

I continued my divergent thoughts with, "However, I thought you were going to ask me the obvious question. The autograph was done with a ballpoint pen and how could I explain that Shakespeare used a Bic pen? Well, a lot of people also don't realize that Shakespeare invented the ballpoint pen. That's why he was so prolific. He had a clandestine technological jump on all the other authors of his day."

I then continued my stream of consciousness ramblings tangent with, "Since we are talking about the great bard, let me also tell you about my own experience in high school English class when we were reading *Hamlet*. My English teacher turned to me and asked. 'Stuart, how would you describe in Elizabethan English a bow-legged farmer standing on a hillside?' I stood up and answered, 'Hark, hark, what manner of men are these that carry their balls in parentheses.' That hark of a lark was followed by a personal invitation to the school's principal's office, again."

Returning to the dubiously signed books, I presented those three copies to my sib on the eve of the celebration of our common birth to add to his growing collection of his home library. I laughed and he howled.

A number of months later I found myself at a book signing of a close personal friend, Charles Bracelen Flood, an accomplished and renowned author. He had just completed his latest superb historical account of Abraham Lincoln with the publication of *1864 Lincoln at the Gates of History.* We chatted and bantered on this 200th anniversary of the Great Emancipator's birth in his native Kentucky.

As he made a personal dedication to my brother I asked, "Bracelen, would you mind if I imposed on you with a special request? Would you sign your name Bracelen "Shorty" Flood and add, P.S. A lot of people don't know that my nickname is Shorty?" He indulged me after I explained the inside family joke. I then sent that book to my brother.

It only seemed appropriate that my fictional autographs appearing in classical great fictional works should be complemented by a non-fictional autograph in a superb non-fictional volume.

Bawbie

My uncle "Bully." whose real name was Billy, was married to my father's only sister. Since she was the only female offspring in a litany of male children she received special status from our family. While all the boys were expected to achieve the best educations and assert themselves independently as well as financially, not so for the only sister. Her ordained goal in life was to be dependent and become a wife and mother. All this to my parent's generation was the norm and contrasts vividly with today's equal gender culture.

My aunt Etta lived in my grandmother's house and she was also responsible for care-taking my grandmother Celia, or whom we always called "Bawbie" which is Yiddish for grandmother. Bawbie couldn't read or write English and since my brothers and I were never taught Yiddish, communication between our two linguistic and cultural generations was limited and mostly non- existent. But we would go along with the charade smiling at everything she said without understanding a word, phrase or thought. Since my parents had made the break with Boston and were well ensconced in New York, our three to four trips yearly to Lynn, Massachusetts where the "family" lived made for exciting and memorable travel adventures.

In appearance Bawbie was a short, heavy set woman of about five feet tall and with gray straight long thinning hair pulled back. The thinning nature of her hair revealed two large pullet egg size bulging cysts on the top of her scalp. I always wondered why my father the dermatologist didn't just remove them from her.

Her face was rounded and her eyes were slanted suggesting a Mongolian heritage making me wonder if as the great hordes of Genghis Khan that conquered much of Russia and which pillaged, destroyed, and ravaged all in their path may have also stopped and took time to engage in other pursuits with the conquered people along their marauding way. My father being the youngest offspring in a traditionally large family made Bawbie seem ancient to my brothers and me.

Bawbie, embarrassed by her lack of education, went to great lengths to hide the depths of her English illiteracy. She could conjure up a few well-rehearsed and memorized English phrases. Since her culture demanded that her life revolve around the family and kitchen, which often meant feeding the men, her language skills mostly related to food. Either not knowing our names or not being able to pronounce them, she referred to my two brothers and me in the collective as "Kindelah" which in Yiddish means children.

Wishing to hide her limited language skills, Bawbie would go to the pantry and retrieve a large can of Campbell's Soup and thoughtfully look at the label and pretend to read it and ask us, "Kindelah, do you vant chicken noodle soup?" We always said "Yes, Bawbie." Chicken soup to transplanted Jews was the culinary equivalent of an antibiotic and was often referred to as Jewish penicillin since it was supposed to cure any malady by which you were afflicted.

The old culture transplanted to the New World seldom dies and often reappears in the kitchen. Since Bawbie had emigrated from Lithuania, one of the Baltic countries of Eastern Europe, many of her culinary talents reflected the Jewish culture of the late nineteenth century from the old country. This translated to my brothers and I being exposed to exotic foods and dishes.

Eight and nine year olds are rarely receptive to the seductive delicacies of a distant, poorly understood culture. Consequently, the subtleties and appreciation of eating Borscht were lost on us. Borscht, also translated from Yiddish, is beet soup. That it was often served cold added, or more properly subtracted, from its taste to the uneducated palate of eight-year-old me.

Another delicacy my brothers and I were forced to endure was gefilte fish, which in Yiddish means stuffed fish. Stuffed with what always concerned me. Usually it meant carp or other bottom dwelling fish that were compressed into balls or cakes and mixed with matzo meal and eggs and then simmered in a broth. Also served cold, my mind always fantasized that some helpless uncooked fish had been unwittingly dredged out of the sewer, then enrolled into the witness protection program of foods to hide its original identity, and then served to unwilling victims - me and my brothers.

Bland in taste and cold to the touch and unknown in content, I would inhale gefilte fish in one gastronomical gasp in hopes that after reaching my gastric juices that my GI tract wouldn't rebel, forcing my mouth to revisit the same process all over again.

As if that weren't enough, there was always breakfast, which meant lox and bagels. Uncooked salmon served on a half bagel smeared and dripping in cream cheese was also at variance with my idealized morning meal. I always managed to avoid eating it by either feigning fullness as an excuse or asking, "Bawbie is there any Campbell's chicken noodle soup left over from yesterday?"

My father had a great love and affection for his mother. Consequently we made the trip to Boston and Lynn three or four times a year. Bawbie lived well into her eighties until she died peacefully at where else but at home on Summer Street in Lynn, Massachusetts when I was twelve.

What Really Happened at Lexington and Concord

My favorite cousin Marcia's oldest daughter had become betrothed, and the wedding was scheduled for the July 4th weekend in Boston, Massachusetts. My wife and I were anxious to attend and made airline connections from Lexington, Kentucky to Boston as soon as the formal invitation arrived via post. The opportunity to reunite with my extended non-nuclear family, whom I seldom saw, for a joyous occasion on our nation's birthday at the site of our country's historic conception was an irresistible magnetic force that pointed my familial and patriotic compass to due northeast.

I speculated as to why her daughter and my second cousin chose that particular holiday weekend. Was the young couple very patriotic and wanted the birth of their marital union to coincide on the anniversary of our nation's birth of a political union? Or was that the only day available? Or as some couples like to do, to have their anniversaries on a holiday since it would be easier to remember which day of the year they married? Or did they just want to get the fireworks going early in their relationship? Regardless of the motivation, off we journeyed to partake, enjoy, and celebrate.

Arriving at the Bluegrass Airport in Lexington, Kentucky, well ahead of the appointed departure time, we were perfunctorily informed by the Delta service agent while the plane was on time it had also been overbooked. His monotone, tape recorder-like voice continued with, "If you are willing to wait for the next flight, Delta will give you each $200 in vouchers for travel over the next year."

Because it meant an additional two-hour delay my wife piped up with, "What are we supposed to do for the next three hours in the airport lounge?" After accessing a number of screens on his computer he then countered with, "I'll tell you what Delta will do. We'll double the vouchers to $400 apiece and drive you by taxi to Cincinnati and upgrade you to first class. Your connecting flight from Cincinnati will actually arrive one hour before your regular Boston flight." "Sure, that sounds fair," I casually responded, suppressing my surprise which was only equal to my excited joy at such unexpected and unheard of airline windfall.

I didn't feel the need to share with him that the original tickets only cost $18 a piece since we had used our Sky Miles to purchase them. We were able to retrieve our already checked bags and quickly entered the waiting cab at the entrance of the airport, and off we went for the ninety mile drive.

Our pilot for the two-hour drive to the Greater Cincinnati airport, which is actually located in northern Kentucky, had long and unkempt hair and was a man about fifty plus. If he had a fear of tattoo needles he obviously had conquered that anxiety. Out of curiosity I interrupted his rambling monologue about whether he should break up with or marry his present girlfriend of three months who was thirty years his junior. "I'm sure you'll figure out what is best for both of you after you both weigh the pros and cons." I tried to answer with a tone of reassurance and concern.

"However, I am a little curious. The distance to Cincinnati is about ninety miles. Do you keep the meter running or do you charge the airlines a flat fee?" "Well, to get their business we give them a discounted fee of $125," was his answer.

He now settled back into his premarital monologue as I settled into a conversation with my wife in an attempt to tune him out. We arrived at the airport without incident and checked our luggage and proceeded to the departure area. I fleetingly wondered if our tattooed, conflicted taxi pilot stud picked up another fare for $125 back to Lexington or did he just solo home alone?

The connection was perfect and the usual voice at the departure counter announced, "First boarding passengers in need of assistance," followed soon by, "We now will board our first class passengers." Having never flown first class before and always choosing to fly steerage, which is euphemistically called economy class, I felt a sense of specialness and privilege as we handed the flight attendant our newly acquired premier first class tickets. She almost had to rip them from my hands, since I was so reluctant to relinquish this one tangible evidence of my newly acquired status.

I often wondered, who are those people flying first class? Are they the super-rich or the super-stupid wasting their financial resources for a one and half hour flight that doesn't get them to their destination any faster than the pedestrian people seated 30 feet behind them but at twice the fare? They always seem to have those little glasses of cocktails and wine in one hand and a cell phone in the other as the economy class anonymous masses pass and stare at them on their way to the rear of the bus. Now I was one of them.

Then the epiphany hit me. They were neither rich nor stupid. They were hapless travelers like me who were bumped from their connecting flight by an incompetent and inefficient airline that was determined to drive itself into premature bankruptcy by taxiing people around the country from airport to airport for $125 a trip and doubling their vouchers and plying them with liquor in the early morning hours.

No wonder they seemed so content and mellow and superior. So I quickly affected that relaxed posture with the little smirk that first class passengers have as the rest of the world passed them, I mean us, by.

Since I didn't have a cell phone to demonstrate my pseudo self importance I started to talk into my pen and pretend that I was discussing something of importance with someone on the other end. My wife, used to my bizarre sense of humor and behavior, didn't even ask the obvious, "What are you doing now talking into your pen?" She just gave me one of those looks and returned to the Sky magazine stowed in the pocket in the equally plush first class seat in front of us.

The attentive and attractive flight attendant now appeared and asked if we wanted anything to drink. Having now finished my imaginary conversation with my pen, I adroitly and in a James Bond-like suave style placed it back casually into my pocket with a sense of flare as only a first class passenger can do with a Bic fine disposable writing instrument embossed with the important message, "Jim's Dry Cleaner - same day service".

She interrupted herself and now asked, "Sir, would you like a damp washcloth?" "A damp washcloth, why would I want a wet washcloth?" I asked. "Sir, your pen has leaked and has spotted your shirt," she replied as I looked down at the black glob of ink on my bright yellow shirt. I plaintively answered to keep up the charade, "That's not my pen that's my phone," and she handed me the washcloth with a very quizzical look on her face. She then responded with, "Well, maybe sir, you should talk into it instead of texting. It may not leak as much."

She now added, "Sir, you might also wish to engage the services of the advertisement on your pen, I mean your phone." Coincidentally, at that same identical moment, my wife must have read something in the Sky magazine that was very, very funny since she broke out into a hysterical fit of uncontrolled laughter. I was beginning to regret all the special attention that first class passengers receive.

We landed shortly at Logan International Airport and retrieved our luggage and headed to the Hertz counter to pick up our pre-arranged car rental. The agent kept staring at the ink glob on my shirt. I said, "My phone leaked." My wife now added, "His phone didn't leak, his brain leaked." We signed our lives away in exchange for the modest economy car and headed to the parking area to start our New England journey.

Since we had arrived over an hour earlier than our scheduled time and since my cousin Marcia, as mother of the bride, was occupied with so much to do before the wedding and we weren't planning to connect with her till much later in the afternoon, Susan and I decided to take a ride to Lexington and then onto Concord and visit the birthplace of the American Revolution on this national birthday weekend.

It was a very hot and humid afternoon with scorching temperatures in the nineties. We arrived at the well preserved wooden bridge where our patriotic ancestors met the British redcoats and where a number of American lives were lost but where also a revolution began. I could only imagine what that confrontation must have seemed like. With camera in hand I managed a number of photos of the wooden arched bridge from different angles. After touring the small gift shop the hour of connecting with my cousin Marcia was fast approaching.

Calling her on the phone, I started the conversation with, "Marcia, you'll never guess where we are at this moment." Semi-surprised she asked, "No, where are you?" "Concord" (KONNchord) I answered. My cousin, the proper Bostonian with the proper Bostonian accent, instinctively corrected me with, "Concord" (KahnKURD pronounced like conquered). "Marcia, not only are we at Concord (KONNchord)," I insisted, "but we just saw a 'minuteman' (Mynoot man)." Again she instantly corrected my pronunciation with "Minuteman" (minitman). "No," I insisted, "it was a minute-man (Mynoot man) It was a small boy about eight years old with a toy revolutionary gun."

A number of months later I found myself at a library function in my home state of Kentucky at Frankfort, the capital. I related this accentual pronunciation adventure to a new acquaintance who happened to be from South Carolina. He now confided that he too had a friend who coincidentally happened to be from New England as well and who was visiting him in his hometown of Concord, (KONNchord) South Carolina. When his friend pronounced his hometown as "Concord" (KahnKURD) with a similar Bostonian accent, he paused and wryly answered his Yankee visitor with, "No, we ain't never been conquered."

What's in a Name?

It was a long and winding Kentucky road that led me to chair the Kentucky Department for Libraries and Archives (KDLA) Advisory Council. It would take another book to fully explain that uncertain journey and curious controversial odyssey. Over twenty-five years ago I, with a core group of concerned citizens, initiated an ambitious project to initiate, develop and nurture a public library for our county. It took ten years of labor and controversy to institute modest public library services for our seventy thousand plus residents.

I spent the following ten years chairing the local library board. Under the careful and concerned scrutiny of the board the library grew and prospered to complete library services, with two main fixed facilities - one located in Richmond, my hometown, and a second in Berea, our craft-oriented, non-metropolis sister town ten miles to the south in Madison County.

In addition a bookmobile serviced those in the more rural areas of the community who couldn't travel to one of the fixed facilities. Both facilities have been renovated, expanded and replaced and serve as an integral part of the educational health of our growing and vibrant community.

Because of this long and controversial experiment, I came to the attention of our state library system and its' most professionally capable and dedicated commissioner, Jim Nelson, who asked me to participate in the planning of the White House Conference on Libraries on the state level in the nineties.

Rash Decisions and Growth Experiences
from the Best Little Warthouse in Kentucky

After chairing one of the subcommittees my name was eventually submitted to the governor for appointment as a lay member to the Kentucky Department for Libraries and Archives, KDLA, Advisory Council. I served in that capacity for a couple of years and was eventually asked to chair the committee, which I proudly subsequently did.

The Kentucky Department for Libraries and Archives operated under the larger umbrella as part of the Education, Arts, and Humanities Cabinet in state government. It was a diverse group of commissions and sub-commissions that rarely interacted with each other within the broad context of that multifaceted cabinet.

To make each department more aware of the others activities, a luncheon was arranged each year in Frankfort at Christmastime. Attended by the commissioner and the chairman of each board this combined social and professional event gave us the annual opportunity to get to know as well as educate each other in a more personal venue. I always looked forward to it.

Each chairman was expected to give a brief progress report to acquaint everyone else in the cabinet with if not their accomplishments at least what their aspirations were. Having attended a number of these over the years, I couldn't recall any of the wonderful endeavors which each commission related from one year to the next. Surmising that no one else's memory was any better than mine I decided to talk about something of parallel significance instead.

I felt if my attempted humorous diversion was well received it might be retained by one or two, but if it fell short of its comical goal - no great loss. No one would recall it or me anyway.

The year was 2000, which in itself doesn't ring a bell unless you're ringing in a new century and millennium. In which case you would be ringing lots of bells. In addition, it was also an election year which pitted the Democratic candidate of Al Gore against the Republican nominee George W. Bush, as well as a third party perpetual candidate of Ralph Nader.

Frankfort, our state capital, wasn't oblivious to the broader stage of national politics. Since Tip O'Neill had articulated the mantra "All politics are local", I took it upon myself to expose my peers to an aspect of the national election that may have escaped their partisan political radar screens.

When my turn came to update, codify, and inform, I explained, "Instead of the usual progress report that is given at this time I would rather like to discuss with you briefly how libraries can aid in the decision making of choosing a presidential candidate for the average citizen during this election year. Considering myself average at best, the following represents my testimony of how I used my local library to help me to decide for whom to vote."

"Since all visual and auditory political ads on the television, radio, and print media seem so partisan and crafted to elicit either anger, fear or some positive political passion from the voting public, I decided to pursue some independent, more objective research source in making up my own mind as to the best candidate."

"So journeying to my own local library in Richmond I proceeded to the reference section in search of *The Random House Unabridged Dictionary* and scoured through it for the definitions of the following words: Bush, Gore, and Nader. This is what I discovered:

"The definition of 'BUSH: 1) a low plant with many branches that arise from or near the ground.' And if you scroll down to definition 11) you find the 'slang (vulgar) pubic hair.' Obviously a definition that only would be remotely entertained to be used during a president's second term and consequently retains little currency for a first run for the presidency."

"When used as an adjective, as in 'bushed', in Canada it means 'mentally unbalanced as a result of prolonged residence in a sparsely inhabited region'. I wonder what is the population of Crawford, Texas? In Australia and New Zealand slang it means 'unable to find one's direction, lost or confused.' Good thing we had that war back in 1776 or we would still be part of the British Commonwealth instead of the Kentucky Commonwealth, and Random House would have undoubtedly also coupled the United States of British America along with the Aussies and the New Zealanders as well in their definition."

"Now turning to the 'G' section, I located the definition of GORE, which has both a noun and a verb form. The noun is defined as: 1) blood that is shed, esp. when clotted. 2) murder, bloodshed, violence, etc. as an example, That movie had too much gore in it.' I wonder if they were referring to *An Inconvenient Truth,* (too much Gore)?"

"The verb form is defined as: '1) to pierce with, as if with a horn or tusk.' In addition there is a third entry in the dictionary for Gore which is 'a city in West Ethiopia,' which incidentally has no electoral votes and consequently won't be visited by either candidate."

"Turning to the 'N' section I was unable to locate any definition for N A D E R. However, there is a definition for N A D I R which is actually out of this world. In astronomy it means: '1) the point on the celestial sphere directly beneath a given position or observer and diametrically opposed to the zenith,' zenith being the highest point or peak in the sky and nadir being the lowest. Skip to definition number 3) and you find a figurative definition - 'the lowest point; point of greatest adversity or despair.' "One of my fundamental beliefs about human beings has been and remains that when a person gives you three reasons for doing or not doing something, reason number three is really number one. I think I'll expand that theory to include certain definitions in *The Random House Unabridged Dictionary* as well."

"Well, my fellow Americans (I always wanted to use that expression in a speech in front of a large audience knowing full well that I would have to delete it from any presentation in Gore, Ethiopia), I eliminated Nader first. Do we really want a candidate who can't even spell his own name correctly and is the lowest point and out of this world?"

"Let me retract that statement because I do not wish to influence you unduly in your own decision making but hope you now understand how your local library services can aid you in making your own personal political decisions in this or any other election year. Thank you all for your time and attention." At which point I departed the podium and returned to my seat with an occasional laughter and chuckle echoing in the background from my peer audience.

Stuart Tobin M.D.

After the adjournment of the luncheon session, former Governor Louis Nunn, who was in attendance, came up to me and proffered, "It's really good to see someone who still has a sense of humor about politics." He proceeded to shake my hand with a sincere sense of conviction accompanied with a large smile on his face. I appreciated his remarks more than my own. As a footnote, his remark was the only one I remembered from so many others made that day. So ended the luncheon, the day, and my political words of humorous wisdom.

Memory Lane

Having developed a number of cherished friendships and close personal relationships with many dedicated and accomplished librarians in many related fields, I felt comfortable asking one of my good and dear friends, Jim Nelson, who was commissioner of the KDLA, if he could help arrange a tour of the National Archives while I was attending an American Academy of Dermatology annual meeting in our nation's capital. Much to my delight, Jim was able to procure a personal tour for me and my wife.

The first week of February of 2006 we arrived to a very cold Washington, D.C. Windblown, with red noses and fingers nearly frozen, my wife and I and our eight-year-old grandson, Tyler, took the subway to the National Archives to be greeted by a docent who was a retired Air Force pilot. He proceeded to take us on a tour of the stacks where our national treasures are archived. My friend Jim had told them of my interest in Thomas Jefferson, and that I was a physician.

An enthusiastic female archivist in the middle of her professional career met us in the stacks. She carried in her arms a host of Civil War personnel records which turned out to be all the Tobins who had served in the Grand Army of the Republic. "We've arranged a little surprise for you and thought you might find a relative who served in the Civil War. Do you recognize any of these names?" she asked.

I looked at the stack of documents with their names carefully scripted and in alphabetical order. I then glanced at her expectant face. "John Tobin, John Tobin," I mused aloud. "Yes, yes, that name does ring a bell. My grandfather used to mention a John Tobin. Of course he used to talk about him serving in the Civil War."

Stuart Tobin M.D.

I confidently expressed. "Well, very good. Here's a chance to learn about your relative," she responded as she surveyed the document and told me about his service.

I didn't have the heart or the nerve to confess that all my relatives arrived in 1881 from the shetls of Russia or the poverty of Poland. Their contact with the American Civil War had been only through textbooks in history class in a Massachusetts secondary school.

"Commissioner Nelson told us all you have done to establish a library in your county and how you have volunteered for the state. He also told us of your medical background and interest in American history so we have a document that we thought you might find interesting." She extracted a tri-folded document with a red string tied around it to keep it secure. Written in perfect script was:

"Surgeon General's Office Washington, D.C. April 27, 1865. Brigadier Genl. J. K. Barnes"
"Reports upon the examination of the body of J. Wilkes Booth, the assassin."
The post mortem autopsy report read as follows:
"Hon: J.M. Stanton
Secretary of War

Sir,
I have the honor to report that in compliance with your orders, assisted by Dr. Woodward, USA, I made at 2 P.M. this day, a post mortem examination of the body of J. Wilkes Booth, lying aboard the Monitor Montauk off the Navy Yards.

The left leg and foot were encased in an appliance of splints and bandages upon the removal of which, a fracture of the fibula (small bone of leg) 3 inches above the ankle joint, accompanied by considerable ecchymoses, was discovered.

The cause of death was a gunshot wound in the neck- the ball entering the sterno-cleido muscle

Rash Decisions and Growth Experiences
from the Best Little Warthouse in Kentucky

2½ inches above the clavicle passing through the bony bridges of fourth and fifth cervical vertebrae - severing the spinal cord and passing out through the body of the sterno-cleido of right side, 3 inches above the clavicle.

Paralysis of the entire body was immediate, and all the horrors of consciousness of suffering and death must have been present to the assassin during the two hours he lingered.

Very Respectfully,
Your Obs.
Servt. J.K. Barnes
Surgeon General "

As she handed me a copy of this remarkable, seldom seen and unique document, I mused to myself what an unusual historical footnote to a singular American tragedy I was witnessing. I felt transported back in time and connected by this authentic archive to an event that had occurred one hundred and forty-one years ago. I also thought that Surgeon General Barnes was undoubtedly a more accomplished politician than an astute clinical physician.

First, realizing that Stanton was the real power in Washington and the government, as well as his immediate superior, he addressed the report to the Secretary of War rather than to the new President Johnson. Certainly Stanton could impact General Barnes's career more than anyone else.

Secondly, he told Stanton what he wanted to hear that Booth's demise was a lingering and a horribly painful one. As any third or fourth year medical student could tell you, a wound resulting in paralysis of the entire body would have left Booth with no feelings or sensations of pain at all. However, the ambiguous last sentence in the report must have fed Stanton's need for revenge.

Thirdly, I wondered had the troops that executed Booth attempted to kill him the same way he had shot Lincoln with a bullet wound to the back of the head. However, at the last moment the actor turned assassin reflexively moved his head resulting in the lethal and fatal wound described above, despite official reports that he was shot while taking refuge in a barn.

Our archivist and guide added, "Please keep a copy of this document as a memory of your trip to the National Archives." I barely had time to acknowledge my gratitude as she continued. "You notice the red string tied around this tri-folded document?" "Yes," I answered. "What we call strings today were referred to as tape in the nineteenth century. Since every document was bound in a red string tape and since there were so many documents to maintain, the expression 'red tape' became commonplace in government as an expression of a slow moving, cumbersome, and inefficient bureaucracy. Also you notice that the report is tri-folded. The filing cabinet had yet to be invented and to store documents they were tri folded and then secured with the red tape and stored in a wooden box."

She then retrieved an archival document encased in a Mylar plastic transparent sleeve. "Commissioner Nelson had told us that you are a great admirer of our third president. I thought you might be interested in this letter from Thomas Jefferson to a War of 1812 veteran petitioning for more benefits from the government for his service to the country. She handed me the letter which went something like this:

> Dear Sir,
> I am utterly surprised and amazed that you still believe that I am President of the United States having been out of office all these years. Consequently I am unable to assist you in your pursuit of additional benefits from the government for your service to our country during the war. In closing I remain absolutely astounded and amazed that you still think I am President.
>
> Very truly yours,
> Thomas Jefferson

Rash Decisions and Growth Experiences
from the Best Little Warthouse in Kentucky

Having read a number of books on Jefferson this was my first encounter with an actual primary source which in itself would have been an extraordinary and exciting event. In addition, it gave me an insight that I hadn't realized concerning Jefferson's keen sense of sarcasm and humor, both of which had escaped my intellectual historical radar scope. As I handed her back the document and thanked her again for her thoroughness and extraordinary effort in making this tour so personal and special for us, she dropped Jefferson's letter. "Oh, my God I dropped Jefferson's letter." She blurted as she instantly bent down to retrieve it from the floor. No harm was done since it was protected by the mylar plastic acid-free resistant sleeve encasing the precious document.

"I have one other document that you might find interesting," she said as she produced a worn and well preserved piece of paper. "This is General George Custer's application to West Point. You will notice that it is signed by his parents. No one could then and still to this day attend West Point Military Academy without their parents consent." I surveyed this document as well, carefully reading every line. I again thanked her for making our venture such an exciting one.   We now left with our docent to continue our tour of the non-public as well as public section of the National Archives. We proceeded to the public area where protected under a thick plate of glass was an engraved copper plate of the Declaration of Independence. Our docent informed us, "During the early part of the nineteenth century many people noticed that the ink on the original Declaration of Independence was beginning to fade. In order to preserve this most valuable national treasure for future generations, the technology of the time required that it be adequately reproduced."

"So the finest engraver and printer of the era was assigned the task. They handed him the original and he rolled it up in a scroll, tucked it under his arm and took it home with him. He kept it for two years as he worked on it almost daily. No one knows exactly how he did it. But every day or so he would unroll the original and engrave it in reverse onto this copper plate. Then he would roll the original back up and shove it back into his desk.

"Do you notice anything unusual about the plate?" he asked. "Yes," I responded, "it looks like someone engraved a word in the

142

middle of the Declaration of Independence." "That's correct. After two years of arduous work when they printed out the first copy it was noticed that he had left out one word. So it was added for accuracy. Also at the bottom left corner of the plate you can read the printer's name engraved. I guess you might consider him as one additional signer of the Declaration of Independence, or at least an editor," our docent added with a touch of humor and a not too well concealed chuckle.

We now proceeded to the great hall where the original Declaration and the Constitution were displayed. We surveyed each document. Our guide now asked, "Do you notice anything unusual about the Bill of Rights?" "No," I answered quizzically, having been stumped. "Well, there are two more amendments than there are actually. This original document was written before it was adopted and two of the original amendments to the Bill of Rights weren't approved. "One amendment which was initially rejected had just recently been passed. It mandated that the Congress could not enact a pay raise to their salaries right after an election."

I guess the nature of politicians remains unchanged in the history of the republic. I wonder if you could ever really enact a selfless, 'for the people' service philosophy instead of a self-service attitude in our politicians. While probably not, you could at least make it more difficult for our elected officials to pursue their self interests with certain checks and balances. Hence, the added amendment two hundred year later.

"Do you notice the founding fathers' likenesses painted around the circular dome and walls? Do you notice anything unusual about any of them?" he now asked. Again stumped, I said "No." See the one man with the peg leg. He's Gouverneur Morris. Gouverneur Morris was the only founding father who was tall enough to look Washington in the eye." Sure enough, he was the tallest figure painted on the wall with of course the exception of George Washington.

That reminded me of a story that I had heard a number of times. One of the original signers had dared Morris to go up to Washington and put his arm around George Washington and greet him informally. He took the dare and placed his hand on Washington's shoulder in a comradely manner. It was met with an ice-like stare that Morris later confided to friends "made me feel like the most insignificant person in the world."

We then proceeded to another section of the building where posted on the wall was a handwritten letter by a nine- or ten-year-old child. It read. "Mr. President, I have never seen a ten dollar green back. Would you send me one?" signed, "Fidel Castro." Our docent explained, "This letter addressed to President Franklin Delano Roosevelt was inadvertently discovered while cataloging Mr. Roosevelt's papers. We thought it might be of interest for people to see it."

I thought to myself if Roosevelt had only sent him the ten dollars it might have converted the lifelong unabashed communist to a Cuban capitalist and would have proved our most cost effective economical foreign aid investment of the 20th century. Oh, well that's just idle rumination and speculation tempered with much hindsight.

Next we were escorted to the archival reproduction room where another librarian and archivist had our grandson Tyler's name added to the original signers of the Declaration of Independence. Thanks to the wizardry of computer technology.

We thanked our docent for this most wonderful and unique, as well as personal tour of our national archives. The upcoming meeting at the Academy of Dermatology became an anticlimax as compared to this once in a lifetime tour. I now understood how people get the "Archive bug" for which there is, thankfully, no cure.

He Tried

Twenty-seven years on the bench, twenty-seven years of dispensing justice in the Circuit Court of Madison County, Kentucky. Considerable stories have been told of his Honor's courtroom which for many became a classroom in the law for the accused, attorneys, and the average citizen sitting on the jury. And a bold and impressive judge he was who would never stand for any theatre in his courtroom of law unless, of course, he was the one on stage. In his flowing black robe he sat behind his judicial bench, authoritative in character, impressive in stature, and always assured of his opinions and not reluctant to articulate them with the fiery force and absolute authority that no one dared question.

Since the circuit encompassed both the city of Richmond in Madison County and the city of Winchester in neighboring Clark County, the JUDGE, as everyone referred to him, would find himself a few days a month in neighboring Winchester. The courtroom being vintage and old lacked the convenience of air conditioning.

It was a hot and muggy Kentucky July afternoon and the temperature in the courtroom added to the very long proceedings of the day. Every window was opened in the hopes that a breeze would waft through relieving the heat and the polluted air of the litigants. The proceedings were as civil as a civil court could be.

The case which seemed simple had been made quite complex by the attorneys representing the litigants. The roof of a new building was porous and leaked. The owner of the building had sued the builder who in turn had sued the roofing company who in turn had sued the architect who in turn had sued the sub-contractor who in turn had sued the sub sub-contractor who in turn had sued the distributor who in turn had sued the manufacturer. Surely, someone was to blame and it was left to the wisdom of the court to sort out the responsible party or parties and affix the penalty and costs.

The attorneys droned on and on with the deft assurance that their defendants were innocent and a miscarriage of justice, or more appropriately any miscarriage of charges, financial that is, should not be heaped on their heads or their client's pocketbooks. If there were to be any transfer of funds it should only be from client to attorney and not to the litigant.

This is what the civil justice system had become. The judge had confided to me on more than one occasion at our weekly lunches, "Stu, 100% of civil law is about money and 95% of criminal law is about money. There is a small 5% of the criminal population that actually performs crime out of passion and stupidity."

The judge, having dined that particular day at Ruby's Café across the street from the courthouse, was beginning to feel the combined effects of his ham sandwich, Ale-8, the heat of the day, and the droning hypnotic litigation of the lawyers. In short, the temptation of a nap kept beckoning him, and his eyes were beginning to succumb and roll.

Suddenly, his right arm under the black robe felt something buzzing his skin. Shaken to his full senses he straightened up in his chair. Just as he did, the wasp that had taken refuge from the summer heat in a complete sense of disrespect for its judicial surroundings, rendered the most pointed testimony of the day and stung his honor. The Judge now let out a roaring, "God Damn!" followed by a second and louder salvo of "God Damn it!" The whole courtroom now reacted.

The little eighty-year-old widow Mrs. Wilby, who out of boredom and loneliness had come to the courtroom for some diversion and company, now fainted. The town drunk, Jamieson, who had laid squatter rights to the back row and had been comfortably snoozing, now awoke and fell off the pew. He abandoned ship, fleeing from the courtroom for his life and leaving a moist trail of processed moon shine in his wake. And the attorney who had been addressing the bench nervously stammered, "Your honor, I withdraw my objection."

Of course the greatest casualty of the proceedings had been the wasp who without benefit of counsel had received the death sentence from the judge somewhere between the first "God" and the last "Damn".

The Judge, now retired, was spending his days in a self-imposed sentence of, "Doing nothing, and it takes me the whole damn day to do it and I never quite get it done." That self deprecating description wasn't quite accurate though. In reality he couldn't "do nothing." He had a very active mind and body and was constantly involved in never completed projects that appeared out of nowhere, and usually that's where they ended - nowhere. An avid reader, cross word puzzle addict, history buff, community involved citizen and local Eastern Kentucky sports fan he had little time "to do nothing."

Rarely at home during the day, he was always involved in something, much to his wife's relief. For she was often heard saying, "I married the Judge for better or for worse but not for lunch, which helps explain why we had a standing weekly luncheon engagement on Mondays or Tuesdays.

Unfortunately, a few years ago while visiting friends one evening, someone had broken into their home and had stolen all the precious jewelry that he had given his spouse over the years. The local constabulary was no more successful in solving this onerous crime than any other that they had investigated. However, they did manage to leave throughout the entire house fingerprint swabbings that took his wife weeks to clean. Neither a fingerprint nor the jewelry or the culprit was ever found.

As April approached, the judge had decided to declare a loss on his taxes for the stolen jewelry. His accountant/lawyer warned him that would probably raise a red flag with everyone's most popular government institution the IRS and invite an audit. "So what?" was his characteristic response. If thieves, villains, murderers, and attorneys didn't intimidate him over his long career, why should the "Infernal Revenue Service"? So dutifully he filed his taxes, claiming the loss of personal property. It wasn't long until the white envelope inviting him to an audit for that year's taxes found its way to his mailbox on High Street in downtown Richmond, Kentucky.

On the appointed day he met with the IRS examiner, an experienced woman, professional and neatly dressed in business attire, who now requested an accounting of the jewelry deductions. He retrieved a shoe box full of checks and receipts. The examiner in a professional and detached tone inquired, "Mr. Chenault, do you have proof of these itemized deductions of lost jewelry?" Without missing a cue and as if back in the courtroom as judge, he grabbed the tax form from her hand listing each one of the pieces of jewelry deductions and demanded as he jabbed at the list with his index finger, "Pick one, any one!" Dutifully, she pointed to one and said, "That one." He whipped open the shoe box and shuffled through the receipts and checks and produced the proof.

"You, see." He proclaimed confidently. "Yes, I do." Used to always being in control he repeated, "Pick another one, any one." Again she picked another piece of jewelry deduction. Again he sorted through the shoe box and retrieved the correct proof. After repeating this same scenario another time she seemed quite satisfied and announced, "I can see there is adequate documentation for these deductions and that will conclude this audit. The IRS is satisfied that your deductions are legitimate."

Well, the judge would have none of it. "No, no pick another," he again demanded. "That won't be necessary, Mr. Chenault, you obviously have plenty of adequate documentation to substantiate your deductions. The IRS will accept your request for a tax deduction as legitimate and correct."

Turning red in the face, he now turned to her and even more angrily barked, "God Damn it, I stayed up half the God damn night sorting through these damn checks. Now I said pick another and I mean it. PICK ANOTHER!!" With her fingers quivering, she picked another. He rummaged through his shoe box again and produced one more check. Now satisfied that he had proven his case he placed the lid on the shoe box and leaned back and smiled a satisfying judicial smile. Case closed. Deductions approved. Refund made. IRS shaken. Justice not delayed. End of story.

Publisher to Physician

I attended high school at a time when summer vacation meant exactly that, a break between the middle of June and early September when school began again. Having reached the mid teen-age years, my parents, like so many survivors of the Depression and the War, felt or rather demanded that their children should and could not waste that time in idle recreation. So each summer I would have to find meaningful employment. It was the summer of 1960 that I started working for Uncle Arthur.

Uncle Arthur, also a product or perhaps more accurately a casualty of the Depression, had acquired through necessity a very frugal and pecuniary approach to life which through years of practice still carried him through all endeavors in his life. Despite his improved and secure economic situation, his lifestyle still remained fixed in and by the 1930s.

Being fifteen years of age and not having experienced the Great Depression, I found his idiosyncrasies curious and in some cases incomprehensible. In his mind he was very generous to me, and I always sensed and appreciated his caring and affectionate nature towards me but marveled at some of his odd behavior.

While in his summer employment he would take me out to lunch occasionally and even more infrequently to dinner at modest restaurants in New York City. At the end of the meal he would remove a small round plastic container from his frayed inner coat pocket, carefully unscrew the top and fill it with table salt from the shaker on the table. He would sometimes do the same with sugar. I always stared in amazement as he repeated this ritual on our occasional dining outings.

His explanation was, "I don't see any reason to waste money buying a whole box of salt or sugar for my small personal needs.

Rash Decisions and Growth Experiences
from the Best Little Warthouse in Kentucky

Since they put these containers out for the patrons, what's the difference if I use the salt or sugar now or later?" End of discussion. I never became a convert to this particular spice philosophy and still buy sugar and salt in bulk packages at the supermarket in the hopes that eventually they would be consumed.

Uncle Arthur was the publisher of a once flourishing and famous book publishing house named Liveright Publishing Corp., which previous to that had been Boni Liveright Publishing Corp. They occupied an office on the fifteenth floor of an aged un-air conditioned skyscraper on Park Avenue South in midtown Manhattan. The elevator had one of those collapsible metal cage fronts that was the only barrier between you and the floors as they whisked by in a monotonous and predictable manner. I do remember the heat and humidity of the New York summers and how difficult it was to concentrate, especially after eating lunch in that stifled oppressive atmosphere.

Lunch usually meant a hot dog and pop from the street vendor with the yellow and blue umbrella at the corner of the building. Since the street vendor didn't speak English and my lunch "hour" really was more like a twenty minute break, in four summers of employment he and I never exchanged any pleasantries. Come to think about it, I don't recall anyone in New York ever exchanging any social banter with casual strangers.

Because I was "learning the business" Uncle Arthur felt a salary would be exorbitant and inappropriate. So I discovered at an early age the meaning of deficit spending, a philosophy which apparently has helped define the American government and the American people since. There must have been more than one Uncle Arthur in our country's past generations.

However, in its day, the company had been very successful, having published *Gentleman Prefer Blondes* by Anita Loos, and Hendrik Van Loon, the great Dutch historian and his most popular book *The Story of Mankind* as well as a host of other non-fiction books by him. Liveright had also published the great Japanese author Akutagayka, whose famous *Rashomon* had been made into a play for television and a thought provoking movie as well. He had also published a host of classic books which were at least popular with libraries that felt the need to have them available for their patrons.

I remember assisting in the mailing room sending many of those books to public libraries all over the country. After all, you never know when some passionate reader from Middlesville, Ohio, will develop the burning desire to read Aristophanes' *Eleven Plays*.

My father had insisted that our family had a personal connection with another ditzy blonde unrelated to Uncle Arthur. He always insisted that Judy Holiday was a relative of ours. Judy Holiday was a glamorous and successful actress of stage and screen who although she didn't play Lorelei, the ditzy southern girl in Loos's *Gentleman Prefer Blondes*, she did play another one in the successful Broadway production of *Born Yesterday*.

Skeptical of this association I asked my dad one day, "How could she be related to us if her name was Holiday? We don't have any relatives named Holiday." He answered confidently, "Holiday is her stage name, her real name is Good." Knowing better than to challenge him any further I just kept my skepticism to myself rather than push the envelope with the obvious question, we don't have any relatives named Good either?

Years later, my older brother Ed, whose interest and infatuation with our family's genealogy had graduated to a full blown obsession, had acquired the ship's log from the boat that our grandfather had immigrated on in 1888. He discovered that our Tobin name had originally been Tov in Hebrew, which translated means good, as recognized in the common expression "Mazel Tov" from *Fiddler on the Roof* and which means Good Luck. So perhaps we did have a Good relationship with Judy Holiday? This seemed to be more of a burning issue with us than it did for distant cousin Judy. I'm quite certain, however, had she in any way acknowledged our presence she would have been granted the accolade of Aunt Judy. To make the familial connection even more tenuous Judy's original Jewish name had been Tuvim which translated is not good but holiday. Well, it does make a good story to tell at the holidays.

Uncle Arthur wasn't really my uncle. He had become a good friend of my parents and they enjoyed a close and personal relationship for years, well before I had even entered this world. I never discovered how they had met. But when my older brother as an infant had become desperately ill with life threatening infantile diarrhea in an era before health insurance, my parents had incurred exorbitant medical expenses that they couldn't pay. Uncle Arthur had come to the rescue and had loaned them the amazing sum of $2,500.

This would account for the "Uncle" appellation. If we had been European royalty we would have bestowed upon him the title Sir, Lord, Baron, Duke, or even King. But that entitlement option wasn't available to the children of eastern European impoverished immigrant Jews from the shetls of Russia. So he became "Uncle" instead. Noble ranks in the good old U.S. of A don't go over well, especially since I had discovered by reading one of Uncle Arthur's publications, *The Story of Mankind* that our nation's origins were focused more in separating us from a monarchy than embracing it.

Anyway, King Arthur had already been taken and would have undoubtedly led to some confusion with his neighbors on the lower east side of Manhattan, which no one would ever mistake for Camelot. Then there would always be the puzzling and lingering question in the public's mind, why was King Arthur hording salt and sugar from a deli restaurant in midtown? So all in all "Uncle" Arthur suited him and us best.

These summer vacation jobs with him continued throughout my entire high school years. I spent time answering the phone and mailing out packages of books and mostly proofreading manuscripts that had been accepted by him for review for publication. By my second summer I was entrusted to reviewing submitted manuscripts by aspiring authors and was horrified that he accepted my opinion about them.

How-to books had become quite popular, and he would extol many times on how successful they had been. Yet he never published any. However, the summa cum laude experience at his publishing house was when he asked me to read Marguerite Wilbur's *Thomas Jefferson, Apostle of Liberty* in the summer of 1962 and write the inside dust jacket review. I have hoped the accomplished author never discovered that the dust jacket had been written by a sixteen-year-old high school student whom she may have failed had she had him in one of her classes.

I can still recite most of that blurb, and it remains my only published piece, although now no longer totally anonymous in nature. The next time you scan a dust jacket blurb in trying to decide whether to purchase the book or not, you might keep this minor footnote of publishing trivia in mind.

I was getting to know the business fairly well and developed if not a love at least an appreciation and major interest in the publishing field. After four summers and now on the payroll, a payroll that now at least covered my commuting railroad ticket and lunches at the hot dog stand, I was in imminent danger of graduating from high school and ready "to move on" - whatever that meant.

Uncle Arthur aware of my situation, one day dropped the bombshell. "Stuart, instead of going off to college, why don't you think about continuing to work for me during the day and attend college at night, say at CCNY. After you graduate you know I am getting much older and you could take over the business. Now you know this has always been a family business and I would like to keep it that way. So I want you to meet my niece."

The following week his niece appeared neither mysteriously nor unexpectedly at the office. I took one look at her and I knew what my answer would be. I didn't realize it at the time but that introduction to his niece was an epiphany of sorts in my doctrine for dating in the future. I became resolved never to date any woman whose left lower extremity weighed more than my entire body weight.

"Uncle Arthur," I confided to him the next day, "We've never really talked about my long term plans and quite honestly I haven't given them as much thought as I perhaps should. But I have decided to go to medical school and follow in my father's footsteps. I'm really sorry to disappoint you and it was really a difficult decision for me to make." I lamented as I lied.

Had I been more imaginative I would have conjured up the lame but plausible excuse that since he was my "uncle" any attachment to his niece would be like an incestuous relationship with my first cousin. However, I'm quite sure a man of such literary knowledge and insight would have found such a claim, if not transparent, at least translucently bogus.

That was my last summer working for him and I didn't see him much after that and always regretted that I didn't keep in touch with him in the future, which is now part of my past. I will always have fond memories of Uncle Arthur and have always missed him. I still keep a set of special shelves in my library packed with books published by Liveright Publishing Corp. and will pull one off the shelf from time to time to read it, although I haven't gotten around to plowing through *The Eleven Plays of Aristophanes*, yet.

Uncle Ben

Uncle Arthur wasn't the only person to receive the non-coveted title of "Uncle" from our family. My cousin Ben also was only known to me and my brothers as Uncle Ben. Uncle Ben had immigrated as a child from Russia, or his parents had. I was never quite clear on that point. However, since he didn't speak with an accent I assume that he was either born here right in the good old US of A or immigrated as a very young child. His parents had died at an early age and he was shuffled from relative to relative as a child with all the love and care that an extended tight knit immigrant family extended to an orphan of its own.

Uncle Ben had traveled the non-traditional route to success, but a success he had become. Shunning the education ladder to which so many of my family and relatives had become addicted, Uncle Ben as a young aspiring entrepreneur had decided to travel a different path. During the Great Depression of the 1920s-30s, he sought his fortune through real estate acquisitions.

He first acquired the Breitmeyer-Tobin building, a local and famous iconic structure in Detroit. He then purchased the Hollenden Hotel in Cleveland. In 1945, he bought the Hollywood Beach Hotel in southern Florida and which became the magnet for beach and sun snowbirds from the northeast. Its name became synonymous with winter Florida vacations.

As the story continued to unfold as told to me by my father, Uncle Ben then, with the partnership of two other men of his same real estate ilk, purchased the Empire State Building, which he partially owned for a number of years. This successful venture allowed him to branch out more independently and he eventually sold his interest in this New York icon.

Rash Decisions and Growth Experiences
from the Best Little Warthouse in Kentucky

With his desire to live in a warmer climate he relocated to Hollywood, Florida. With his hotel becoming a very successful enterprise, he accumulated more and more wealth. Realizing that South Florida was becoming a magnet for growth, he became involved in real estate and accumulated even greater wealth.

With keener competition in the hotel industry he eventually sold The Hollywood Beach Hotel. Ironically, the mecca for leisure and fun was converted into a Baptist Bible College. He now became heavily involved in philanthropy and contributed large sums of money to Jewish and other charities, earning the recognition and acknowledgement as well as numerous accolades from many prominent citizens for his charitable works as a great man of society.

In addition to his Florida residence he maintained a suite at the Hampshire House in New York City close to Central Park. The Hampshire House was one of those exorbitantly expensive exclusive apartment hotels in Manhattan. One Saturday evening in the late 1950s when I was ten or eleven years old, Uncle Ben invited the whole family to dinner at the Hampshire House.

This became my first brush with exposure to a life style I had only seen in movies or had read about in newspapers. In preparation for the big event, my mother gathered my brothers and me together and informed us that although Ben was our distant cousin because he was so wealthy we should refer to him as "Uncle" Ben. From that day forward he remained Uncle in mind, thought and pocket book. Dressed in our Sunday best, which for Jews was our Saturday best, off we went for dinner to the Big Apple and a rendezvous with caviar and upper culture cuisine.

My recollections of that evening were of a handsomely tailored and tall man with an outgoing and jovial personality who relished entertaining his less fortunate family. Standing over six feet tall and with rosy red cheeks and his hair fashionably slicked back and an encompassing smile that never seemed to leave his round and jovial face, he made a singular impression that has stayed with me till this day. His two children, slightly older than my brothers and me, also were very expensively dressed.

When it came time to order dinner I was shocked as I looked at the prices on the menu. I ordered the cheapest item as did my brothers. My shock turned to apoplexy when my young cousin sitting opposite me at the dining table with the neatly pressed and starched linen table cloth ordered a peanut butter and jelly sandwich for the incredible exorbitant cost of five dollars and then only ate half of it. I couldn't believe that I was witnessing such an incredible profligate waste of money, not to mention of Peter Pan chunky peanut butter and Welch's Concord grape jelly.

I didn't hear or have any contact with Uncle Ben until I had returned to New York for my dermatology residency many years later. One day while walking from New York University Medical Center to Grand Central Station to catch the commuter special, the same local train that I had taken so many times before while working for Uncle Arthur to Westchester, I picked up the *New York Post*. There, plastered on the front page, was a huge headline with a full page photograph announcing that prominent hotelier and real estate magnet and philanthropist, Ben Tobin, age sixty-one, had been scammed by his newly acquired wife and former showgirl thirty years his junior. Unannounced, she had unlocked his safe, emptied it, left him, and then sued him for divorce.

About a year after my father had died, which wasn't too long after Uncle Ben's recent divorce, he invited my mother out for dinner. She told me that he was still as elegant as ever but she felt uncomfortable with the Damon Runyon chaperone who was Uncle Ben's bodyguard with the bulging coat pocket.

I lost sight of Uncle Ben for another thirty years until he was in his early nineties when he died. My brother sent me his obituary from the *New York Times* which extolled all his accomplishments and philanthropic activities.

It's About Time

One good thing about living in a small Kentucky community is everybody knows everybody else. Of course the bad thing about it is everybody knows everybody else.

Joe owns a watch shop in Richmond and if you have any timepiece of any vintage or type that needs repair, Joe is the person you go to. An experienced, thoroughly competent, and all around pleasant guy, Joe can fix anything that has a second, minute or hour hand attached to it. His shop on Water Street in downtown Richmond is an old clapboard cream colored house complete with dark brown shutters. A sign that announces Joe's Watch Shop sways in the breeze. His parking lot in front can accommodate two cars concurrently but more sequentially if you time your visit just right.

From time to time I wander to Joe's to get a battery replacement in the umpteenth consecutive Elgin wristwatch that my wife has bought me for my most recent birthday. As I perused my own collection of wristwatches I wondered if perhaps I should open my own used watch shop. Letting my fantasy carry me one step further, I even decided on a pun name for it, *Stu's Second Hand Shop*. However, I passed on the thought since neither my house nor my wrist was zoned as commercial.

As Confucius would say, "A man who has one watch knows what time it is. A man who has two watches is never quite sure." I really doubt that Confucius said that since he died long before any hand held timepieces were invented. However, I have adapted the same pattern of logic to my patients when confused by a diagnosis or treatment approach.

Often when a patient appeared in my office for a second opinion or was just referred by another physician and my diagnosis or treatment varied from their other physician, I invoked the all wise and knowing Confucius with, "A patient who has one doctor knows what is wrong with him. A patient who has two doctors is never quite sure." It sounds wise on the surface and since I'm a "superficial" physician that was deep enough for me.

One day while visiting with Joe to replace one of those watch's battery, I spied in his long glass covered presentation case which ran the length of his shop a cache of pocket watches. Joe had already expertly repaired a pocket watch of mine that belonged in our family and a watch that other repair tinkers had said couldn't be fixed.

"Joe, do you have any old pocket watches for sale?"

"Well, Doc, as a matter of fact I do." He went back to the dark cavernous labyrinth of his repair shop and produced a 14K gold pocket watch that was 111 years old and in multiple pieces which more resembled a jigsaw puzzle than a functioning timepiece. "This is a nice one and I hate to melt it down for just the gold value. I would rather sell it to someone who will give it a good home."

I'm wondering what constitutes a "good home." Are there watch social workers who show up unannounced at your house to inspect the premises to be sure that the timepiece will have a chance of being adequately nurtured, wound, and preserved for another 100 years. Do they check the humidity and temperature control in your home? Are you entitled to an appeal if rejected as unsuitable? I decided since Joe didn't ask me any questions that I qualified as a "good home."

As I examined the pocket watch, despite it being in a jumble of pieces, it had a very attractive alabaster face with each of the 12 hour numbers surrounded in a fine delicate gold circle with an ornamental delicate lace like gold minute and hour hand. Inset at the 6:00 hour sat a second miniature clock face with a sweeping second hand. This beautiful pocket watch had a gold cover that snapped open and shut as well as a back cover also of 14K gold that when opened revealed the engraved inscription in flowing script:

Mother
to
Elmhurst D. Prescott

"Joe, who was Elmhurst D. Prescott?" I curiously inquired.

Just as quickly Joe answered with a smirk. "He was Mrs. Prescott's son."

"You know Joe you're almost as a big a wise guy as me." Well, enough of that for the genealogy of the watch. Good thing we weren't on The Antique Road Show in which the value would be affected by documented history.

"How much do you want for the watch, Joe?"

Joe retrieved a small precision scale from the dark chambers of his shop and set the watch's gold cover and back on it and weighed it. He then produced the daily quote for gold and did some mental mathematic gyrations. After pondering for a moment he said. "Given the weight of the 14K gold and the price of gold now and then to repair the watch a fair price would be $800 dollars."

"Eight hundred dollars?!?!" I exclaimed. "What do you think I am, a rich doctor? Just joking Joe. I'll take it. Do you want me to pay you now or when I return to pick it up?"

"When you pick it up will be okay, Doc."

"When will you have it ready, Joe?"

"Give me about three weeks to fix it."

"Okay, see you then."

As I turned to leave he handed me a ragged brown wrinkled receipt with the price written on it.

As it is in Kentucky, 3 weeks usually means at least 6 weeks in other cultures' time frame. So 6 or 7 weeks later I showed up at his shop to claim the watch.

"Joe, I'm here to get my watch."

"Well, doc, I've been swamped and haven't had a chance to fix it yet."

"Okay Joe, but it has been over a month and a half and I was expecting it to be done by now."

"I know but I just haven't had time to repair it.

Are you going to need it by Christmas as a present for some-one or is it just for you?"

"It's just for me."

"Then there isn't any real deadline or rush."

"While I don't technically have a deadline I was kind of hoping that you would have had one," I added.

"Well, give me another month. Oh, by the way the price of gold has gone up considerably to an all time high since you were here last, and I'm going to lose money on our deal compared to today's gold prices."

"Gee, Joe I'm sorry the price of gold has gone up but we made a deal and agreed on the price. The price was fixed on the price of gold at the time and it was already high. With a little luck the price of gold will drop when I return in a few weeks and you'll feel better about the deal."

"Okay," he said as I left.

Another Kentucky month goes by and I stopped by to pick up the watch eight weeks later.

"Joe, I bet you don't have to guess why I'm here. How's the watch look?" One look at his face and I knew the watch looked the same as it did the last two times I had been in the shop.

"Doc, I've been really swamped and I'm the only one here. People filter in and out all day, and I have a stack of watches to fix and just haven't had the time to work on it. You know the price of gold has gone up again to even higher than the last time you were in."

"Gees, Joe, I would love to get the watch before it celebrates its bicentennial. Look Joe whether the price of gold has gone up or down, and I've been hoping that the price would have gone down, we still made a deal and I know you are a decent and honest man and will fix the watch as we agreed."

"I realize it must be painful to fix and sell a watch that you could make more money on now. However, we both know that when you purchased the unassembled watch that the price of gold was considerably less and that you're not losing money on your investment. You're not just making as much of a profit as you would like."

Rash Decisions and Growth Experiences
from the Best Little Warthouse in Kentucky

"I'm sure it must also warm the cockles of your heart to think here I'm selling a watch to this damn rich doctor who is rolling in dough and that I'm just a poor watchmaker eking out a living. That has to be doubly painful for you." I hope he realized the validity of my hyperbole.

"Doc, I had been thinking of offering you a $100 to let me out of the deal before the price of gold drops again."

"Joe, I don't want a $100. I want the watch."

"Okay, doc. Come back in another month."

I return in 4 weeks x 2 for the next episode in our soap opera out-of-pocket watch drama.

"Hey Joe, guess why I'm here." Not knowing what to expect now.

"Doc, I have a surprise for you. I finished the watch." He brought out the now assembled timepiece and it was absolutely lovingly restored.

"I shined it up and it's working beautifully." As he wound it and I put it to my ear to listen to the exquisite mechanics of a bygone era of over 100 years ago now ticking in perfect harmony with non-Kentucky time.

As I handed him the $800 we had agreed on he mentioned that the price of gold was holding about the same.

"Isn't it a beauty Doc?"

"Joe, it certainly is and you have performed the perfect restoration that everyone in the county knows that you're capable of. You're certainly a vanishing breed and a singular unique craftsman and an accomplished artisan of a bygone era."

"I'm glad you like it. You know doc, I was thinking that a beautiful watch like that needs a lovely gold chain and fob to go with it. I just happen to have one I think that you would like."

He withdrew to his inner sanctuary and retrieved a gold chain with an unusual handmade fob with Colorado inscribed in gold and with mountains in the background.

"Doc, this is a very unusual piece, and I have never seen one quite like it. It's all handmade and it would go with the watch really well."

"Joe, how much do you want for it?" I casually asked. He retrieved his little scale and carefully weighed it. He then did some mental mathematical gyrations and said, "If you take the price of gold today and add on the cost of repair, you know it needs to be repaired, the gold links are coming apart and if you wear it the chain will fall apart. Hmmm, I could let you have it for $750 and have it fixed in about a month."

I'm thinking haven't I've been here before? In the words of Yogi Berra, who may have been as great a prophet as Confucius, "It seems like déjà vu all over again." Is this going to be another time after time?

"Joe, let me think about it and I'll get back to you in a timely manner if I decide to take it. Thanks for the wonderful restoration of the Elmhurst D. Prescott, whoever he was, pocket watch, and in the paraphrased words of Benjamin Franklin, whom I think was a contemporary of Confucius, if 'time is money', we've both lost a golden opportunity and need to 'watch' our alchemy more carefully in the future." Whatever that means.

"Joe, Gotta run. It's about time I left."

Candy Goes Cuckoo?

The summer of 1980 seemed a wonderful time to take that British vacation I always wanted. The Jefferson County Medical Society had sent me a slick glossy brochure for a two week excursion to Ireland, Scotland, and England. What a wonderful opportunity to sample a smorgasbord of countries in such a small time frame. This was the era of traveling that embraced the great American vacation philosophy of squeeze as many places into as short a time span as possible for as little money as you can. It was a different city every day and a different country every 72 hours. So I quickly signed up for the "If this Is Sunday This Must Be Scotland" tour, etc., etc.

Sponsored by the Jefferson County Medical Society of Louisville, Kentucky, through a reputable touring company, every day was laid out with a specific itinerary and a very tight schedule. To keep all the wheels turning and the schedule met, the XYZ Touring Company provided us with a tour guide to keep us on schedule, on time, and together. Ours was Candy, an attractive post-college pre-commitment-to-life American young woman who could express her independence and maintain her freedom by traveling with a bunch of dotty, old, and aspiring-to-be-old physicians and their spouses (of which I belonged to the latter). So off we went, passport in one hand, tour guide in the other, and 35 mm camera dangling around my neck.

Our first stop was the gorgeous emerald isle of Ireland. Landing in Dublin we had a dizzying tour of the city and environs including a visit to Trinity College, with a 90-second viewing of the *Book of Kells* followed by a bus tour of the glorious and colorful doors of the Irish townhouses.

Stuart Tobin M.D.

Following in the footsteps of the great Irish poets, I almost felt inspired to read their great works. A feeling, however, that passed as quickly as the tour. Then, by bus, we darted to many quaint little picture postcard shamrock hamlets and villages with their thatched roof houses all surrounded by the glorious shades of greens of the lush Erin Isles countryside, bathed in liquid sunshine. Arriving at Blarney Castle I hiked to the top of the highest turret in a foggy mist. This was the equivalent of climbing a seven-story building just to kiss the famous Blarney Stone.

The origin of the word blarney derived not from the Irish but the English and a very noteworthy English lady, in fact, none other than Queen Elizabeth I. During her reign she became enchanted and amused by the noble and entertaining story teller Lord Blarney, whose ancestral castle we visited. One day, noting his absence from court she remarked, "Where is my Blarney? I miss my Blarney." The appellation stuck and became fixed and synonymous with Irish wit, humor, and exaggeration ever since.

To claim the bragging rights to having massaged your lips to the cold wet stone, one had to lie on your back and lean and extend your neck and head to kiss the stone while an ancient Irishman as old as the stone itself held your feet so you wouldn't plummet the hundreds of feet below, which would have undoubtedly left your lips permanently adhered to a not so nearly as famous stone at the base of the castle.

Since this is the Mecca for all who love to embellish and embroider their comical cloth, I happily made the pilgrimage and successfully made the trip in the twelve and a half minutes allotted for this tourist stop.

Then off we sped to a woolen mill and then to Waterford, which relieved us of the anxiety of carrying a lot of excess money in our not so bulging pockets for the remainder of the tour. Who said the ancient science of alchemy had died? We successfully converted, with the help of our spouses, gold to glass in a mere fifteen minutes.

Seventy-two hours were now up so off to Scotland we scurried. We crossed by air the Irish Sea according to the Irish map at the Shannon airport, but upon landing it was labeled the Celtic Sea by the English map in the airport.

Arriving at a quaint border town we stopped to dine for lunch. I remember the waiter inquiring as to how we enjoyed the cuisine. The recent sojourn to Lord Blarney's castle, still vivid in my frontal lobe, I replied without a moments hesitation, "Sir, this is undoubtedly the finest meal I have ever had in the entire country of Scotland." Realizing that our American tour group had just crossed the Scottish border, he asked, "Sir, how many meals have you had in Scotland?" Not nearly as confidently I answered, "This is the first. However, it is the standard by which all the others will have to be measured." I lamely added.

Back into the bus we loaded ourselves for the race to Edinburgh, arriving on time. The next day we toured the city and traveled the Golden Mile which is the causeway from Edinburgh Castle to Holyroodhouse, the Queen's official residence in Scotland. While roughly a mile in distance and while Roger Banister, the Scots physician, was the first to break the four minute mile, our tour guide allotted us only slightly more than two hundred and forty seconds to traverse the cobbled stone route.

The street is peppered with wonderful little shops and historic homes including that of Robert Burns, or at least one in which he had temporary residence. All is going well and as planned. Then events, unpredictable events, started to unfold.

Nestling into our four star hotel in Edinburgh, our little band of forty or so American physicians and our spouses settled down to a pleasant dinner, which now ranked as the second best meal I had ever had in Scotland, although I was the only one in the troop who held steadfast to that culinary belief.

Expecting another whirlwind day tomorrow we all decided to retire early and get a good night's sleep. Just as I was entering that wonderful relaxing dreamy stage 1 of sleep, at ten o'clock my phone rang. Who could be calling me at this hour I wondered? Picking up the receiver I immediately recognized Candy, our tour guide. She sounded very agitated and anxious. "What's wrong?" I asked. "I can't discuss it over the phone. You need to come up to my room now." "Can't it wait till tomorrow?" I asked. "No, you need to come to my room right now," she pleaded.

So I quickly got dressed and headed to her room. She seemed very anxious and fearful. "What's wrong?" I asked. She pointed to the ceiling. There was the same type of ceiling fan that was in my room. Unlike America, the Scots have a conspicuous rather than a hidden wire running from the fan to the wall where it disappears. She then whispers into my ear that the fan is "bugged" and that our conversation was being monitored. "Who would want to monitor our conversation?" I asked incredulously. Then she dropped the bombshell, "The IRA."

In the 80s, the whole of the British Isles was experiencing the convulsion known as "The Troubles" which was the unrest that translated into bombings and killings committed by the Irish Republican Army which was rebelling at the occupation by the English in northern Ireland, the Catholics against the Protestants, the green against the orange, and so on. While most of the turmoil was centered in Northern Ireland there had been a spilling over into the rest of the British Isles as well. While in the Republic of Ireland, I saw signs and notices posted on telephone poles attesting to the anger against the Queen and the British government. One could not be totally unaware of the possibility of an incident occurring anywhere in the United Kingdom, which apparently wasn't quite as united as its name and the tourist office led us to believe in their attractive, colored, shiny brochures.

She continued, "The IRA plans to bomb the train that we are taking tomorrow to London." "What?" I gasped. "The IRA plans to bomb our train tomorrow and the people working at the front desk are in on it." She quietly but anxiously whispered. "I needed to tell you this. I didn't know who else to tell?" she pleaded plaintively. "Well, let me think about this." I answered quizzically and confused. My curiosity had gotten the better of me. So I wandered down to the front desk and engaged the clerks in meaningless conversation, as they gave me an equally quizzical look, especially when I inquired about the Troubles spilling into Scotland.

I stayed up half the night trying to make some sense of what she had said. Candy had seemed so reliable and sensible and possessed all those qualities you expect from a competent tour director. Yet her accusations seemed so farfetched and improbable. Where did she get this information? Could it possibly be true? Could we be in danger? Should I report it to some authority? Why didn't she report it to the authorities? Should I report Candy to the authorities? Why did she confide in me? Why would the IRA want to blow up a bunch of Americans in Scotland?

It just didn't make any sense. Sense or not the questions kept racing through my mind all night. Time stops for no one and the next morning came too quickly or too slowly. It was hard to distinguish. As any man of action in a similar situation would do, I decided the best course to take was inaction and would await my/our destiny to unfold around me rather than to actively seize the moment to affect its outcome.

We ate a quick and early breakfast and took the arranged bus to the railroad station. As we arrived at the platform to board the fast train to London, Candy refused to allow us to board. She kept making excuses and giving us reasons why we shouldn't. The ticket master told us with a very exasperated and irritated voice that "if we didn't board in the next few minutes the train was going to leave without us."

Should we board or not? Everyone seemed confused and didn't understand why we weren't already in our assigned seats. All of a sudden there appeared out of seemingly nowhere three emergency medics who placed Candy in a straight jacket and whisked her off in an ambulance as if on cue from some movie. What a bizarre coincidence I thought.

The ticket master announced again with a very irritating and authoritative tone of voice, "If you don't get on the train right now you will be stranded in Edinburgh." Everyone in a near panic hurried onto the train in the confusion. I was about to do the same when I spied Candy's briefcase sitting by itself on the platform. I quickly turned around and grabbed it and just made it to the train as it started to move. The briefcase contained all our passports which she carried for our safekeeping.

Candy quickly became the exclusive topic of conversation and I began hearing bits and pieces of information from some of my

168

fellow travelers. One related that she had seen her in the bar consuming large quantities of alcohol and another said that she had been not sleeping well and had been taking amphetamines to stay alert during the day. Cozying up to one of the psychiatrists I confided in him my strange and bizarre encounter with her the night before and wondered how he would piece all this together.

He confidently deduced that she had had a drug induced psychosis and had become acutely paranoid. As it is with most paranoid thought patterns there is enough reality intermixed with the fantasy that it became difficult to ferret out fact from fiction. "She must have reported her delusional thoughts to the tour service who then arranged for the medical intervention?" he proffered.

That all seemed reasonable as we sped 100 miles an hour on our four-hour ride from Edinburgh to London. "Of course, all that makes a lot of sense," I told the psychiatrist, "unless we get blown up on the trip in the next four hours. I think I'll wait until we reach London before sharing that piece of information with the rest of our tour group."

We arrived on time and without incident. Whew, went my heart. I then safely at dinner confided the rest of the story to my colleagues, followed by my observation to the waiter that this was undoubtedly the finest meal I had ever had in England.

Later that evening I called the emergency number of the tour group who told me that they didn't have anyone to replace Candy and that they couldn't or wouldn't divulge any personal information on an employee. So I never did discover what happened to her and only hoped that she eventually recovered and became healthy again or was released unharmed by her unknown captors.

If I were writing a fictional spy thriller would that be the ending, or had Candy been kidnapped by the IRA because there was non-fiction in what we thought was bogus? Was there an incendiary device on our train that failed to detonate and went undetected? It was awfully coincidental that the men with the straight jacket arrived at that exact moment when they did as if they had been following her every move. In America someone could not be seized on the street or in her case off the train platform as she was for presumed mental health issues and it would require 2 physicians to deem her incompetent for any type of involuntary commitment. Could the British secret service have staged the whole event because in some way Candy had stumbled onto some clandestine sinister scheme or that she was an agent that had gone wild? It all seemed so bizarre.

****

Thirty years later I returned to the west of Ireland for another escorted tour with my wife. The picturesque countryside was even more beautiful than I had remembered. We saw all the usual and planned sights without mishap or misplaced tour guide. The last day of the tour our guide asked each person to compose a limerick to present to the group. I composed two. The first was a more respectable one and the second a bit more bawdy and more properly told in a pub under the influence of the local Guinness. Against my wife's advice I recited both.

The first:
The Brits to Erin did travel
To instruct the Irish rabble
But accents so queer
Affected by beer
Stiff upper lips unraveled

The second:
A gray haired nobleman's phallus
Yearned for a virginal chalice
Horizontal endeavors abound
Which led to an abdomen round
And triplets a born at the palace

A woman on our tour confronted me afterwards and self-righteously and indignantly accosted me. "Sir, you are a dirty old man." I immediately countered with, "Madam, you are mistaken. I'm a DOMIT." What's a domit?" She asked confused. "A dirty old man in training," I confidently answered.

The Red Glove Revue

A few years after opening my private practice in Richmond, Kentucky, one of our local charitable organizations decided to have a fund raiser for a worthwhile cause in the community. They contracted with a national organization that would provide the format, music, choreography, scenery and costumes for a designated fee of a stage production of the *Red Glove Revue*. To defer additional expense, people in the community would volunteer to provide the talent. Any excess monies would go directly to the local charity.

I, with a few of my friends, thought we could sneak into the production under the guise of low level talent. Since when I sing in the shower the hot water goes off in protest, I auditioned for a comedy bit part instead of a solo vocal one. I was placed into one of the filler vaudeville comedy routines that were placed in between the singing and dancing acts from a number of popular Broadway shows.

After reviewing the canned humor I confided to my good friend Bill, who was going to be one of the other joggers in our little troupe, that I thought I could write better material than those provided. I cajoled the others into allowing me to give it a try. We casually and serendipitously substituted my creative humor for one of the generic canned ones already provided.

I concocted the following scenario that we performed once and only once on opening night. Two joggers ran out onto the stage and the first said:

"Did you hear that the local bank president has quit his job?"

The second jogger straight man asked, "No, what's he doing now?"

"He's gone into the novelty business."

Rash Decisions and Growth Experiences
from the Best Little Warthouse in Kentucky

"What's he making?" asked the straight man

"He's making wooden signs to hang over people's bed posts."

"What do they say?"

"Substantial penalty for early withdrawal."

The mini scene received a lot of laughs. However, one prudish mother in the audience indignantly complained that her senior in high school son had heard it and that it was inappropriate for his virgin ears.

The manager of the production, succumbing to the one squeaky wheel instead of the carloads of laughter, put the brakes on our skit, derailing it from the second performance the following night. I felt that was an unwarranted substantial penalty resulting in an early withdrawal of pointed bedroom humor from the show.

SCHOOL DAYS

Bed, Breakfast and Beyond

Having graduated from high school I was fortunate enough to matriculate to the University of Pennsylvania. As a freshman I was confronted with all those mandated pre major courses an undergraduate finds himself compelled to take as dictated by the college's curriculum. The "100 and 101" courses that have become the source of humor after you have completed them but while enrolled take on the features more of a cumbersome but painfully surmountable hurdle. For the instructors and professors who are forced to teach them they prove to be more a compulsory boring bane and burden, the albatross of academia that the administration had hung around their neck.

I can recall one English professor who expressed his frustration "that teaching English 101 was more like irrigating deserts rather than pruning jungles." Another professor sarcastically remarked, "It took me almost five minutes to read some of your composition papers. I wish you had spent that much time in writing them." The commitment and enthusiasm on both sides of the classroom often lacked global warming temperatures.

The fall semester of 1964 found sophomore me enrolled in Introduction to World Religions, a survey course of the 100 genre. It met once a week for a two-hour time slot from 9:00 to 11:00 a.m. On one of those mornings I forgot to set my alarm clock and overslept. I hurriedly dressed and raced across campus. However, my appetite for a morning glass of orange juice was rapidly supplanting my thirst for knowledge of the world religions. So I decided to detour to the girl's dormitory whose cafeteria was coed for an institutional breakfast.

Settling down to a bowl of cold Cheerios bathed in homogenized whole milk and toast with marmalade and butter with a glass of frozen concentrate orange juice whose concentration seemed

Stuart Tobin M.D.

much greater than my own, I spied another delinquent fellow class-mate also eating breakfast. With rectangular plastic tray in hand I approached her and asked if I could join her for breakfast. She smiled, so I sat down.

The conversation quickly turned to the class we were both missing. "I overslept." she confided. "Well, so did I," I added. "There's going to be a lot of make-up if we miss the whole class and there is still over an hour left in the lecture. Since he gives a break in the middle of the two hour class, if we go over there now we can go in after the break and can catch at least one-half of his lecture," I confidently deduced. She readily agreed to the plan. I quickly gulped down the last sip of my OJ while she finished her coffee. We raced across the street to the ancient ivy decked Bennett Hall.

One of the older buildings on campus, it boasted an impressive stairwell and much wooden paneling as well as creaky classroom oak doors. The lecture hall was an elongated rectangular shaped classroom with two of those towering glass paneled doors, one in the front and the other in the back. As we waited for the expected break, it became apparent quickly that he wasn't going to give one that day. "I guess he's fallen in love with his voice more than usual and isn't going to stop talking," I quipped and then added quickly, "look, there are two empty seats in the last row in the back. Why don't we just open the back door and quietly just slip into those two seats for the second half of his lecture. No one will even notice that we are late," I assured her. "Sounds like a plan," my coconspirator readily agreed.

On my quietest tip toes I gently turned the brass solid antique door knob and pushed open the wooden door. As we entered the classroom the three un-oiled hinges began to squeak with a deafening roar as if they hadn't been moved in a hundred years.

The professor stopped lecturing and the one hundred and twenty-five students turned to see what the commotion was followed by dead silence. All eyes transfixed on us, and my compatriot in crime and delinquent classmate became as unhinged and as verbal as the door as she embarrassingly blurted out to everyone, "I overslept! I overslept!" To which I immediately added confidently, "I can vouch for that." My affirming testimony did little to comfort her for her pretty alabaster cheeks became even more embarrassingly crimson.

Melted Chocolate and Bing Cherries

      Entering my final year of college required some thought into "the future," which meant "What are you going to do after graduation?" Since I had managed to delay any commitments both socially, personally, as well as professionally for the past four years, I was faced with the dreaded graduation deadline. The tentacles of graduate school began beckoning. Not really committed to any passionate desire for any particular graduate training program and since my dad was a dermatologist, my older brother had just been accepted to medical school, and my twin was sending off applications to medical school, I decided to let the medical octopus grab me, rather than vice versa. With a good academic honors record from an Ivy League college coupled with adequate and convincing scores on the MCAT qualifying entrance exam for medical school, off went applications in search of a medical degree. Invitations for interviews quickly followed. One of the first was from the newly envisioned Hershey Medical Center in Hershey, Pennsylvania.

      Geography was kind enough to place Hershey, Pennsylvania a relatively close distance to Philadelphia, and the chocolate magnate of the world had decided to pour some of his sweet assets into the founding of a medical school. As chance would have it the Hershey Medical School was accepting enrollment for the first class, to which I could matriculate. Since I already had a sweet tooth, and the definition of sweets to me had always meant chocolate, I decided to make the bus trip to the Mecca for all chocolatiers for an interview. Yes, by bus.

Stuart Tobin M.D.

My parents had invested in a Vespa motor scooter as transportation for me and my brothers to and from campus. However, the thought of trusting my life to a bicycle with a stepped up lawn mower motor whose speed could occasionally top 40 mph on a windy day if the wind came from behind and you were going downhill to the Pennsylvania Turnpike seemed more risky than scaling Himalayan mountains peaks in Bermuda shorts and flip flops. So I took the Greyhound.

Since construction of the anticipated new medical school was well underway, although not completed, I was taken into a house right across from the huge steel superstructure with a frame that was daily growing to become the arc-shaped state-of-the-art contemporary medical complex that it is today. The administration while awaiting their new housing was temporarily relocated in an old rambling 1930s home. I was ushered into a well decorated, cherry paneled library with a huge imposing wooden desk befitting the Dean of the Medical School.

In a wing back leather chair sat a gentle and impressive grandfatherly, distinguished figure of a physician whose eyes told of energy and excitement and whose stately shock of gray mane spoke of experience and wisdom. He was so cordial and pleasant that he made me feel instantly comfortable and relaxed. Because of the unique circumstances with developing a new medical institution, he seemed very anxious to reassure me that none of the first year's new medical classes' education would be compromised by the construction. He elaborately detailed the plans that the administration had developed so that construction would parallel the medical students' needs.

The basic science labs and classrooms would be the first to be completed and were well ahead of the appointed schedule, followed by the clinics and hospital construction, which would be completed in time to accommodate the last two clinical years of medical school. The case was well made, and the more I listened the less skeptical I became, until.........

Simultaneously, a sudden flash of light coupled with the sound of a huge explosion rocked the house, the interview, and both of us. We both reflexively turned to the window to see the entire steel superstructure engulfed in a wall of flames. Apparently, a workman with an acetylene torch had ignited a propane cylinder which in turn produced this conflagration. The magnitude of this event was not lost on either of us. As the fire grew in intensity and strength, the flame in his eyes that had just seemed so strong was now waning and becoming extinguished. He slumped into his chair, despondent and seemingly unable to act. I walked over to him and put my hand on his shoulder and blurted out, "Sir, I'm sure everything will eventually turn out all right." That was the best and the most I could manage.

The Dean's door now swung open, and a fortyish slender man who identified himself as an anatomy professor exploded into the room and very agitatedly and excitedly shouted, "Does anybody have a camera? We need to take photos for insurance purposes." He repeated his request again and again as if by doing so a camera would appear. As I glanced at the Dean, slumped in his chair, insurance photos seemed to be a low priority.

So it is with a sudden unexpected crisis; do we react differently or is it the same, with a profound sense of shock and inaction or overreaction? Sensing that the interview was over, as well as my aspirations to attend The Hershey School of Medicine, I made my way back to the Greyhound bus station for a contemplative ride to a far and distant land called West Virginia, my next destination for a medical school interview.

....

An acquaintance of mine from high school was attending the West Virginia University Medical School in Morgantown, and he had suggested that it would be worth a look. Well, I thought if he had been accepted I probably could be as well. A piece of intelligence that had escaped my academic radar screen was that my friend, who was not particularly academically gifted, had a father who owned coal mines in the embattled state.

I sent off a snail mail application which resulted in the present bus ride. Back in the sixties, all mail was snail mail and also there wasn't an abundance of applicants to medical school with a

Stuart Tobin M.D.

social science background and quasi minor in English. Most applicants had majored either in the biological or physical sciences, and their communications skills were better adapted to slide rules and chemical symbols from the periodic table than the articulated word. Encouraged and flattered by this recognition, as well as the interview request, I found myself traversing the winding and desolate mountain roads of Appalachia, arriving to a darkened Morgantown the night before the interview.

The morning daylight brought the town and medical center into focus. First impressions, which as time would prove, became lasting impressions. Morgantown was small and hilly, but the medical complex seemed quite impressive and modern and new, with state-of-the-art hardware and buildings which bristled with bright, florescent lit, clean classrooms and immaculate, antiseptic lecture amphitheaters. The contrast seemed highlighted in my mind since Penn, so steeped in tradition, had ivy on the walls, dark antiqued wooden paneled commons, and ancient classrooms which I'm sure the custodians had been instructed to place dust into rather than remove to maintain the Ivy tradition of ancient academic continuity and enduring, educational preppy permanence.

The next morning, after a whirlwind tour of this spic and span facility with a third year medical student, I was invited into a small but clean, yet cluttered office where stood one of those metal collapsible folding tables with the simulated wooden veneer Formica top that one sees so often at church bazaars, picnics, and wedding receptions. Opposite me under the glare of those florescent lights sat two men in neatly, industrially pressed, long white lab coats that are epidemic in hospitals and medical centers.

Despite this most important event of my academic life that was about to unfold, the only thought that skipped across my mind was do the manufacturers of those metal tables really believe that people think those tops are real wood? I decided not to share this recent superficial insight with these two men whom I didn't know and who were about to interview me, an interview that as it progressed took on the semblance of a Monty Python inquisition.

The tall, thin Mutt-like anorexic character, white lab coat with his finely manicured beard which offset his reflective scalp that had a yellow green glow under those lights, introduced himself as a professor of anatomy. The shorter and more rotund Jeff-like character announced that he too was a professor, but of pathology. Instead of concentrating on my academic credentials and medical aspirations and motivations, they both, as if by a prearranged script, decided to focus on two unrelated areas of interest to them - my unusual academic background and my geographic venue, having been born and raised in and around New York City. While seeming odd, it became surreally strange.

"Mr. Tobin," began the slender anatomist, "I notice that you don't have a traditional science background like most of our applicants but are more rooted in the social sciences." Nothing gets by this guy, I muse to myself, being careful not to allow my body language to betray my thought. He continued, "Tell me Mr. Tobin, who was Washington Irving?"

I had grown up (as far as anyone can say a twenty year old is grown up) in Mt. Vernon, New York, which lies the same number of miles as my years in age from Irvington, New York, where Washington Irving lived and wrote along the Hudson River. I once visited his homestead, Sunnyside, while in high school, not so much out of literary intellectual curiosity but rather as a response to roaring male hormones in an attempt to impress a pretty girl who wanted to see the great author's home.

I decided to spin a tale of my own, perhaps not as literary eloquent as the great American author in question could but which would be at least classified by the Dewey Decimal system to the same area of the library where most of his fictional works could be found.

"Yes, sir!" I enthusiastically piqued. "Washington Irving, one of America's greatest and earliest of writers, lived along the Hudson River and authored many short stories of fiction well known and beloved by many generations since." Not having read any of his works, I did remember seeing on television a black and white Disney cartoon adaptation of one of his short stories, *The Legend of Sleepy Hollow,* whose images of Ichabod Crane riding for his life from the headless horseman were now racing through my own head at a furious pace. Sensing, or at least hoping, that their knowledge of the legendary great author was even more anemic than mine, I asked innocently, attempting to turn the Formica wooden simulated tables on them, "Have you ever been to his home?" "No" they both cautiously responded. Even more innocently I injected, "Well, if you ever have the opportunity to visit it, you will gain insight into his vivid imagination and fertile sense of humor." At the same time hoping that they wouldn't gather insight into my own less fertile vivid imagination.

"His home," I continued "is a patchwork of fanciful gingerbread architecture complete with a tower and a mis-inscribed date etched into the cornerstone of his house, misleading people into believing that his home is really much older than it really is. If you tour the interior, you will see his small closet-like bedroom with a thick and dark heavy drape to keep out the unwanted night air from the Hudson River that is but a small stone's throw from his property."

"One can imagine how the moonlight would cast all types of unusual shadows, prompting his imagination which would consequently be transcribed into his characters. You should go; it will enrich your appreciation of his wonderful writings," of course none of which I had read, I added even more innocently but with an air of literary assurance and certainty.

Now it was time for round two from the other white lab coat who now seemed so anxious to pounce. The pathology professor burst out sarcastically with a non-disguised air of arrogance and assuredness that he could trip me up.

"Mr. Tobin, you are from New York City, tell me who is Rudolph Bing?" as an air of self satisfaction migrated across his entire face. Luck must be on my side in Medical Jeopardy today I thought. My mother, who was an opera singer and who had trained at the Julliard School of Music, would drag her unwilling children, of which I was one, to the Metropolitan Opera House every Friday evening where we had an annual subscription to a box to listen to the pain of opera. As a teenager I neither understood nor appreciated the opera and the culture it was supposed to convey on me. Fortunately, I have managed to carry this attitude into adulthood till the present day.

Rash Decisions and Growth Experiences
from the Best Little Warthouse in Kentucky

In one of those auditory as well as emotionally painful out-ings, she introduced me to Mr. Rudolph Bing, a tall tuxedoed man with a regal bearing who was the Manager and Impresario of the prestigious Metropolitan Opera. By this time, Washington Irving's sense of fiction was well entrenched as a theme in my thoughts. Without batting an eye and as if on cue I answered, "Which Rudolph Bing? Do you mean the Rudolph Bing who is the famed manager and impresario of the prestigious Metropolitan Opera in New York City, or do you mean the Rudolph Bing who is the curator of the American National Museum in Washington, D.C?" I now answered smugly. That concluded the interview, which in turn concluded my once in a life time adventure to Morgantown. I walked back to the bus station for a different type of contemplative return trip to Phila-delphia.

A few months later I received a rejection letter from the West Virginia University Medical School. To this day I have won-dered if my medical inquisitors ever discovered that there is no American National Museum in Washington, D.C. or anywhere else for that matter except, of course, in the medical meanderings of my mischievous mind or perhaps in the public library under the Dewey Decimal system not too far away from the fictional works of Wash-ington Irving.

Considering fictional works, why would I want to attend a school whose state is GPS impaired and consequently fictionally misnamed anyway? One look at a map will clearly show that most of the state lies north of Virginia and some of Virginia is even west of West Virginia. Shouldn't the state be more appropriately named North Virginia? This would follow the precedents of North and South Carolina and the Dakotas.

Who's Interviewing Whom?

As a senior in high school my sole inculcated ambition was to ascend the academic ladder as quickly and as high as possible, having descended from second generation Jewish immigrants from the old country. Regardless of how much reverence was reserved for Jehovah, the real unspoken focus of worship for our family was the god of education who would eventually lead me to a high level of a professional degree. This was the cultural tradition I lived, ate, and breathed in the second decade of my life of the last century in the last millennium, nostalgically referred to as "The Sixties."

As one would expect, matriculation to college was not any more a choice than the previously mentioned bodily functions of breathing, eating or living. Not only was college expected and demanded, but positioning myself to enter the best and most prestigious of universities remained my enduring and passionate goal, or at least my parent's. Why attend a community college when I could enter a four-year institution, and why attend a state university when private, more expensive, as well as prestigious schools beckoned? And why choose any private school when the Ivy League could be attained?

So that these expectations would not be lost on me, my mother started giving me solo academic subliminal messages for nine months prior to my birth in utero. Those academic messages crescendoed as a parental duet after my delivery with my father now chiming in. The lyrics and verse remained the same for the next seventeen years of my life. During the waking hours of the day they resonated as studying and homework and at night became my mid-summer night, as well as all the other seasons, academic dream.

As a senior in Mt. Vernon Public High School situated in the 'shruburbs' of New York City, I found myself competing with hundreds or perhaps thousands of other students with similar backgrounds who were receiving the same cultural prodding from their parents as well. Hence arose academic competition.

Sports, which have become the lifeblood of succeeding generations, paled against the fierce, mostly non-contact sport of academic competition. The only reason why anyone of my culture would sacrifice critical study time for football would be so that you could gain a five yard edge in matriculating to the academic gridiron by appearing "well rounded." Weighing 135 lbs, there was no way I was going to be "well rounded."

So a flurry of applications to middle and upper echelon universities and colleges as well as the finest Ivy League schools were sent off by post, or what would be today labeled as 'snail' mail. However, in the 1960s, many old and entrenched "traditions" or prejudices of quota policies for entrance into the finest schools still lingered. The academic playing field was not equal, or level, everywhere.

The Civil Rights movement, which would eventually give maybe not all, but most, an equal opportunity when applying to college, was yet to happen. Quota systems for minorities deprived many of my generation access to those sought after schools that favored sons of gentlemen often referred to as WASPS (White Anglo Saxon Protestants.)

Lest this logic not be lost on me, I had heard numerous stories of how my parents and my generation were denied access to those colleges and universities, having to settle for similar educations at the state institutions which embraced intellectual achievement as an asset among a minority rather than as a liability and consequently didn't discriminate.

Much to my surprise and amazement, a snail mail invitation for an interview arrived in early fall from an Ivy League school that was well known to have an entrenched quota system. A very small number of students of my Jewish minority group would be accepted and the competition was always very stiff. To prepare for the interview I needed the proper equipment, which meant wearing the Ivy League uniform.

184

Stuart Tobin M.D.

The next day, off to the local haberdasher we journeyed to buy the appropriate tweedy sports coat with matching khaki cuffed pants, blue button down oxford cloth long sleeve shirt, and matching paisley tie. To complete the look a pair of oxford colored penny loafers without the Abe Lincolns were purchased as well. To give them the appearance that they weren't obtained for this special occasion I wore them daily, going out of my way to scuff the leather on the toes. I even wore them to bed in hopes that my restless leg syndrome would add miles to their appearance of authenticity and longevity.

My mother, who grew up in the Depression, always spent more time concerned about the future than the present as she lived in the past. When it came to buying clothes she ascribed to the one size too large fitting philosophy. "Always buy your clothes one size too big and you will grow into it." I sensed that this interview must have been very, very important to her as well for it was the only time in her life she ever abandoned the purchase of the large clothes for the small boy philosophy.

The appointed day finally arrived, and off we drove to the interview, arriving well ahead of the scheduled 2:30 interview time. Although quite nervous, I prepared myself to appear as relaxed as possible. Crowded into a small waiting room were a group of mostly blond and well groomed young students with finely chiseled Anglican facial features and Celtic skin, all my age but with the aura of prep school about them. While we were from the same universe attempting matriculation to the same university, I felt strangely out of orbit and from a different cultural solar system.

Ushered into the interview room I found myself confronting an older version of the group I had just left. With thinner blond hair and gray mixed in and with scattered wrinkles, they retained the same facial features with the fairest of skin.

That sense of difference and being in an alien academic land struck me hard and convincingly. No matter how many similarities there were, similarities in language, speech, academic accomplishments, knowledge, the marked and most pronounced difference of ethnic background became the defining and delineating issue at this moment. I sensed it in them and knew it for myself.

185

Rash Decisions and Growth Experiences
from the Best Little Warthouse in Kentucky

The usual barrage of standard questions followed. "Why do you wish to attend our finest of universities? What studies do you plan to pursue?" Etc. etc., followed by a review of my academic record followed by a summing up of...... "Mr. Tobin, we have many excellent students like you with academic credentials similar to yours and with a similar background, why should we accept you instead of them?"

I had been told by many friends that this was typical of the question reserved for minorities which really translated to "Why should we accept you over another Jew like yourself since we have only limited spaces for your kind."

I stared at those faces, those unemotional and stone-like countenances, who expected a reply that they undoubtedly had heard from so many like myself in one form or another before. Suddenly, my response became, if not transparent, at least translucent.

"That is an excellent question but if you pardon me not the one I wish to address. Who is really being interviewed today? Is it me or is it also you? You have the opportunity that you may or may not recognize to act on my admission as you would for any other applicant. While I stand in front of you for your decision, you stand in front of yourselves in the conscience of your own minds and spirit of your own hearts to make a fair and unbiased decision."

"Some of your early graduates were also the founding fathers of our Constitution, a constitution that insured a Bill of Rights for all of this land equally. Do you not have an obligation to honor their heritage by honoring the rights and freedoms they fought for so long ago? Is that not your university's obligatory charge? So while you sit here in judgment of me, you will be making a judgment about yourselves. This could be an opportunity for both of us."

I restrained myself from adding something to the effect of give me liberty or give me death. The situation didn't seem to warrant such a drastic choice. My mother, given to drama, might have added it, however, had she been in the room. Anyway, they thanked me in a very polite and gentlemanly way, and I made my exit. That concluded the long awaited interview which had consumed my thoughts and mind for weeks. By this time the blue collared button down shirt had perspiration marks and creases in it, and the tweedy jacket just didn't seem quite as preppy now.

Two months later an envelope arrived by snail mail, an envelope with the brightly colored and heavily embossed emblem of that fine, prestigious and ancient Ivy League university in the upper left hand corner. Before piercing the outer protective shiny white covering to read the vellum announcement of acceptance or rejection inside, a smile crept over my face.

VD and Me

During my first of three years of residency specialty training I was assigned to dermatopathology to review and study slides of skin biopsies. As fate would have it, NYU had just acquired a new section chair to head that department. Dr. Bernard Ackerman possessed an extraordinary dazzling intellect which leaped from mountain top to mountain top while other professors struggled to escape from the academic valleys. His curious and incessantly active mind coupled with his enormous energy and proficient teaching skills provided an electric presence in the classroom, lecture amphitheatres, and the clinic areas. Towering at over six feet three inches tall he commanded respect and attention wherever he went. If the rest of us operated on conventional energy, Bernie's was nuclear. By the luck of the draw I became the first resident assigned to work with him at NYU. Everyone wanted to meet and interact with this most unusual and accomplished dynamic star in our specialty.

One afternoon while reviewing and discussing the slides of the day through the Medusa multi-headed microscope of Bernie's own ingenious design, one of the more senior and experienced professors wandered by to ask Bernie's counsel on a baffling case he had just admitted the day before. Bernie immediately leaped out of his chair and announced, "Why are we just sitting here discussing this case? Let's go right now and see the patient." We now found ourselves running and struggling to keep pace with him as he sprinted to the elevators. As we rode to the fifteenth floor, Bernie and Jerry, the clinical professor, turned to me and said, "Let's have Tobin do the initial evaluation and see what his diagnosis is." Me? The only enlightenment as a first year resident that I could possibly shed would be 10 watts of questionable dull illumination and 150 watts of embarrassment, I thought to myself as my heart began to race from a sudden influx of adrenalin.

As we entered the patient's room to examine the enigma rash, we encountered a mid twenties man approximately five foot ten and weighing about one hundred and eighty pounds. He sported a very bushy jet black beard and copious long black curly hair and was dressed in the traditional non flattering hospital gown.

As I began to examine the skin lesions I engaged him in casual conversation and discovered that he was a short order cook at a medium sized in-and-out restaurant. This predated the "fast food" nomenclature and culture which has become so ubiquitous and popular today. He certainly had the aura of someone who was streetwise and had been literally and figuratively around the block.

The rash itself and the reason for our presence was a half dozen or so of one to two inch circular crusted and deeply eroded scabs on his torso. The first impression that entered my meager dermatological mental library mind was some form of impetigo, a bacterial and common infection of the skin which caused similar scabbing and crusting on the skin.

However, I reasoned that such an easy pedestrian diagnosis could not be correct. So what could it be I nervously pondered, a young, virile looking food handler who gives the impression of having had a lot of worldly experiences with those types of lesions. The only diagnosis that came to mind was a very rare form of a sexually transmitted disease resulting from the pursuit of various horizontal endeavors. So I blurted out my diagnosis, "Rupioid Syphilis," which was greeted by a duet of laughter from both of the senior attending profs. Up goes the embarrassment titer and down goes the self esteem titer.

"Have you done a VDRL serology (the screening test for syphilis)?" I asked defensively trying to deflect my rising embarrassment with a forced calm and professional tone in my voice. "No," Jerry answered at the same time still laughing. Well, they continued to huddle discussing an assortment of other infectious as well as non-contagious diagnoses but the moment overcame me and I didn't hear a word they said. Bernie added that he thought it could be one of a few different diseases the best way to narrow the differential clinical possibilities would be to perform a biopsy and "Let's humor Tobin and order the VDRL."

The next day when Bernie reviewed the biopsy specimen he exploded in surprise, "Look at all those plasma cells, Tobin was right! It's Rupioid Syphilis." That afternoon the blood test came back positive and with an extremely high titer indicating active disease. The only person who was more shocked than they was me, although I decided not to confide that to them. While the patient lost his Rupioid syphilitic rash with a heavy infusion of penicillin, I gained a new nickname 'Rup' for the rest of my residency. I guess it could have been worse; they could have decided on VD or Syphlitic Stu.

Rup, after completing his rotation with Bernie, found himself assigned to the very floor where the short order cook had spent his hospitalized confinement. As resident on the attending wing of dermatology, I assisted the professors in the care of their inpatients. Some had more impatience than others.

All My Problems Are Behind Me

Dr. Baer, Chairman of the department and a legend in our field, had admitted a private patient for care on the University Hospital dermatology ward. At the time, as a first year resident, I was assigned as the inpatient house officer. Since the great man was expected on rounds the next morning I decided to forego watching *Wheel of Fortune* and bone up on the case instead. So I reviewed the patient's history, evaluation, treatment, and the world's literature on his unusual disease so I could impress the chief with my recently acquired academic and temporarily encyclopedic knowledge about this important case.

So when he arrived on rounds the next morning I felt prepared for any esoteric question he might have. Dr. Baer arrived promptly at the appointed and expected time, reviewed the chart and lab data, and turned to me and asked his one and only question about this exotic case. "Stuart, did the patient have a bowel movement?" WHAT?!?!?! I'm screaming in my mind. What does that have to do with the disease? How the hell do I know if the patient had a bowel movement? I do know, however, that I'm about to have one. He repeated the question a little louder and a more forcefully, "Did the patient have a bowel movement?" "Ah, ah, I don't know, Dr. Baer." I stammered. "Hmmm," was all he said and he then disappeared into the room and asked the patient the same question. The patient appeared to be much more knowledgeable on this particular subject than I and answered clearly and accurately, "Yes." Dr. Baer then examined the patient and wrote a note in the chart and told me what the day's plan was. He exited without further comment, leaving me to wonder if all my problems were behind me or was the end in sight?

Old Lace

As my training preceded so did my competency. Now ensconced as senior and chief resident of NYU's dermatology program I found myself responding to consults from other services. One month while rotating through Bellevue Hospital I received a request to examine a patient on the psychiatric ward. Bellevue has always had a reputation nationally and even internationally for its psychiatric in-service, for over a century rivaling even that of Bedlam Hospital of London as a center for the mentally ill.

Even today when one mentions Bellevue Hospital, apparitions of the incurably psychotic and the permanently institutionalized mentally ill surface. I wandered those dark and dingy poorly lighted ancient hallways that connect the large open fifty bed wards illuminated with single light bulb green open chandeliers hanging from the 20 feet ceilings. Hallways that would seem to go on endlessly from one end of the hospital to the other in this oldest of city hospital institutions in America. Finding my way eventually to the locked and very secure psychiatric ward, I gained entrance by ringing an ancient rasping rusted buzzer and eventually located the patient who needed the dermatological consult.

He was a cooperative and unkempt man in his forties who did not make any eye contact. He had that flat affect seen so often in psychiatric depressed patients. The reasons for the consult were for unexplainable skin and mouth findings. Examination of his mouth revealed a dark gray line along the gums and his fingernails had unusual transverse white lines. The most unique and characteristically striking findings of all were multiple thick callous like pits on his palms. While losing his hair, it wasn't the male pattern seen so commonly in men but rather a diffuse uneven patchy loss throughout the entire scalp.

Stuart Tobin M.D.

After completing the exam I searched for the psychiatric resident in charge to discuss my findings. He was extremely busy and overworked but granted me a moment to listen. I now inquired why this man was institutionalized and the nature of his psychiatric disorder. "Oh, he's paranoid, he has this obsession that someone is trying to kill him." He responded in a hurried manner anxious to get on with his pressing duties. "Well," I interjected, "he has all the clinical features associated with chronic and acute arsenic ingestion! Maybe he's right; someone is trying to kill him. You might want to look into his history more closely." I concluded.

Crying Wolf

While a resident in dermatology at the Skin and Cancer Unit of New York University from 1972-1975, I lived in an apartment building on the fourteenth floor a few blocks from the medical center, allowing me to easily walk to and from my training program. NYU had the largest dermatology program in the city and we coordinated care not only at the University Hospital but also ran the dermatology services at Bellevue as well as the Manhattan Veterans Hospital. All in all, our service had over a hundred dermatological inpatient beds as well as extensive outpatient clinics and related services.

Having relocated from Kentucky where I had completed my medical internship I experienced a reverse social readjustment even though I had been born in the Big Apple. As much a reverse cultural shock as it was for me, it became even more difficult and challenging for my German Shepherd, Lupus, which in Latin means wolf and in dermatology refers to a skin condition whose mask-like features resemble those of a wolf. Lupus was much more used to the open green and wooded spaces of Kentucky than the concrete and steel vertical confines of urban Manhattan.

After a few months of residency, my loyal and occasionally obedient dog started to act odd. He wouldn't eat, became lethargic, and his activity level diminished. After a few days of this changed and unexplained behavior I became very concerned about his health and decided to spare no effort or energy to discover what was wrong with my ailing pet.

I borrowed a few laboratory vials from the Bellevue Laboratory and drew blood samples from my canine patient and submitted them to the lab under my own name. The next day I received an urgent page from the laboratory. I called and the perplexed technician told me that my blood smear was the most unusual that she had ever seen. There were white blood cells that she didn't recognize and there were over 65% eosinophils, allergic cells, in the smear, where the normal range was less than 5%.

Of course I wasn't as nearly perplexed and confused as she was, recognizing that such a reaction in a dog could only mean a worm infestation. So I thanked her for her concern and making me aware of the situation. Then I explained nonchalantly that I had never been totally free of parasites and worms since returning from Vietnam, which in turn aborted any further inquiry from her. So off to the veterinarian I dragged my loved one for a de-worming followed by a quick return to health.

Dodging the Bullet

As a resident in dermatology at New York University's Skin and Cancer Center, I like my fellow peers had the opportunity to learn from academics as well as established practitioners in the community, which meant talented physicians from New York City and the suburbs. One of those outstanding non full time professors was Norman Orentreich who was an innovator and pioneer in cosmetic dermatology. He invented the hair transplant procedure with the Orentreich punch. Actually, historically, the first successful hair transplant was by an American pioneer on the frontier who survived an Indian scalping and replaced his severed top back on his own head. While controversy often surrounds those on the cutting edge, Norm was a brilliant courageous physician who taught me much.

Norm's reputation was not just national but international as well. The ruler of Morocco, King Hassan II, while visiting in New York City had brought one of his cherished wives from his harem to Norm for cosmetic work. He was so impressed with the results that he invited Norm to travel to Morocco, along with his staff, to work on some of his other wives. They flew first class to Paris and were met by the King's private jet which whisked the New York City dermatology entourage to Rabat. For a week he treated them for an assortment of skin issues.

The King was again even more pleased with the outcome. If there were eventually more heirs to the throne as a result of Norm's work I'm unable to speculate. It wasn't but a short time later in 1971 that the King was to celebrate a milestone forty-second birthday and in royal fashion that meant a huge gathering and festivities. Norm received a special invitation to attend and was to be seated with other physicians at the royal shindig. Norm, however, had promised his

196

son that he would help him study for the college entrance exams that same weekend and declined the invitation.

Well the event took place without Norm's presence with much food, entertainment, and pomp in a huge tent lined with pillows and non-flying Arabian carpets in the desert. All proceeded well until a group of uninvited and inappropriately dressed guests attempted a coup d' etat. The day's festivities were abruptly interrupted by renegade machine gunfire that strafed the tent. Among the casualties were all the medical personnel at the table which Norm would have been sitting.

Norm continued the story with, " the king with the aid of his security detail and troops who quickly appeared regained control of the chaotic situation and put down the coup attempt." The unintended consequence of Norm dodging that bullet was that a host of young dermatologists in training benefited for many years afterwards from his on hands teaching and superior medical knowledge.

As a footnote, a second failed attempt on the King's life was an assault by renegade Air Force jets that attacked the same plane that Norm had been on. "The quick witted King got on a broadcasting radio band and announced during the aerial attack that 'the King has been killed.' This false statement stopped the attack and the King quickly regained control of the situation and the kingdom as well with royalist troops subduing and killing the insurgents." They were unable to bring it down.

I wonder if the II after the King's name represents the successful survival of two coups d' etat, kind of like notches on a gun handle? If there is any moral to this tale it might be: If anyone ever offers you a kingship you might consider that three strikes and you're out in any ballgame.

The Penn College Reunion

Forty years after graduating from college, my Ivy League alma mater, University of Pennsylvania, invited me back for a nostalgic reunion with my classmates. I'm sure thousands of other graduates received an equally personal request. Anyway, not so vivid memories filtered through the prism of time blinded my rational senses and I succumbed to the lure of nostalgia. Nostalgia is defined in the Tobin dictionary as "Returning to your college, etc. reunion to visit with all the friends that you never had." So my wife and I made plans to visit Philadelphia for the not so long awaited class bash.

Closing my dermatology practice and making arrangements for my peers to cover my patients, I started to plan for the reunion. With the aid of the internet and Travelocity.com we booked hotel room and airplane tickets on the cheap to fly economy class which should be more appropriately named "steerage and storage". That captures more aptly the bitter essence of modern day air travel. All of which was quite tolerable because the light at the end of the traveling tunnel was the college memories of my sophomoric past. Departing from Lexington, Kentucky to Charlotte, North Carolina and making the connection to Philadelphia we landed in the city of Brotherly Shove without adventure and more importantly without lost luggage.

"Lost luggage" according to the airplane industry dictionary can only be applied after forty-eight hours and until then your bags are only "delayed". I'm quite sure that is very comforting to someone on a weekend visit without a change of underwear because their jockey shorts are "delayed" in Charlotte, North Carolina rather than lost in Philadelphia.

Picking up our one not delayed suitcase we exited the terminal to taxi to our hotel. My good friend and neighbor back in Kentucky who had recently returned from a business venture to Philly told me that the airport ride would be exactly $26.50. As the cabbie loaded our one bag into the trunk I casually inquired about the fare. His answer, "$26.50, sir." As the Holiday Inn commercials used to say, "The best surprise is no surprise." The trip into town seemed more relaxed than my infrequent taxicab rides into urban America where I would usually keep one eye on the frenetic traffic and the other anxiously on the metronome like ticking meter.

One of the great unexplained mysteries of life is why do those taxicab meters advance in cost when you're stuck dead still in traffic and your charges are only supposed to be tied to distance traveled?

Famished and since our hotel room at the Club Quarters wouldn't be ready for an hour we dined at Davio's, the hotel's restaurant, to a wonderful treat of Chilean sea bass. Since our reunion party wasn't planned to start until 6:30 later that evening we decided to change and head over for a walk down college nostalgia lane.

Dressed in a red wine blush colored shirt with a red and blue striped Penn tie and khaki slacks with a blue sports coat, I felt dated, dressed and determined as we departed by cab for the short ride in distance, but long in memory, to the University from which I had graduated forty years previously.

It was a gorgeous spring May day and the azaleas were in full magenta bloom. Locust Street was now Locust Walk and without the rush of traffic the atmosphere added a beauty and tranquility to my nostalgic wanderings.

I fleetingly wondered why the University administration hadn't named the path Locust Lane which would have given it a more iambic poetic resonance. But of course Locust Lane sounded too much like an aggressive female reporter for a large metropolis newspaper who had a crush on a guy wearing a cape and tights and who was flying around town pursuing truth and justice and preserving the American way. It could have worked, however, I mused since his suit was red and blue, the school colors.

Just as this thought left my mind, my feet led me to a realistic life size bronze statue of Ben Franklin sitting on a bench reading the *Gazette*. I grabbed a quick snap of our University's founder and heard a female voice behind me ask, "Would you like me to take a picture of you and Ben sitting together?"

Surprised that anyone would notice an old fart alum meandering around campus I spun around to answer a pert, blond young graduate student. "Yes, that would be great." As she focused and snapped my photo I wryly observed, "You know Ben and I were classmates. No, that's not actually correct. He was really the year behind me." She smiled a genuine smile, laughed a genuine laugh, and handed me my pocket digital Canon camera back. I thanked her for her kindness and continued my walk down Locust Walk without encountering a Locust tree or the Locust plague or an aggressive female news reporter.

However, I did encounter a well tailored man about my age in an expensive gray suede sports coat with a very trendy silk tie, fashionable black pants, and a mod contemporary hair style as well as appearing quite fit as well as trim approaching from the other direction. Our eyes engaged at the same moment and there was something so familiar about him.

He broke into a smile and said, "Stu? Stu Tobin?" "It's me, Eddie Cohen." Of course Eddie Cohen, my freshman year roommate. Eyeing him from modern coif to shiny black leather toe I pronounced, "Eddie, you look terrific. I hope life is as good and successful for you as you appear?" "I'm so excited." he burst out. "We just bought the Washington Nationals," as he handed me his business card with the Washington National baseball logo embossed announcing Edward L Cohen, Principal Owner.

Stuart Tobin M.D.

The word principal caught my eye as well as my thought. The only other principal I had ever met prior to Eddie had been Mr. Blunt, the principal of my elementary school, whom I had been introduced to in the fifth grade by my music teacher after I claimed that I was related to Beethoven, whose first name I had insisted was Bay and last name was Tobin. Of course our name had been altered through translation and time I had protested to Mr. Blunt.

Mr. Blunt, the other principal in my life, wasn't impressed by my imaginary family musical genealogy and invited me to spend some time in detention. I had omitted that piece of educational foot-note trivia from my Penn college application from the space marked other pertinent information.

I then said to Eddie, "I can see that life is really good for you and I'm very happy for you." Although not having followed base-ball for years I assumed that the Washington Nationals was a major league team in D.C. If I had been on *Jeopardy* I would have guessed that the Washington Redskins were still defending our nation's cap-ital and my second guess would have been the Washington Sena-tors.

"Stu, what do you do?" he now asked. I straightened up and beaming with pride and grabbing my antique Penn tie in my out-dated 60's college preppy outfit, I answered with great poise and confidence peppered with an air of pride, "Eddie, I own the Best Little Warthouse in Kentucky."

His blank stare was quickly transformed into a quizzical look. Thinking better than to probe he quickly diverted my attention by introducing me to his son who now was a freshman at Penn, as we had been forty four years before. We exchanged pleasantries and off he went as I did as well. As we parted I did hand him one of my own business cards revealing my rash profession which would have explained my Warthouse connection.

Since half past the sixth hour was now fast approaching, Susan and I headed over to the Van Pelt Library for our class of '67 reunion. I remarked to my wife. "If this isn't the greatest irony, I spent four years studying in this damn library and our class decided to have the reunion there." Fortunately I didn't experience either an episode of post-traumatic stress disorder or a mild panic attack on entering the building. We headed to the rare book room to be greeted by all the friends that I never had. (Footnote: for further explanation refer to the Tobin Dictionary under nostalgia.)

Standing in the congested chamber I found myself confronting someone whom I had no idea as to who he was. But he had been in my class. Since we were all jammed together as in a packed subway car and were unable to escape each other's presence I introduced myself. "Hi, I'm Stuart Tobin also here for our class reunion." He introduced himself as well.

To keep the conversation going I asked the open ended question, "So what have you been doing the last forty or so years?" He responded with, "Well, I've been in retirement for the last few years commuting between my homes." He continued, "However, I received a phone call from my old business partner who was elected Governor of New Jersey and he asked me if I would head up the Economic Cabinet for the state. So I came out of retirement to help him out," as he shrugged his shoulders.

"What do you do?" he now asked with an air of politeness peppered with a genuine interest. I straightened my red and blue tie, beamed with pride and burst out with, "I own the Best Little Warthouse in Kentucky." That's my story and I'm sticking to it. Politely smiling and despite the very crowded room he managed to navigate to the other end of the room as far away as possible lest a photograph appear in his political future with the owner of the Best Little Warthouse in Kentucky. He left so quickly I didn't have time to give him my last business card. So I casually tossed it into a fishbowl filled with other classmates' business cards sitting on a vacant table.

Susan turned to me and asked more than just a little annoyed, "Why do you keep telling people that ridiculous story about owning the best little warthouse in Kentucky rather than that you're a successful, respected dermatologist, on the faculty at the medical school and an involved community civic leader?" "Beautiful, I'm here to have fun this weekend and humor is on a higher plane than the truth at least for these next two days."

Stimulated by my antiquarian rare book surroundings, I attempted to paraphrase a famous quote that I remembered from freshman English adding, "Humor (Beauty) is truth and truth humor

Stuart Tobin M.D.

(beauty). That is all you know and all ye need to know." To be honest I didn't understand those quixotic lines back in English 101 and time as well as my literary background has done little to enlighten me. Although my paraphrase made less sense to me than John Keats' original poem, *"Ode on a Grecian Urn"*, I figured it would at least get her off my back for the moment. She gave me one of those exasperated looks followed by a sigh of resignation. I knew I was safe at least for a little while longer to continue my humorous charade.

We soon adjourned to the ground floor for a buffet dinner and dancing to the Oldies which all of us in our class remembered when they were Newies. Since I love to dance, Susan and I bounded onto the dance floor and east coast swinged to some great old tunes of the sixties. The first song the DJ played was *"Run Around Sue,"* one of our favorites.

Since Susan had injured her arm and couldn't dance as much as I wanted, I asked one of the undergraduate student monitors assigned to keep an eye on the old fogies to be sure we didn't wander off and get lost to dance. She seemed anxious to get on the dance floor and off we went.

I couldn't help but notice that the Secretary of the Economic Cabinet watched me twirling this young attractive coed and I wondered, hmm could he be thinking that I was recruiting for my business? So I gave him a knowing wink in hopes that it would add fire to his embering thoughts. The evening ended and Susan and I taxied back to the hotel.

The next morning found us back on campus for a lunch under the class tent followed by the parade of classes. Sitting on an easel was the blown up class check of contributions made that year by our class of '67. I was totally amazed at the amount made by some 400 plus of my classmates. The check was for over 36 million and seven hundred thousand plus dollars. I was even more amazed when I was asked to carry this lottery size check in the Parade of Classes by one of the student monitors with whom I had danced the night before. "Sure, I'd be happy to carry the check." Well, this was a potential humorous opportunity I just couldn't pass up.

Rash Decisions and Growth Experiences
from the Best Little Warthouse in Kentucky

As we assembled class by class and with the check in hand or more appropriately two hands, we preceded to Locust Walk, aka Locust Street, aka Locust Lane. As we marched I shouted to anyone who would listen, "Alms for the rich, alms for the rich." I heard someone behind me say, "Now, that's really funny." Of course that only encouraged me to be more audible and less creative. One of my classmates came up to me and asked incredulously "Is that what our class gave this year?" I answered in my most condescending tone, "I can tell by your voice that you weren't the one who sent in the 30 million dollar check." However, I quickly added in a confiding whisper, "If I had known that we had raised that much money, I wouldn't have sent in my ten dollar donation either."

I then turned to the class behind us and boasted as a third grader might, "Our check is bigger that your check." (Nanny nanny boo-hoo). Another classmate came over and asked, "Is that a real check?" "Nah," I quipped, "I've already been to one of the local banks to try to cash it and have the funds transferred to a country without extradition to the U.S. They wouldn't do it."

I then got a 20 watt idea and started asking people around me. "Does anyone have a magic marker? I want to put a '1' in front of the 36." No one came up with one but a few did search their pockets in anticipation of co-conspiring in a college prank.

As we proceeded down the parade route I shouted a new 20 "Watt"er, "It's in Euros, not dollars." Someone along the parade route shouted back, "Why not pounds?" As we approached the reviewing stand where sat with the greatest dignity, Amy Gutman, the President of the University and the oldest Penn grad, as well as Paul Williams, a member of our own class and head of the Alumni Association. I proceeded to do a little dance and repeat all my remarks to the amusement or embarrassment of all. So ended the parade and our reunion.

So who didn't show up for the reunion? Donald Trump, a Wharton graduate, wasn't in our class but was the year behind ours. I guess that would have made him and Ben Franklin, who also was also a no show, fellow classmates. Had the big Donald been in attendance I wondered how he would have reacted to my quip, "that our check is bigger than yours." Would that become a challenge for him or would it be an inspiration for a Rosie O'Donnell diatribe?

Candice Bergen, also a member of the class of '67, was a no show. Actually she departed the dear Old red and blue at the end of her freshman year for greener pastures. However, she remains a noted and valued honorary re-instated member of the class of '67. Andrea Mitchell, chief capitol, and white house correspondent on the NBC evening news and wife of the former head of the Fed Alan Greenspan, didn't make it either. I guess covering the Capitol in D.C. was a higher priority than carrying the capital in the Penn Parade. As a footnote, she did make it to the 45th reunion and gave a splendid private talk to our class on her 40 plus years in journalism and presented each of us with a copy of her fascinating chronicled autobiography, *Talking Back to Presidents, Dictators, and Assorted Scoundrels*.

Another notable no show was Arnie Klein, dermatologist to the stars. His personal connection with Elizabeth Taylor, Sharon Stone, Carrie Fisher and many other Hollywood notables occasionally pops up in the tabloid and non-tabloid media. Arnie achieved his fifteen minutes x 2 fame as Michael Jackson's dermatologist. Because of his close personal relationship with the King of Pop and the tragic circumstances surrounding Jackson's death, Arnie was on many of the talk shows, including Alan King as well as appearing in the print media.

Being a fellow dermatologist I followed his national exposure with more than casual curiosity. I "Pennsively" thought about the different paths we had taken. When we both finished dermatology residencies at the same time, Arnie headed to California to treat the stars in Beverly Hills while I headed to moonshine Kentucky to treat the Hill Billies. I believe I made the better decision.

As we left the dear old venerable Ivy League campus I wondered what the 50th reunion would be like and, hmm, would my name be inadvertently omitted from the next invitation list? Well, maybe I'll be able to send the old alma mater a $30 million check by then. We'll both be happy if they don't try to cash it.

Rash Decisions and Growth Experiences
from the Best Little Warthouse in Kentucky

Arriving home the following day I was greeted by a phone call from a member of the University Reunion Planning Committee to inform me that my business card advertising the Best Little Warthouse in Kentucky had been picked out of a fish bowl at random. I had won a beautiful dark navy blue blanket with PENN embroidered in red on it. It arrived the following week. I was now glad that the Cabinet Secretary hadn't lingered to take my last business card the night of the reunion.

YOU'RE IN THE ARMY NOW

A Major in the Army
and a General Nuisance

During my years in residency training, the Vietnam War, which technically was not a war, was raging in Southeast Asia. Since the Army needed specialists and since I was hoping to complete my residency training before entering military service, the Army had agreed to defer my induction. This was called the Berry Program. Unbeknownst to me I was to be one of the last Berries picked from the military bush.

Every year while in my residency training program I would receive during the summer a very official letter from the Department of Defense. They would read similarly: "Congratulations, Stuart Tobin, on entering military service. You are being promoted to the rank of 2nd Lieutenant in the U.S. Army." The following year I received another letter addressed to 2nd Lieutenant Stuart Tobin which read, "Congratulations, because of your performance over the last year you are being promoted to the rank of 1st Lieutenant." The next summer another letter arrived announcing that because of my excellent performance I was being promoted to the rank of Captain. Just as I was completing my third and last year of residency training the final letter arrived announcing my promotion to the rank of Major as well as notice of induction into service.

I'm thinking to myself the only contact I have had with the military these past three years have been those letters of promotion. Hmmm. I guess once I've entered active duty and really start performing my duties I'll probably be promoted to General or something higher. So in the summer of 1975 I traded my white residency coat for Army green.

The military had sent all specialists a request form to list their assignment preference. Since my inclination was to eventually practice and live in Kentucky, I had listed my choices as #1 Fort Campbell on the Kentucky-Tennessee border, #2 Fort Knox near Louisville, and then some other post in Arizona which sounded exotic. My assignment came back as some place I had never heard of, Ft. Stewart in the swamps of southern Georgia. The best sense I could make of it was that my first name and the post's last name were similar (Stuart and Stewart). This was my initial, but not my last, encounter with military logic.

Since all the residents in New York knew one another, I by mere chance had run into a peer at another training program who seemed quite depressed and glum when he told me that his preferences had also been ignored and that he had been assigned to some place in the middle of nowhere, Ft. Campbell, my first choice. That ended the illusion that we could choose our location assignment.

While serving in the largest Health Maintenance Organization (HMO) in America, the United States Army from 1975-77, I now found myself the only and the best dermatologist at my namesake post and attached to the 24th Infantry Division and the 75th Ranger Battalion as medical support.

This was the first year of the volunteer Army and the Army found itself in a dilemma. Volunteer physicians would be paid up to four times what drafted physicians would be compensated. Since I like many of my peers were obligated under the old draft system and had been deferred for active duty until we completed our residency specialty training, the military had to figure out how to circumvent the new pay scale.

So the anonymous upper echelons came up with the innovative and clever solution of labeling us as OBVs, **obligatory volunteers,** and therefore relegating us to the pay of a draftee. The result of which found me scrambling for the nearest Webster's to review the definition of oxymoron.

Rash Decisions and Growth Experiences
from the Best Little Warthouse in Kentucky

The second enigma the Army encountered with me personally was my name. Apparently it is unacceptable in the military not to have a middle name. The abridged name of Stuart Tobin resulted from the fact that when my dear mother found herself pregnant with me in 1945 she stopped her prenatal visits because her obstetrician, who was a friend of the family, accused her of eating too much and gaining too much weight.

Consequently, the fact that I was sharing cramped quarters with my twin brother escaped both their attention until time of delivery. Since the hospital had a rule that all newborns needed to be named within twenty-four hours of delivery, she divided the name in two, leaving each of us without a middle name.

The Army found my shortened name unacceptable and apparently some form of threat to national security. Consequently the Department of Defense conferred on me the middle name, "NMN" (No Middle Name and pronounced nimin). All my military documents read Stuart NMN Tobin. Fortunately for me, even in the deep South where nicknames are such commonplace, no one had decided to call me nimin. Comfortably ensconced in my role as military dermatologist, I with my new name and rank labored through the day screening troops at sick call at 7:00 every morning, followed by a full day's clinic, attending to active duty personnel, dependents, and retired military.

One extremely hot summer morning, a very proper and serious minded JAG (Judge Advocates General, which is the legal arm of the military) officer appeared at my clinic carrying a black and quite bulging briefcase. I greeted him, "Good morning, Captain, what can I do for you?" He proceeded to tell me that he was here on official business. "What official business brings you to my clinic?" curiously I inquired. "Well, Major, we're bringing court martial proceedings against an enlisted man that you have seen in your clinic." He answered.

He then related the story that over the past number of months that the Military Police had been investigating some unusual occurrences at the officer's stable on post. One week they discovered that the padlock had been broken off. Another week the stable door was inexplicably left open and the officers' horses were wandering about unattended. A few weeks later they found a horse with its tail cut off.

The MPs increased surveillance of the barn and in the middle of the night they caught the enlisted man in question engaging in alleged non-consensual relations with the general's horse. While the military code of behavior is quite clear about fraternization between enlisted personnel and officers, the code governing officers' animals is a horse of another color. The general apparently didn't approve and the wheels of military justice began to turn.

He continued to tell me why I had been drawn into these proceedings. Since I had seen the soldier in my clinic for jock itch, a type of yeast infection, months prior to the night in question, the prosecutors wanted to know if I could testify at the court martial proceedings that he had acquired the skin affliction from the mare and therefore providing evidence of repeated prior offences.

I now found myself staring at a black and white photograph of the victim in her stall. She didn't appear particularly upset and there was no clear evidence of post-traumatic stress disorder that I could detect. I explained to him, "Yeast infections are so ubiquitous that it would be impossible to tie his rash to the horse, I mean the victim." Having watched the TV show *MASH* for years, I had a particular bond with the irreverent Hawkeye Pierce. Since I can resist anything except temptation it now seemed a good time to exercise that bond with a touch of acerbic humor.

A number of thoughts were now galloping through my mind which I decided to articulate. "How do you know the soldier wasn't seduced by the attractive white and lonely general's mare? She does have something of a reputation on post and look at that gleam in her eye." pointing to the photo. And wouldn't it be his word against her ney? Why had the victim waited so long to report the incident and were there any signs of resistance, and wasn't she at 1500 lbs able to defend herself? And of course she was naked." I continued. Apparently my observations were not convincing and he left more confused than amused, well certainly not as amused as I. The case as I learned weeks later, however, was eventually dropped.

Later that year the General of the military post marched into my clinic with a skin problem and wanted my advice. He looked at me and with all the authority of a man in charge and said, "Young man, do you know what that means?" as he pointed to the star on his collar. "Yes, sir," I shot back, "you can always trust your car to the man who wears the star, the Texaco, Texaco star," mimicking a gasoline commercial popular at the time. Lucky for me he had a sense of humor and laughed.

While ninety-five percent of my time, effort, and energies while stationed at Ft. Stewart, Ga. for two years revolved about my own dermatology specialty, medical military protocol obligated me to perform general medical duties as MOD, medical officer of the day. This in reality translated to manning the emergency room for twenty-four hours every few weeks.

On one of those occasions, on a Sunday morning, an enlisted soldier came in with an injury to his right arm. After the corpsman performed triage I entered the small white draped partitioned area to inspect and treat his problem. Sitting on a small cot was a young nineteen-year-old soldier with the epidemic military crew cut and wearing his camouflaged khaki fatigues. Despite his camouflaged uniform I was able to locate him.

He removed his shirt. As I examined him there was a small crusted bloody wound on the outside of his upper arm where the triceps muscle is located and a smaller area also bleeding on the inner side of the arm as well as a red linear streak burn area across his chest. There was no nerve injury and he had full range of motion of the entire extremity and function seemed to be perfectly intact.

I turned to him and asked him what happened. "Sir, I was at home and getting ready to have some tea and the teapot exploded causing this injury, sir." In the military the prefix and suffix of every sentence or thought is always the same, "sir," when an enlisted man engages an officer in conversation.

You always know when a soldier has completed his communication with you because you have heard the word sir twice. I studied this young man and he seemed to become more anxious as I just stood there looking at him. "Tell me young man, was it a 22 caliber or 25 caliber teapot that exploded?" I asked.

He just looked at me now not knowing if he should tell me the truth. "Soldier, I can't give you the best and proper treatment unless I know exactly what happened. So why don't you just tell me what really happened." I continued in a non-threatening concerned manner and gentle tone in my voice.

"Well, Sir, the truth is my girlfriend and I were driving on the Interstate and we got into a fight. Well, she just kept getting madder and madder, and she finally reached into her pocketbook and pulled out a small 25 caliber handgun and reached over and shot me. I was kind of scared it would get infected or something so I came over here, sir."

I'm now standing there imagining the scene to myself. He's driving at least 70 miles per hour on the Interstate with both hands on the steering wheel, and she can't be more than two feet from him when she decides to shoot him. The bullet passes through the soft tissue of the outside of his right triceps and exits out the inner side of the arm missing every vital structure in that extremity and grazes across his chest leaving the red streak and then harmlessly exits out the window.

How fortunate *they* are that she is an incredibly inaccurate marksman. If the angle of the trajectory had been one or two degrees different instead of missing his chest it would have entered his thoracic cavity lodging into the lung and/or the heart or aorta and probably would have killed him. Of course if he had died or even just passed out from shock from a non fatal wound, the car is still traveling 70 miles an hour but without benefit of a conscious driver or controlled direction. The consequences of her decision would have become apparent rather quickly as the car's trajectory would have become as precarious as that of the bullet.

I turned to him and asked, "Soldier, did your girlfriend ever consider what may have happened to her if she hadn't missed?" "Sir, no, sir" he answered. "Well, you might run that thought up her poor impulse control flagpole and see if she salutes it. But you might be sure she doesn't have her pocketbook nearby when you ask her." I had the corpsman clean, debride, and dress the wound. I placed him on prophylactic antibiotics as well as light duty, told him to return to sick call later that week for follow-up, and secretly prayed that he would find another girlfriend, as we dermatologists would say, who didn't have an 'itchy' trigger finger.

Veteran Medicine

My respect and bond with the military did not end with my termination of active duty in 1977. Now relocated and practicing in my own private solo practice in Richmond, Kentucky, I found myself accepting a position as a consultant to the Lexington Veterans Hospital which held clinic twice a month on Friday afternoons.

This gave me an opportunity to reconnect with veterans and also a venue to teach medical students. Teaching has been and continues to be one of my great passions and love and has provided me with many intangible rewards in preparing a new generation of physicians for their own medical careers. Despite my official status as a consultant, no one had ever bothered to issue me an identification badge. Since the problems of security were not as prominent as they are today, no one, including myself, seemed to care. Most of the patients knew they were seeing a dermatologist, and whether my name was on a name plate, or not, never seemed to be a concern.

One of those afternoons which always presented with more patients than time, I examined a retired vet with an uncomfortable and recurrent itchy psoriasis eruption. He had those large salmon colored and white thick scaling lesions that left a trail of flakes wherever he went. The eruption was extensive and covered much of his torso as well as his arms and legs and involved his entire scalp as well.

I explained to the students why this was a classical presentation of psoriasis and how easy it should be for them to diagnose such patients in the future. Since I had not seen him before, I proceeded to take a more extensive history about his condition. He told me that he had seen another dermatologist for the same condition about three or four years ago.

Stuart Tobin M.D.

So I asked him what that dermatologist had told him about his condition and what treatment had been given. He explained that the dermatologist had diagnosed him with an infection of the skin and had given him antibiotic creams to apply. I was absolutely dumbfounded. Every dermatologist easily recognizes and can diagnosis psoriasis and initiate the standard therapeutic treatment. I'm wondering to myself who is this peer who made the wrong diagnosis of such a simple case and who also instituted the wrong treatment? I caved in and asked. "Do you remember the dermatologist you had seen for this same condition in the past?" "Yes, I didn't like him, and he didn't get me any better so I thought I'd go to the VA and get some real help and it would be a lot cheaper too," he responded. "Who was it?" I asked. "It was a dermatologist in Richmond, a Dr. Tobin," he answered.

The medical students now broke down in waves of laughter as one of them informed him that he was now seeing the same Dr. Tobin again. Flashbacks filled my mind, especially from an old and experienced medical mentor who had taught me years before, that of all the information that you gather in making a diagnosis of a patient the part you should least pay attention to as credible was the history. Most patients just don't remember things accurately. I wondered if I should pass that same medical pearl onto these young student doctors at that moment or wait for a less self serving opportunity. When the clinic ended that afternoon I hurriedly headed over to administration to get an official name tag identification badge.

MEDICAL MENTORING AND MEANDERING

The Jock with the Itch

My dermatology office in Richmond, Kentucky lies about thirty road miles from the University of Kentucky Medical Center where I had experienced some of my own medical training. My medical internship in 1971-72 was located geographically and temporally between medical school graduation from Missouri and dermatology residency in New York. Since my internship the expansion of the medical curriculum at the University of Kentucky has allowed fourth year medical students and residents to apprentice in private practitioners' offices through the Area Health Education Center (AHEC) program,.

Richmond, located in the Southern AHEC area, lies on I-75 due south of Lexington and is a short commute for students. Many young physicians and student doctors over the years have made the trek to my office for a learning experience. I always delighted in teaching students in a preceptor and mentor environment. My patients seemed to enjoy and accept them as well.

Kitty, president of her medical school class, very bright, independent and self-assured as well as tall, blond, and attractive, elected to spend a month with me. Like so many other aspiring physicians, her quick grasp of basic dermatological concepts derived from a natural intelligence coupled with a keen desire to learn as much as possible, made for a rewarding experience for both mentor and student. Since my teaching philosophy embraces the belief that learning is more likely to be retained if the student is involved in the direct care of the patient, I always make a special attempt to have the young student doctors interact in the clinical setting with my patients rathrer than just shadowing me.

217

Rash Decisions and Growth Experiences
from the Best Little Warthouse in Kentucky

This particular morning a young strapping and muscular young man in his early twenties came in with a complaint of breaking out in his groin. After receiving his permission to have the medical student participate in his care, we entered the exam room where he had removed all his clothing with the exception of his jockey shorts.

He had well developed pectoral muscles as well as abs and strong well defined arm muscles, the type of body structure that comes from doing heavy manual labor. I proceeded to examine the patient's rash which had all the findings of tinea cruris, or what is commonly known as jock itch. And itch it did.

I proceeded to explain to Kitty why the eruption fitted so well with the arc shaped, ring-like pink pattern hugging the inner thigh and sparing the genitalia, and the nature of the fine white scaling edge which gave "ring worm" its name. We discussed with him the nuances of his condition and treatment options as well as the nature of recurrence and what measures he might undertake to prevent it from coming back as frequently.

I wasn't sure how much of this he was absorbing but Kitty seemed to be learning a lot. After relating all this information about his condition he hesitated just for a moment, seemingly bewildered as to what to do next. He then turned to Kitty while standing in his jockey short underwear and asked, "What should I do now?" Kitty as if on stage cue turned to him and answered, "You can either get dressed or I can stuff dollar bills into your underwear."

Well he apparently made the wrong decision and put on his clothing. Kitty has since gone onto a residency in Medicine and Pediatrics and has become an extraordinary medical asset to her community.

Digging in the Dermis
and the Dirt

Doug spent a month with me while he was completing his last year of medical school. Doug, who actually grew up in our small community of Richmond, had already established a reputation and presence while in college at Eastern Kentucky University as a talented and accomplished collegiate swimmer.

This interest has persisted through today as he competed internationally in the Masters swimming competition. He had converted his home into an aquatic center complete with a standard size swimming pool as well as a lap pool, a resistance pool, and as well as a child's pool for his kids. All are housed in a mammoth glass enclosed and steel structure aquanasium attached to the rear of his home in central Florida allowing him to practice year round. His property also backs up to a lake as well.

While rotating through my office Doug always had an expansive smile that was dwarfed by his deep and resonant pitched laugh. His sense of humor was securely attached to both. While he was in college one of the first true reality shows was *Real People,* which made its way to Kentucky.

Doug had decided to compete and ventured to the Kentucky River at Boonesboro, where Daniel Boone established the second permanent settlement in Kentucky. He appeared dressed with a mask and cape as well as Speedo bathing suit and announced that he would walk across the mighty Kentucky River in a homemade Styrofoam aquatic skis that did not have the benefit of either scientific design or testing.

Rash Decisions and Growth Experiences
from the Best Little Warthouse in Kentucky

Having engineered the entire contraption for this TV occasion, he had glued it together two days before in his dad's garage. With a powerful muscular stride and momentum and cameras rolling he sallied forth into the river. His powerful leg muscles and initial thrust defied all the rules of physics for about ten yards at which point the laws of science caught up with him. He promptly sank with the weight of the wet cape pulling him down. Because of his enormous strength and swimming talents he overcame both gravity and current to return to his disembarkation point, wetter but not really wiser, but at least captured on celluloid for the benefit and amusement of the great TV wasteland.

At the time of his rotation with me I traveled to Lexington every other Friday as the Consultant to the Veterans Hospital and Doug would travel with me to be joined with other medical students from his class who would participate in the care of our veterans.

Since Doug had spent more time in dermatology with me than these other students, I delegated him more responsibility. Since the clinic was usually overbooked with patients who had waited months for an appointment I was spread pretty thin, which often translated into more delegation than supervision. This particular day was just one of those days, and more. Doug had assisted me in my office performing skin cancer surgeries and had proven himself quite capable in the art of removal and suturing the skin back together, often referred to as excision and closure. I asked him if he felt comfortable in excising a straightforward skin cancer on a patient's arm.

He jumped at the opportunity and I told him to get started and I would return to check on him in a few minutes. Student after student, as well as patient after patient, monopolized more time than I had expected. I finally caught up with him. I entered the minor operating room and leaned over the surgically draped site and found an expertly excised and reconstructed skin cancer surgery worthy of any practitioner.

Doug, after completing his medical degree, would keep in touch with me from time to time and still does. One day he appeared unexpectedly at my bimonthly Friday afternoon clinics at the Veterans Hospital while I was instructing a number of fourth year medical students. Innocently he asked if I would look at a rash he developed and get my opinion. Knowing Doug as well as I did, I suspected that this was some form of medical trap and that he was setting me up. He raised his right pants leg and asked what did I think the eruption was? He had a circular brownish and resolving red sharply demarcated series of linear bands wrapping around his ankle and lower leg. The trap had been set and he wanted to see if he could catch me. I turned to the medical students and decided to play Dr. Sherlock "Cutis" Holmes with him and said, "This is a puzzling but interesting case, let's see if we can figure out what is wrong with our young colleague."

"First, as we look at Dr. Doug we notice that he is quite muscular and physically fit and athletic. Also he has a definite tan, which is unusual for someone to have in Kentucky during the month of February. Consequently, we would assume that he has recently traveled somewhere to a much warmer climate. Where might someone like him go?" I asked rhetorically. "Florida would be most likely. What would someone so athletic be doing in Florida at this time of year? Probably swimming, and where might he swim?" I kept answering my own rhetorical questions. "The ocean, of course. Since the rash is pinkish brown we can safely assume that it's about two weeks old and resolving."

"The circular line like nature would suggest a contact reaction. So it would only be logical to conclude that while swimming off the Florida Atlantic coast our young medical friend came in contact with a Portuguese Man of War who wrapped its poisonous tentacles around his ankle and leg causing the reaction that is now improving. I would also surmise from the diameter of the tentacle marks that the Portuguese Man of War was either a female or young male." I confidently concluded.

"So, Doug what happened to you?" I asked as "innocently" as he had asked me. He laughed his all encompassing and embracing good natured laugh and said, "That's exactly what happened!"

As the clinic progressed late into the afternoon an inpatient on a gurney was brought to the examining room with multiple linear scabs and crusts on his legs. Every question asked of him was met with a wall of mute dead silence.

Rash Decisions and Growth Experiences
from the Best Little Warthouse in Kentucky

"How long have you had the eruption?" one student asked. Nothing in response. "Is it painful or does it itch?" asked another. Silence again. Another wanted to know if he had ingested any new medications and still nothing from the unresponsive older man who lay there on the gurney in a horizontal stupor of silence.

Still feeling my deductive dermatology detective oats from my interaction with Doug, I started to explain the findings to the students. "What the ward physicians were calling a rash are in reality scratch marks. The scratches are so deep and crusted because of either a psychiatric fixation or intense pruritus (itching)," I suggested.

I continued, "As you study the lesions they are all linear and straight line. The linear nature could only mean that they are self-induced lesions. Now if you look a little more carefully you will notice that the direction of the linear deep erosions on the left leg are perfectly vertical while the ones on the right lower limb travel in an oblique 45 degree angle and direction. All of this would suggest that he used only his left hand to do all the scratching. "Consequently, we can safely assume that he is left handed." I now pronounced proudly.

The mute patient's eyes opened and he bolted straight up on the stretcher and uttered the one and only phrase of communication during our entire evaluation in a feeble but audible trailing voice, "I'm right handed." before falling back into a catatonic state.

Doug now practices dermatology in Florida and has become an exemplar credit to our specialty and will always be a special person in my life. Doug has always had a sense of humor as well as an imagination that skips from one humorous peak to another. When he was dating his soon to be wife in Florida, she accompanied him on one his antique outings.

While retrieving an artifact from a store the owner asked him, "Doug, don't you also have an interest in old maps?" "Yes", Doug replied. He continued, "Wait here a minute, I have one that just came in and it's of this area of Florida." Doug looked at the map and became intrigued and asked how much would it be and purchased it.

When they returned to his home Doug examined the map more closely with a magnifying lens and noticed a small "X" etched on the map. He did some calculations and to his amazement determined that the "X" was actually in his back yard. So he turned to his girlfriend and announced, "Let's dig up the backyard and see what's buried there."

"Doug, you're crazy, we're not going to dig up a whole backyard on a whimsy inaccurate old map," she responded. "Ok, ok," he said, "but I am going to get out my metal detector and see if anything shows up!" Off to the garage he darted and then to the backyard with the metal detector buzzing and his skeptical girlfriend in tow.

After a few minutes of searching the detector goes ballistic with the arrow indicator, bouncing around in a wild and positive way. He ran into the garage in search of a shovel and started digging frantically through the Florida dirt which anywhere else in the world would be called sand. After going about one and a half feet his shovel contacted something hard and metallic.

By now his girlfriend's skepticism has been converted to curiosity and possibly even borderline interest. Well at least her arms were no longer crossed and the smirk of disbelief had left her face. He not so carefully dug out an old rusty metallic box and now her borderline interest had become genuine curious enthusiasm. He flipped open the rusty lid and there to greet her was an exquisite diamond ring and he turned to her and asked on bended knee, "Will you marry me?" After he recovered from the traumatic shovel injury inflicted to his head she said "Yes!"

Barbie, Beethoven, and Churchill (The BBC)

Many medical students pass through my office and assist me in the surgical procedures I perform on my patients for removal mostly of skin cancers. Since their level of training is on the lower curve of learning they are always anxious to assist and to learn. As it is in most similar situations there is bound to be a harmless error or two that will occur.

After years of practice with so many students, I have discovered that the medical student's favorite word in the operating room is "Oops" and is often heard while we are operating on an awake patient under local anesthesia. Since these patients are anxious enough, hearing the word "oops" may not be reassuring.

The "oops" word was usually pronounced when the student may have placed a suture too far from the preceding one or when they may have inadvertently cut a suture they were attempting to tie. In any event, their pronouncement of "oops" has never led to me saying or feeling "oops" in turn. When this does occur, I always turn to the patient who is draped and unable to see what is transpiring and ask them, "Mr. Smith, what does 'oops' mean to you?" They always respond with variations of "has something gone wrong, doc? It doesn't sound good."

I then explain what the oops was all about and that there is no need for alarm or concern and that we are replacing one stitch that just didn't look as good as we wanted it, etc. The only time that I experienced the "oops" expression myself with a medical student

224

was when I opened the door to my consultation room to discover a female medical student breast feeding her baby, at which time I uttered "Oops!" before doing a one hundred and eighty and exiting.

While so many students have proven themselves to be knowledgeable and accomplished in the arts and fields of medical science, this depth does not always extend to other areas of education. I was mentoring a fourth year female student who had proven, as had many of her peers, to have gathered an extensive and in-depth command of multiple areas of medicine.

We spent much time discussing cases and the nuances of the practice of dermatology and she performed as well as any other. I had a musical stereo system installed in my office which received only two radio stations for whatever technical reasons that escape me. One of those two stations was the local university NPR station.

The hospital is located on land donated by the university, and the university radio station was visible from my office window and was located across an empty landfill a few mere yards from my clinic. This may account for why my little stereo system could pick up this and only this station. At the time NPR radio played classical music throughout the day and evening and remained a constant background presence in my exam rooms.

Most of my patients, even many who do not share the same appreciation for Mozart, Bach, Brahms, Mendelssohn and Schubert that I do, found the music tranquilizing. Listening to it defused some of their anxiety from being in a physician's office. Playing the classics had the added benefit of reaping revenge on adolescents who because of some faulty neurological wiring often mistake noise for music and feel the need to amplify their misjudgments for everyone else to hear, especially on local streets and behind you when stopped at a red light.

During one of our patient interactions Beethoven's Fifth Symphony echoed through the exam room with its characteristic opening chord of dit dit dit dah, dit dit dit dah. I guess I was feeling particularly pedantic and trivial oriented that day. There is no one more trivial than myself. I interrupted myself to ask her if she knew what that opening chord did to help the British win the Second World War?

Rash Decisions and Growth Experiences
from the Best Little Warthouse in Kentucky

"No." she replied. I would have been very disappointed if she had answered yes. So the opening was there and I leaped in. "Dit, dit, dit, dah is the same as dot, dot, dot, dash in Morse code, which is the letter V," I informed her. "During World War II when the outcome of the war was in doubt and the British were under aerial bombardment from both German bombers and rockets, Winston Churchill would travel around the country with great confidence with cigar erect in his mouth and his hand raised with his index and third digit pointing to the sky forming the shape of a "V" for Victory to buoy the nation's spirit. The "V" for Victory became his trademark. The BBC radio would play the opening bar of Beethoven's Fifth as an auditory translation of this visual cue to inspire the people of the nation," I triumphantly added. My medical student seemed confused, or at least her body language seemed not comprehending it all.

"You do know who Winston Churchill was?" I asked her. "Wasn't he vice President of the United States or something like that?" She hesitantly answered. While medicine was going to be her profession, the likelihood of seeing her on Jeopardy was fading fast. "Who was he?" She asked. "I'm not going to answer that right now. Your homework assignment is to come back tomorrow and tell me who he was," I instructed her. The next day she did. I don't know how much dermatology she retained after leaving her rotation with me but perhaps remembering Winston Churchill instead of Dr. Tobin wasn't a bad trade off.

The Ten Things They Don't Teach You in Medical School

I'll skip Rule Number 1for now, but I'll get back to it.

Rule Number 2: You're Really Not a Physician but a Server in the Medical Restaurant.

During training you're given the subliminal as well as overt message that you are captain of the medical ship navigating the patient on a course of health. However, many times you find yourself one on one with the patient's personal request taking precedent over your own well intentioned medical plan.

As a server in the dermatologist restaurant I repeatedly encounter patient after patient who will request a certain treatment. "My friend has acne and they used product X and it made them a lot better and I want to try it too."

I'm thinking to myself that's not what I originally planned to give them but it's on the dermatological ala carte standard of care menu. We could start off with that and see how they respond.

Or frequently patients will present with a high level of concern about a mole or growth on their skin and no matter how much you try to reassure them of its harmless nature they will not be satisfied until you do a biopsy.

You perform the biopsy to give them the reassurance that they need. It inevitably comes back as expected but the patient now feels that their issue has been addressed completely and consequently you receive the accolade of a "good doctor". They will now return to see you when some other medical issue arises.

Patient control over physician decision making has not been lost on the pharmaceutical industry. When I first started in practice the drug companies funneled much of their financial resources targeting only physicians. The marketing logic that prevailed in the industry was all prescription medications are dispensed by licensed physicians. Consequently, by targeting that relatively small population of practicing physicians they could gain a substantial share of the market.

Recently, the drug makers have had the financial epiphany realizing the extraordinary control that the consumer can exercise over the physician in his prescribing. They now spend gazillions of dollars targeting the public with TV commercials, ads in the print media, and radio spots.

The TV medication ads can be divided into two categories: 1) Vertical Medications and 2) Horizontal Medications. Vertical medications would include statin drugs, cardiovascular meds, pulmonary meds, as well as those for prostate enlargement. "Ask your doctor about Zocor, Lipitor, Crestor etc. or Caduet and for your asthma, Advair, Omnaris, etc. to keep you healthy." Other vertical meds include Avodart or Flomax and others for prostate enlargement.

Once you have achieved vertical health status with those meds you can now graduate onto the horizontal medications like Viagra, Cialis, or Levitra to improve your horizontal quality of life issues. Almost every other television commercial in prime evening hours touts some new drug and its particular benefits.

Yes, despite your superb, lengthy, demanding, and critically supervised and superior medical education, you will find yourself many times the server in the medical restaurant as the patient picks and chooses off the medical menu. And no matter how good a server you are the patient will never leave you a tip.

Rule Number 3: See the Patients Before They Get Better on Their Own.

Despite the logarithmic explosion in technology and advances in contemporary medical research there are still many acute illnesses that just run their natural course and we add little to affect the outcome.

Many of the acute skin eruptions just go away with time. Drug eruptions, acute cutaneous viral exanthems, pityriasis rosea, erythema multiforme, and on and on goes the list. So it is for all medical and primary care specialties. Pediatricians and primary care physicians are bombarded daily with infants and children with fevers of unknown origin that self cure.

We may intervene with drug therapy to shorten the duration of the disease or to make the patient more comfortable, but often they do little to really affect the outcome.

If you really want to enhance your prestige with your patients you have to see them before their acute disease self-remits and they get better on their own so you can claim credit for their improvement. Moral of the story - keep your waiting time short which leads into our next rule.

Rule Number 4: The Most Valued Prescription a Physician Can Dispense Is Reassurance.

Despite the almost daily breakthrough of this drug or new treatment approach, the most important and frequent prescription any physician can prescribe for a patient is reassurance. Reassurance that things are going to be all right or that at least we're going to work together to achieve the best possible outcome.

That translates into talking to the patient. Almost every patient presents with a sense that their symptoms represent the worst possible medical scenario leading to a disastrous outcome, yet they cling to hope. This is a rough translation of the old adage - people fear the worst and hope for the best.

I have had patients present time and time again with chronic skin conditions like psoriasis, recurrent eczema, and even acne like conditions who were sure they had cancer. Every patient who presents with a growth of any kind has cancer in the back or more likely the front of their minds.

Unless you confront this anxiety, you've done your patient and yourself a disservice. Often, I will start the consultation with, "Let's first start off with what you don't have. None of your skin conditions or growths has any of the typical features of skin cancer. Now let's spend some time discussing what you do have."

Defusing the patient's real anxiety through some form of reassurance allows them to follow your treatment plan more compliantly and with greater success. Sometimes reassurance takes the form of an explanation as to the nature of their disease or condition so they can have a more realistic insight as to what to expect. Always at the core of every explanation and treatment plan lays the theme of reassurance of physician and patient connected working together.

Rule Number 5: You're a Good Physician If You Don't Find Anything Wrong with the Patient.

A physician's entire medical education revolves around learning as much as possible about many disease entities and diagnosing and undertaking treatment plans for each one. The more exotic and rare the diagnosis, the practitioner experiences a greater sense of satisfaction and accomplishment, as well as pride in deciphering the symptoms into a recognizable medical entity.

This concept is ingrained into all physicians at all levels of training. Consequently, it is not at all surprising that the mantra behavior of all specialties and primary care is to diagnose, diagnose something wrong with the patient. Conversely, if you don't find something wrong with the patient you are some form of a failure.

If you have ever had the fortune of being a patient and presenting yourself to a peer physician for evaluation you quickly learn the patient's perspective that they don't want you to find anything wrong with them. You will quickly discover that your status from the patient's perspective remains equally as high even if you didn't discover the sixth reported case in the literature of "phallus genitalis abnormus" - whatever that is.

I always remember an elderly patient from the mountains of Estill County confiding in me that the reason he seldom sought medical evaluation was because, "Those damn doctors keep looking and looking to find something wrong with you and aren't satisfied until they do. Then they got you and won't let go."

Rule Number 6: When All Else Fails, Listen to the Patient, They May Be Telling You Something Important.

Every house officer early in his training discovers the changing history that the patient spins. They tell one story to the medical student, another to the intern and resident, and finally a totally different monologue to the attending. The evolving and changing history sometimes reaches mythical proportions.

Consequently, one learns to discount the information that patients often relate in connection to their disease if it doesn't fit with the clinical evidence or presentation.

Our cause and effect culture dictates that there must have been a specific cause that triggered off a particular illness. Frequently, my own patients will relate that their psoriasis only began after eating at a particular Italian restaurant, or that their skin cancer appeared right after they changed laundry detergent. It only becomes natural to relegate the history to low priority in the hierarchy of clinical assessment, lab tests, etc., in assessing the patient's diagnosis.

However, sometimes even the most experienced physician can be surprised. I hadn't been in private practice but a couple of years when an elderly woman came to the office and preceded to show me the innumerable seborrheic keratoses (harmless warty barnacles) that covered her entire torso. There were hundreds. She pointed to one on her chest and demanded, "Take that one off. None of the others bother me but I don't want that one on me anymore. Take it off." Invoking rule #2 I immediately complied with her request. To my utter astonishment it turned out to be an early melanoma.

So when everything else fails you might want to listen to the patient they may be trying to tell you something important. But only if everything else fails.

Rule Number 7: The Patient Is Smarter Than You.

Just because you have at your disposal a vast armada of technical as well as clinical information, data, and expertise doesn't mean that you are smarter than your patient. The way you present yourself and that information will betray more about yourself and the kind of physician you are than most physicians acknowledge or even realize.

The physician's body language is more telling than any spoken word. Over 80% of all human communication is done with body language. Yet so many practitioners seem oblivious to this form of communication. The flat affect, lack of eye contact, and monotone voice that was so commonly associated with psychiatric disorders seem to be spreading like an epidemic flu virus in medical practitioners' interactions with their patients.

Patient after patient has complained to me about "the physician didn't seem interested in me. He seemed just concerned about getting out as fast as he could. He had his back to me the whole time he was in the exam room."

Another patient once confided to me, "At least you're not like the last dermatologist I saw, Dr. Door Knob." Curious, I asked, "What do you mean Dr. Door Knob?" "The whole time he was in the room with me his hand never left the door knob. He couldn't wait to get out of the room and away from me," he replied.

If you're in a rush, the patient will know it. If you're distracted, the patient will know it. If you're not interested or engaged, the patient will know it. He will know it just the way you know your parent or spouse is upset or angry with you without ever uttering an audible word. Will your body language impact on patient care. You bet it will.

Rule Number 8: Every Patient Wants to Like Their Physician.

I cannot think of any other profession in which the client places so much positive trust in their professional. The cards are stacked in our favor from the get go. I've never seen a patient who didn't want to bond and trust me. That doesn't mean the relationship ended that way. However, initially we have the peculiar advantage of having the "customer" on our side.

As a practitioner all you have to do is give the patient an opportunity to like you. A kind word, a sensitive observation, a smile, eye contact, and even a little humor becomes the logarithmic factor that creates the positive bond with your patients. This spills over in greater patient compliance and more successful outcomes.

Rule Number 9: Death and Dying Is One of the Last Growth Industries in America.

In 2007, the country experienced the greatest recession/depression since the Great Depression of 1929. A recession is defined as when your neighbor loses his job. A depression is defined as to when you lose your job. Unemployment rose to greater than 10%. The banking industry almost imploded, the housing market collapsed, the automobile industry accelerated into disaster.

The disease of recession which spread like an economic plague was unable to substantially infect the medical economy which has remained mostly immune. Fifteen percent of the entire national economy is related to health care. The amounts of money that are expended on Medicare, private insurance, hospitalizations, long term care, the pharmaceutical industry, and other areas of medicine each year has shown disproportionate growth as compared to the national economic trends. This is reflected in the cost of health care having risen faster and higher than other sectors of the economy.

Health care is the most insulated and growing area of the service related industries in America. Death and dying is one of the last growth industries in the good old U.S. of A.

Rule Number 1: There Needs to Be More Humor in Medicine.
Patients need to laugh, and physicians need to laugh too.

Rule Number 10: The Thematic Model that Modern Medicine Follows Is that of the Pimp, the Prostitute, and the John.
See next chapter!

The Pimp, the Prostitute, and the John

Having practiced medicine and dermatology or external medicine for over thirty years as compared to my medical colleagues who practice internal medicine, I try to be sensitive to changing trends in medical care. What some people refer to as a life perspective. Of course to have a perspective on anything there must be some form of comparison, which in my case relates more to a temporal accounting rather than jumping from intellectual peak to peak, which is done by those with exceptional and dazzling intellects. I'll let the more brilliant practitioners with their keen and insipid minds make those deductions.

My questionably wise and non prophetic conclusions are those tempered by time as I look back in an attempt to look forward and say something, if not profound, at least that would be retained by someone somewhere for more than ten minutes. The following statement smacks of repetitive contempt that is made frequently but is relegated to old fools. I'm hesitant to utter it but it will serve its purpose, and those who read it might, no not might, but will definitely arouse hostility directed at an old fool who just doesn't get it. So here it is from an old fool who just doesn't get it. The younger generation has lost it and doesn't have the same moral medical values that my generation had. Or when I was your age, my young medical colleague,……..I was twenty-seven.

Now that I have inflamed and antagonized an entire generation let's add that the greed need in medicine is not age specific. Many of my contemporaries of all ages are driven more by income outcomes than by their moral compass. So what great and previously

234

unarticulated trend can I reveal that no one else has already expounded upon. The model I would use to describe how medical trends and advances develop in today's culture is that of the *Pimp*, the *Prostitute*, and the *John.*

The pimps are the drug companies and the manufacturers of medical equipment whose gigantic and megalithic profits are more obscene than those of the giant international oil companies. The scenario that plays out in medicine today follows these broad strokes regardless of what specialty you practice. The pimps develop a new drug or invent a new medical device which they tout as likely to improve the delivery of medical care, which it certainly may do.

This new expensive breakthrough has to be approved and marketed. So the pimps go to the prostitutes who are the researchers and the leaders of the medical field.

They approach the "giants" of medicine with the following proposition. We have developed a new drug or a new machine which will do this or that and we want you to become our consultant and do trials on it to see if it is really as good as we think. We'll pay you money to do the research and compensate you for your time and fly you here and there to conduct this study or that trial at your institution, etc.

Since it is in the nature of a researcher to research, and since the cost is going to be underwritten, the offer is infrequently refused. So the research prostitutes do their controlled investigations. Lo and behold it works or most of it works or it seems to work a little better or if not better a little differently than the other guys. Off goes the study to be submitted for publication in a prestigious medical journal or better yet a popularly read magazine or newspaper.

The prostitutes are then sent by the pimps to spread the word. So off to international and national and regional medical specialty meetings they go to teach and update the Johns, who like me are the practicing physicians serving the public. While the content of the message is different from product to product the theme is always the same. If you want to be practicing standard of care and up to date medicine you must now use this particular drug or this particular device. We are the leaders in the field and you should

Rash Decisions and Growth Experiences
from the Best Little Warthouse in Kentucky

"follow our lead" and prescribe this medication or now use that latest technological gizmo or you will be practicing inferior not up to date care.

No one wants to be accused of falling behind so we Johns fall in line. In case we Johns miss the message, there are the armies of drug detail people who parade into every physician's office with the good news and samples of the new wonder drug. It's no coincidence that they all look like they stepped out of Vogue or GQ, appearing stylishly dressed and young and very attractive carrying in one hand their products and in the other a box of doughnuts. And what may one ask is the significance of the Krispy Kremes in the south or their northern cousins counter parts, Dunkin Donuts?

Since we're on the subject of donuts, let's evaluate the irresistible temptation of the chocolate or sugar coated carbs and saturated fats on medicine in a non nutritional venue. While attending the American Academy of Dermatology annual meeting, which by the way was well infiltrated with pimps at the trade section and many prostitutes lecturing, this particular John managed to find himself seated at the annual business meeting. This concave usually features some ethical lectures on the do's and don'ts of our profession.

At this particular session the official academy officer lectured us on the dangers and unethical practice of accepting donuts from drug representatives regardless of whether they were Krispy Kremes or of the Dunkin Donuts variety. As I exited the lecture hall I found myself balancing the nutritional and ethical value of donuts. I, who am obsessive about my weight and who exercises three times a week and who eats a salad every day for lunch and adheres to a strict low fat and cholesterol diet, have a weakness in my nutritional chain of armor for chocolate and donuts. Combining the two together becomes for me, as Oscar Wilde so eloquently expressed in his play *Lady Windemere's Fan,* "I can resist anything except temptation." If I knew the world was going to end tomorrow I would go to Dunkin Donuts tonight.

While engaged in deep thought as I wandered the caverns and escalators of the Moscone San Francisco Convention Center, providence, or more accurately my feet, led me to the official display of the American Academy of Dermatology acknowledging those platinum, gold, silver and bronze contributors to the AAD. Of course anything that is expressed by the Holy Grail plus three precious metals in our capitalistic culture relates to financial contributions.

Listed in alphabetical format were the pimps that populated all those display booths in the trade area. A new question now arose in my already fatigued moral and donut stimulated mind. Why was the Academy warning me not to accept a $4.99 box of donuts while it was proper for them to receive over 2 million dollars from those same pimp drug companies and makers of durable medical goods? It's a rhetorical question. As with all other rhetorical questions, the question is more illuminating than the answer.

The safe and unsatisfying self-serving answer to this moral dilemma would be if the Academy can accept that much money I can surely accept a box of donuts, or what is good for the goose is good for the gander, or two wrongs could possibly be manipulated to be a right. The perhaps better response is: Well, they may accept the money, but on the smaller scale of personal conviction I won't accept the donuts. However, I find my moral code eroding as I ponder, ah, unless there's a chocolate covered cake donut in that box of twelve assorted jellies and glazed.....Hmm, I might just take one. Surely it won't hurt.

Ashes to Ashes

While most of my medical intern year was on site at the University of Kentucky Albert B. Chandler Medical Center in 1971-72, I was required to spend two rotations at other medical facilities. One was in the small eastern Appalachian community of Morehead, Ky. at the St. Claire's Medical Center which serviced indigent and mountain folk.

I have often wondered why almost every large medical fixed facility is always named "Center?" Would that not indicate that there are medical facilities that aren't the center and should consequently be named periphery. Has anyone ever seen or would you entertain taking your medical problems to a medical periphery. Yes, my medical facility is not a center but is on the non-cutting edge or periphery. It was a warm and not quite yet hot Kentucky summer and my obligation fell during the month of June. As I made rounds in the hospital with my medical mentor, the same artifact kept greeting me in every room. It was a fixture that I had not seen anywhere else in any hospital before nor ever since. It intrigued me as much the hundredth time I saw it as it did the first.

On every bedside stand table in every patient room of that small and rural hospital medical center stood an oil can painted either jet black or bright red with a small funnel attached to the top. This unique device was in effect an ashtray that had been donated to the hospital. That in itself was an irony that would have caught my attention. In addition on each ashtray were two identical gold labels, one on the front the other on the back accompanied by an inked drawing of the funeral chapel. Under the name came the advertisement, "Air-Conditioned Ambulance Service-Radio Dispatched Oxygen Equipped" I guess the funeral hearse was not air conditioned for apparent reasons.

The irony of an ashtray in a hospital enabling patients who were already hospitalized for smoke related illnesses of lung cancer and pulmonary as well as cardiac diseases to smoke more easily was hypocritical in itself. Coupled with an advertisement for the combined services of an ambulance and funeral parlor bordered on black comedy.

The message seemed to be if you come to the hospital for a respiratory or cardiovascular disease it was not only all right to smoke but you were encouraged and enabled to do so. If you survived that go around and needed to return call the oxygen equipped ambulance service and if you didn't survive you had one stop shopping with the funeral home, all on one ashtray by your hospital bedside. I have never seen since or before such successful hypocritical marketing chuptza by any business. The tobacco giants could learn a thing or two from the funeral home in promoting their products.

I felt that type of cultural marketing irony had to be preserved and documented. One afternoon after rounds I sneaked into an unoccupied patient room and placed a black oil can ashtray under my white intern lab coat and absconded with this cultural iconic treasure. It has remained a prize possession and on display in my library for the past thirty three years and triggers smoky nostalgic medical memories of Morehead, Kentucky in the summer of 1972.

The Shoe on the Other Foot

I arrived at my office to perform an early surgery on a Thursday morning. However, the young lady with the curable Melanoma was actually scheduled later that day. Noticing a bright yellow sticky note on my desk requesting a consult at the hospital, I with this unexpected free time decided to wander over across the street to see this inpatient .

The patient, a delightful aging, educated, articulate and well-mannered man in his eighties had become dependent on crutches reducing his mobility and confining him to a wheelchair and bed. All of which led to a stubborn pressure sore or ulcer on his buttocks. Although we had discussed numerous times in the recent past the importance of relieving the pressure to the area with an inflated donut which he would sit on while in his wheelchair, the recent flare arose from his supine position from lying in the bed on his back.

The long-term care facility had difficulty in keeping him propped on his side with two hour turnings to relieve the pressure over his sacrum. As chance and good chance as it may be, when I walked into his semi private room, his primary care physician was attending to him. Rick has been a colleague of mine for many years and was an excellent internist. He and his family had a small farm just outside of town and a number of years ago he called me on a Saturday morning to come over to help him repair a barbed wire fence to keep his cattle from wandering off the farm.

As everyone knows collegial, over educated medical professionals are cheaper help than transients or migrant workers on quick notice on Saturday mornings for the gentleman farmer. We now talked about different approaches to heal our common patient's bedsore. I suggested that we re-institute promogram with an occlusive duoderm dressing which has worked successfully in the past for many of my patients. Also, if we were to sew a tennis ball into the back of his shirt that would act as a good prompt to keep him off his

240

back and to lie on his side. After discussing the case we both wandered back to the nursing station to do the dreaded paperwork in the non-digital era.

At the nursing work station was our resident nephrologist already engaged in his own documenting of care for one of his patients. Upon seeing us his whole face lit up and he anxiously started talking to us about his own recent medical predicament and experience. "A few weeks ago, I developed this incredible pain on the top of my foot. I never had so much pain in my life!" he announced excitedly. "Every time I would touch the side of my leg that would trigger the pain on my foot," he continued. "Although I continued to work, my ability to concentrate and think was really impaired by the pain which was so intense. So I saw our orthopedist, who took me to the OR and removed a Schwannoma, nerve growth tumor from my leg," as he now pulled up his pants leg to demonstrate the proud red badge of courage in the form of a linear dark brown healing scar.

"What instant relief I had. As soon as it was removed, the pain went instantly away. I couldn't believe it. It certainly has made me a believer in the incapacitation of pain. The next time a patient tells me that they have incredible pain I am going to listen more attentively and sympathetically," he concluded. This personal medical adventure in turn jump started Rick's memory of his own encounter as a patient shifting him from detached objective professional experienced physician to excited animated patient in testimonial gossip mode.

"Let me tell you what happened to me shortly before I opened my own private practice in Richmond quite a number of years ago," He excitedly gasped. "I didn't know anyone in the medical community and I had just completed my training. I suddenly developed pain in my abdomen and the pain not only persisted but intensified over the days to come. So my wife prodded me to go to the ER where I was diagnosed by the emergency physician as having a kidney stone. Although I didn't know what was wrong with me, I did know it wasn't a kidney stone. As I was walking down the hospital's hallways I ran into a janitor who had done some work for me and I told him about my pain." He said, "Doc, I think you have a

ruptured appendix." I answered him with "Naw, it couldn't be a ruptured appendix. It would hurt a lot more that it did."

"Well the pain continued and worsened, so back to the emergency room I returned the next day. They had the greatest trouble
locating a surgeon to see me and finally they found one who immediately operated on me to repair my ruptured appendix and treat the
peritonitis that has set in."

A beam of satisfaction came over Rick's face as to the irony
and humor of how he too had survived as a patient. How could I let
this opportunity pass without me bonding and sharing my own personal medical experience with my colleagues whose admission of
vulnerability and brush with the other side of the medical street they
had just related.

"A few years back after exercising and running on the tread-
mill, I began having pain in my right sole. So I mentioned it to my
internist on a routine check-up. He examined me and discovered a
mild peripheral neuropathy. So off to the lab I went for every blood
test in the book. On follow-up he triumphantly announces that I
don't have any rare macroglobulinemia or undiagnosed diabetes and
that all my tests were normal."

While pleased to hear that I'm not going to be the only person in the county to die from a rare zebra disease, I still find myself
in patient mode with the pain in my foot unabated. So I asked him,
"Jim, why is my foot still hurting?" "Well, I'm not sure," he
answered. "But my own foot was hurting a couple of years back, so I
went to John's Running Shop in Lexington and bought a pair of
Mephisto Shoes and the pain stopped. Why don't you go down there
and buy a pair of those great shoes?" he asked as he pointed down to
his own feet to the pair he had on.

So that weekend I drove the twenty five miles to Lexington
and arrived at John's Running Shop. I casually mentioned to the
shoe salesman that my foot had been hurting under the second and
third toe, I failed to mention that I am a physician and had already
sought medical evaluation for my ailment and pain. He examined the
area and pressed on the spot. "Is that where it hurts?" he asked.
"Yes," I responded. I think you have the classical presentation of a
neuroma. Why don't you get some mole skin at Walmart and make a

little support cushion and place it behind the painful area," he suggested.

I thanked him for his advice and bought the shoes which not only turned out to be advertised as the most comfortable shoes in the world but also apparently the most expensive ones in the known universe as well.

So Monday morning I called our experienced local orthopedic surgeon for an appointment. He accommodated me with an appointment right away. I deliberately neglected to tell him all the history that led up to this not so serendipitous visit but rather just went for the jugular. "Tom, I think I have a neuroma in my foot," I proudly announced as if the diagnosis was all my own. He removed my sock and palpated the area on the sole of my foot and announced, "Stu, you indeed do have a neuroma in your foot. I can feel it. I could surgically remove it but a lot of patients get symptomatic relief by placing a support pad just behind the area on a cushion insert."

He retrieved from his supply room a couple of metatarsal mounds to place in my shoe. "Why don't you try these first?" Well, every time I took a step with those mounds I felt like I was stepping on a mini mountain. It was as annoying as the neuroma. So I decided to follow the shoe salesman suggestion and went to Walmart to purchase some mole skin. I cut and fashioned it into a custom made support pad and placed it into the sole of the shoe. The pain went away instantly and has stayed away for a year or so. I felt like a sole survivor as I removed my shoe to show my peers. I quickly added as they stared at my sock-less foot. "I hope you two won't mind if I bare my sole to you."

Each of us have ventilated our own confessions of misadventures of physicians turned patients and laymen turned physicians. With our own personal badges of courage, we departed from each other to undertake our professional care of our patients in each of our specialties. Having now walked on both sides of the professional street as patient and physician we each have gathered insight about our patients. These personal experiences in turn have made each of us a little more sensitive and understanding and consequently more empathetic physicians.

Good Judgment Comes from Experience, Experience Comes from Bad Judgment

My most memorable medical mentoring experience was my own and evolved from a rotation I had while just starting my senior year in Medical School at the University of Missouri at Columbia. As a fourth year student I was entitled to an elective four-week rotation allowing me to spend time away from the medical center apprenticed to a general practitioner.

Many of my peer classmates had suggested that time spent with a particular general practitioner in the northern part of the state would yield unique opportunities for doing procedures and direct hands on patient care. I anxiously and quickly signed up.

I found myself arriving on July 1st 1970 to a small and isolated rural northern Missouri town of about 1500 inhabitants serviced by a small but clean and efficient twenty bed hospital staffed by the Sisters of St. Francis of Assisi, all of whom were immigrants and nuns from Austria. They wore the black and white traditional habit. My little immaculately clean and furnished room was located in the convent and every day fresh flowers were placed on the small end table at my bedside and frequently I would find freshly baked cookies there as well.

Upon arriving at the hospital I searched out my new mentor, a tall and serious yet overworked primary care physician in his early forties with dark hair combed straight back. I reached out my hand in a gesture of friendly greeting and announced that I was his new medical student for the next four weeks.

Stuart Tobin M.D.

His pressured response was neither one of greeting or dread but of expediency. Without even introducing himself or questioning me as to my name, he bottom lined me with, "Have you had OB (Obstetrics)?" "Yes," I answered half uncertainly and fully bewildered. "Well, there's a woman in the delivery suite dilated and effaced, deliver her and then meet me at the clinic across the street, I'm running late," he replied as he briskly walked off.

This was a lot more autonomy and independence than I expected or was accustomed to, but I had had OB and I had delivered a few babies under the supervision of the OB residents, and I felt that I could do an uncomplicated delivery. Surely he wouldn't be asking me to deliver a complicated one, I mused. Off I went to confront a young nineteen or twenty-year-old mother in stirrups, and just as I walked into the delivery suite the newborn decided to give me more of an animated greeting than my mentor had.

After performing the delivery, ligating the cord, and removing the placenta and checking the newborn's status and performing the episiotomy, I made my way to an overcrowded and hectic clinic populated by men with muscle and joint injuries, expecting women for prenatal exams, children with coughing and sneezing, and the elderly with that resignation written on their faces clutching zip lock bags full of multiple medications.

Every morning for the next week and a half, I would meet my mentor for rounds at the hospital at eight o'clock where he always had six to ten hospitalized patients with uncontrolled diabetes, others with pneumonia, or hypertension or congested heart failure, and other usually uncomplicated but serious medical problems.

We would discuss each case and he would share his insights and experience with me. Then off to the afternoon clinic we hurried to see an exhausting 50 to 75 patients in an afternoon. It was well into the second week of this unrelenting and busy schedule that just as unexpectedly as our first encounter he turned to me and announced, "You know I usually like to take a little time off in the summer and go fishing. Why don't you run things for me while I'm gone?" At the time I hadn't mastered the insight that good judgment comes from experience and that experience comes from bad judgment.

Rash Decisions and Growth Experiences
from the Best Little Warthouse in Kentucky

As a fourth year medical student I was just interested in experience, experience and more experience. The opportunity to perform what I had been studying in theory for the past three plus years overwhelmed my common sense. Without thinking, it had to be without thinking, I responded, "Sure." That casual "sure" answer that doesn't anticipate that a situation could arise that I wasn't prepared to handle, the type of "sure" that came more from ignorance than from good judgment. The type of "sure" that originated from bad judgment that is clouded by an insatiable desire to do procedures and perform primary care. No sooner had I uttered those four letters, he was gone without a forwarding address or phone number.

The next few days while very hectic were uneventful. I already knew the treatment plans of the inpatients, and I had wonderful assistance from the dedicated and knowledgeable nuns who treated me very kindly. The afternoons, while tiring, were uncomplicated - treating respiratory infections, allergies, hypertension, supervising diabetics, and refilling prescriptions for established patients. So this pace continued for the next three days. Nothing unusual or unexpected occurred until.....

While making rounds the fourth morning a nurse came running over to me and with a great sense of urgency in her voice said, "Some woman just called from across the street and said that her husband looked just terrible and someone had to see him right away." Guess who that someone was. So I said confidently, "Let's go over and see what the problem is." Off we hurried across the street and down a block to enter a modest one story wooden clapboard home so common to rural northern Missouri.

Lying on a sofa that was too small for his six foot farmer frame was a man in his late fifties who appeared cold and clammy and was clutching his belly and chest. As soon as he saw me he uttered his chief complaint, "If I could just have a good shit I would feel better."

I immediately turned to the nurse and said, "Check his blood pressure!" After two attempts, she frantically said, "Doctor, I can't get a blood pressure." I grabbed the cuff and carefully inflated it as I had done so many times before as a student and listened intently over the brachial artery with my stethoscope pressed against the arm listening for those familiar bass like beating sounds I had heard so many times before. "He has a blood pressure it's 40 over 0!" I triumphantly announced.

Forty over zero I thought, he's in shock. I'm in shock. The reality of the situation hit me hard and strong. There was no one else but me to handle this medical crisis. "We can't do anything for him here. We need to get him over to the hospital emergency room!" I said. The small and sparsely equipped ambulance finally appeared across the street and we raced to the emergency room to evaluate and undertake his care.

What could be causing his shock, I kept asking myself. He's diaphoretic and clammy and clutching his chest, It must be cardiogenic shock I reasoned. He has low blood pressure because the heart pump isn't working, isn't working because of a myocardial infarction or heart attack, I conjecture.

We immediately hooked him to an EKG and I had enough medical training to recognize an acute MI which showed up on the tracing. I started to bolt out of the emergency room and one of the nun nurses grabbed me by the arm and said, "Where are you going doctor, the patient is in here?!" "I have to get my *Washington Manual*, sister. I have never seen a case of cardiogenic shock, and I have never had any cardiology training," I blurted out. The *Washington Manual*, which could be found at the time in most interns front white coat pocket, is a cookbook on how to treat emergency situations. This certainly qualified as one, and I needed help.

I raced back to my little sanctuary room and retrieved my spiral manual and bolted back to the ER. I flipped open to the section on cardiogenic shock and to this day those two pages remain emblazoned and embedded in my mind. The book said the first thing you need to do is raise the blood pressure and the drug of choice to accomplish it was Isuprel. "Nurse," I barked, "place an ampule of Isuprel into D5W and run it intravenously!" The nun responded, "Doctor, we don't have that drug." Incredulously, I said, "You, don't have that drug? It says right here in the book that is the drug we need to use. What do you mean God dammit you don't have it!" "We don't have it," again she repeated. I also knew that

Rash Decisions and Growth Experiences
from the Best Little Warthouse in Kentucky

I'm going to catch it later from the nuns for my use of an uncensored obscenity.

I scanned down the page and the next paragraph said the drug of second choice would be Levophed. I pointed to that drug, which I also had never heard of and stabbed at the name and asked, "Sister do we have that one?" "Yes," she replied. "Let's try it," I responded. After a few more tense moments she announced, "His blood pressure is up to 90/50 and then after more infusion of Levophed his pressure rose to a normal 120/80.

I continue to read on and the manual then instructs me that you have to check for cardiac arrhythmias which if present they can make the heart beat in an inefficient manner. The manual instructed that the treatment for these arrhythmias would be intravenous xylocaine. As I rescanned the EKG tracing, sure enough he had a severe arrhythmia leading to complete heart block. So in goes the xylocaine and out goes the arrhythmia.

Continuing the cookbook instructions, the manual suggested that supplemental oxygen be given to increase the oxygen content to the blood. On goes the green tubing with a flow of 6 liters per minute and the patient becomes pinker. Don't forget to relieve the patient's chest pain with morphine I'm reminded in the next paragraph. I now infuse slowly a dosage of morphine to prevent respiratory arrest as the medical emergency manual now instructed. Also get a chest x-ray the manual reminds me. A portable chest x-ray is obtained. After a half hour of this incredible tension, the patient has converted to normal sinus heart rhythm and his blood pressure had remained normal. He is pink and well oxygenated and is resting comfortably, at least more comfortably than I am.

The last paragraph of my little manual, which by now has risen to medical biblical doctrinal status in my mind, says that the survival rate from cardiogenic shock is only 20 percent. We have beaten the odds or have we? I turned to one of the nuns and said, "Find my mentor and tell him his fishing vacation is over. I can't do this anymore. It's just too stressful for me!" Finally, a wave of sanity came over me. He quickly retuned, and we resumed our usual relationship for the remainder of my apprenticeship.

Stuart Tobin M.D.

The patient continued to have a rocky course and remained too unstable to transfer to a larger medical center. I was awoken three nights later to be informed by the nuns that the patient had succumbed in the middle of the night despite all our heroic measures.

It's interesting about a tsunami of insanity. Sometimes after it hits the sands of time the wave quickly disappears and is easily forgotten. Just like the defendant in a legal case who claims temporary insanity, we who are normal can sometimes suffer from temporary insanity and forget the turbulent waters we have just sailed through and look out at the peaceful untroubled sea of the future and again feel adventurous and confident. It was time for me to learn again what I had just recently forgotten.

About a week later I was having lunch in the hospital's small cafeteria and the only other person there was the town's only general surgeon. He was a short man with wavy gray hair and a prominent nose and dark olive complexioned skin. He had been born in Greece and for reasons I never learned had settled in this small town.

He was self-assured and gentle and seemed to like me. I sat down next to him and we began to talk. He told me that he could never get used to the accent of those wonderful Austrian nurses. Every time he heard their German accent it would send chills down his spine. I asked why.

He confided to me, "As a child growing up in Greece the country was occupied by the Nazis, and one afternoon while hiding on a hill near the center of my small village the Germans had rounded up a group of about half dozen people and marched them to the center of the town square and executed them before my eyes. One of them was my uncle." Post traumatic stress syndrome hadn't been recognized yet as a psychiatric entity. As I look back he certainly suffered from it. He seemed relieved having ventilated and confided in me. We began talking medical talk and he causally asked me if I had any interest in surgery. I told him I had interest in doing and learning as much as I could. That was my charge as a medical student.

Rash Decisions and Growth Experiences
from the Best Little Warthouse in Kentucky

"Well, I have a young woman with abdominal pain in her lower right quadrant and I think she has appendicitis. Have you ever taken out an appendix?" he asked. "No," I answered. "Would you like to remove one?" he continued. "Sure," I answered without thinking. You would think that by this time the word "sure" would induce post traumatic stress syndrome for me, but the chance to do a major surgery again blinded my common sense. We walked to the major surgery suite and after a thorough surgical scrub we donned sterile gowns, masks, and gloves and entered the sanctity of the OR.

He handed me the scalpel and carefully instructed me on where to make the incision over McBurney's point and guided me as we passed through overlying muscles and fascia entering the unfamiliar territory of the abdomen. He helped me examine the large intestine as we searched for the appendix.

Carefully I dissected the appendix, separating it from the intestine, and began under his patient supervision to repair and close the defect and suture back the invaded tissue and overlying muscles one layer over another until I finally closed the skin.

He complimented me on my technique and suturing, and the sense of satisfaction that passed over me at the time has rarely been experienced since. I spent a few more days in my final rotation working with my mentor and returned to Columbia and to the Medical Center having felt a new level of maturity and confidence and most importantly a respect for the boundaries of good medical judgment.

Anachronistic Misnomers in Medicine

Every morning at the office the phone is ringing off the hook! Ringing off the hook, an expression that must be utterly bewildering to a younger generation who never saw, or perhaps better expressed heard a telephone truly ring. Truly ring because at one time in a distant universe far away there actually was a bell that rang announcing a phone call. Today's phones don't ring, they beep, buzz or rattle. Cell phones are even more removed audibly since they play some form of a irritating ditty to make their presence known. Perhaps a more appropriate expression for this phenomenon would be instead of the phone is ringing, the phone is singing. But is it really correct to impart to a mechanical device the ability to "sing"? Should not "singing" remain the preserve of humans, birds and other life forms with some mode of true vocal chords? A new word is needed to accurately reflect this changing cultural phenomenon. I would like to place into nomination the word "songing." My cell phone is "songing" sounds more resonant anyway.

Teaching old dogs new tricks has rarely been successful in the world of lexicography. So what more likely happens when we encounter a new meaning for an old term is we just add another definition to the existing word. Definition number fifteen in the Random House Unabridged Dictionary for the verb ring would eventually become the act of noise produced when a telephone has an incoming call. All bets are off, however, if you have call waiting because the same definition would have to appear under the word beep.

Rash Decisions and Growth Experiences
from the Best Little Warthouse in Kentucky

So it is with the English language that we would rather add definitions to old words rather than create new ones. Let's not even broach the expression to "dial" a number when every phone, landline or cell, has buttons to push. No one truly dials a phone number anymore and haven't for years. The contemporary generation's only encounter with the word "dial" would be in the supermarket in the soap aisle! Consequently, I'll get off my soap box about the word dial.

So every morning at the office the phone is songing off the hook. Yet where is the hook? When telephones had true bells they also had true hooks on which the ear receiver rested while not in use. The ear piece, because of the volume and wavelength of the ringing bell, would also visually vibrate. Hence the phone would almost literally ring off the hook. Landline telephone receivers, if you can find one today, rest on a cradle and not a hook. So the correct expression should be the phone is songing off the cradle. Misnomers are as rampant in the medical field as they are in the general language. Never questioned and never challenged they exist and persist indefinitely as familiar landmarks in our twisted medical lexicography.

In dermatology one of the most common skin rashes that physicians and the lay public know well is Poison Ivy. The term utterly defies all logic and is classically misnamed. The two common skin reactions that patients manifest are either toxic reactions or allergic reaction. The designation toxic is used for chemical or poisonous reactions that have encountered the skin and caused a severe irritant reaction as seen with acids or alkali. These reactions happen in everyone exposed to the chemical or toxin. Poisons produce toxic reactions. Poison Ivy, the rash, however, is not a toxic or poisonous reaction but is instead a truly allergic reaction.

People are either allergic to poison ivy or they are not. The reaction that it produces in the allergic individual is considered the classic model of delayed allergic hypersensitivity reaction that defines all contact allergic reactions in our specialty. It is not a toxic poisonous reaction and consequently is misnamed. The correct name should be Allergic Ivy. Yet this is never mentioned even in our specialty in any of the volumes and textbooks of our scientific literature.

252

Stuart Tobin M.D.

And what about the name Ivy? Is poison ivy a true ivy? My botanist friends tell me that it may not be the best classification as well. So if not of the poison variety and not in the Ivy genus, then what name should reflect this common skin rash? I would like to submit into nomination, to be ignored by perhaps everyone except me, the name Allergic Rhus Oleoresin Dermatitis. Even my professional colleagues wince when I mention it. Let's turn our attention to another misnamed disease.

Herpes in Greek means to creep. Herpes Zoster or "shingles" is caused by the same virus as chickenpox or what we refer to as the Varicella Zoster virus. After exposure to the chickenpox virus the body stores up the memory as well as some of the virus and later in life, for some known or unknown reason, that same virus which has remained dormant and inactive becomes revitalized and attacks one specific nerve. Patients develop pain because of the inflammation around that one nerve, and it appears as large fluid filled blisters that "creep" along one nerve or dermatome to which it has attacked. The most common location is usually around the chest area,, afflicting one of the thoracic or lumbar nerves.

Also in the category of Herpes viruses is the common cold sore or the Herpes Simplex I virus that most commonly appears attached to one of the nerves around the mouth. Another related variation is the similar Herpes Simplex II virus that usually attacks the male or female genitalia and has considerable emotional overtones and stigma associated with it because of its sexual transmission nature and frequent reoccurrence, which brings us back to the changing nature of the English language. The Greek verb herpes, which means "to creep", has now been altered to the English nominative noun form to "the creep gave it to me."

Influenza, the common respiratory virus that has plagued mankind for centuries, was well documented in medieval times. While the correct cause was unknown, the medical and scientific intellects of the time were not unaware of this repeated seasonal respiratory plague.

In the winter months, a respiratory disease that would afflict and kill so many people across Europe with severe coughing, fever, and breathing impairment, reappeared yearly. In an attempt to explain this more rationally and medically, the great physicians and intellects of the time in medieval Europe consulted the most advanced science and technology of their era - astrology.

After much pondering and plotting and time measurements of when the disease peaked, they came to the conclusion that this incapacitating respiratory ailment only developed when certain stars were in a certain alignment. Hence it was this alignment that caused or influenced the disease. Influenza in Latin means the influence and consequently became associated with the influence of the stars. While we retain the same name for the disease as our ancient predecessors, the cause has been more accurately ascribed to a mini microorganism virus viewed under the electron microscope rather than as small lighted dots in the night sky as seen through a reflecting telescope.

One would think that with that type of medical advanced insight, coupled with yearly new vaccines, would come a more appropriate name that reflects the etiology of this devastating respiratory ailment. None, however, seems on the horizon, or shall we say "in the stars."

Malapropisms are even more abundant in the medical field since the lay public has become more knowledgeable and involved in the decision making process. Especially with internet - anyone with access to the web can tap into an encyclopedic reservoir of medical knowledge in relative depth and width any time of the day or night. As patients present their questions and relate their findings in an office setting there have been quite a number of mis-mangled medical malapropisms.

One day while attending patients in my itinerant Wednesday office in Somerset, Kentucky, (which lies fifty miles south and slightly west of Richmond), a fortyish-old woman presented with an embarrassing chief complaint, "that she had a breaking out in her *public* hair." Without a moment's hesitation I asked her what she did for a living, or was it a "loving"?

Patients quite cognizant of the rising cost of medicines have a fairly good understanding of the difference between trade name drugs and the less expensive generic chemical equivalents. However, I was taken aback by an older Medicare patient who requested, "That

254

Stuart Tobin M.D.

I don't want that expensive trade name medicine, Doc, I want a *sub-scription* to that *genetic* medicine."

Subscription is a word that I hear almost weekly in the office when patients want a prescription. I've heard that alternative mala-propism so often that it has cross linked into my own subliminal synaptic psyche. Last summer I found myself renewing my *pre-scription* to *Time* magazine.

Life is too Commercial

Performing the same procedure over and over again leads to a sense of routine. This happens with anyone who performs repetitive activities in the workplace. Auto mechanics, blue collar workers on assembly lines, and maintenance personnel are all well aware of this mental cruise control. What may appear as unusual and unique to the new practitioner of the art translates to experience and routine in someone who has performed it innumerable times.

This also occurs in medicine and surgery. The routine repeated procedure loses its excitement and uniqueness when performed so often. Your cerebrum is controlling your hand movements with a lower level of anxiety. While the young and less experienced physician will be engaged and excited on performing a new procedure the more seasoned one while just as committed to as good an outcome doesn't obsess over it between cases. Your mind then begins to wander to unrelated thoughts. Countless surgical procedures over my professional lifespan has led me into this meandering mental mode.

Operating on a quiet, stone faced countenance and non-communicative mountain man for a skin cancer on his face, I attempted to engage him in conversation or ply some of my humor but to no avail. None of it was having the desired effect. It was as if I had anesthetized his whole body instead of just the local surgical area. I sensed for this particular patient golden silence was more soothing and less distracting than a slick silver tongue. So I drifted into a sense of quiet matching his own. Consequently I found myself embracing the 'if you can't beat them you might as well join them' philosophy.

After completing the case, I found my quiet mode of introspection led me wandering from one thought to another. Thinking about the rerun television program I had seen the night before, I also began to recycle in my mind the commercials that were peppered throughout the program. Many of them were so cleverly done. I wondered if I could write anything of that caliber. The following images began to merge and gel in my mind.

A photograph of the planet Mars appeared as the opening scene in my imaginary commercial. A very handsome male like Ben Affleck or Tom Cruise is on the red planet. He is then transported through space to the driver's seat of an unknown convertible automobile parked on a romantic beach setting. A gorgeous woman who is on the planet Venus is now also transported through time and space and ends up in the passenger seat next to him. They look at each other and make a cosmic romantic connection.

The convertible, which until now has not been identified, takes off from the beach into the beautiful blue Pacific sky. You can now see it's a sleek Saturn sporty vehicle. A soothing and resonant voice can now be heard narrating, "Whether you're a man from Mars or a woman from Venus, if you want a driving experience that's out of this world, get yourself into orbit with a SATURN."

All the time in the background music is playing from Mozart's Jupiter symphony or a Space Odyssey or some other appropriate celestial musical piece.

Since I'm given to some obsessive compulsive behavior, commercials and cars seemed fixed in my mind. I found myself musing again with the following advertising fantasy.

Saturn and all its competitors are lined up on a dusty and dirty rural racetrack. They all are gunning their engines in anticipation of a competitive race. The camera now focuses on a hand with a starting gun. The gun goes off with a plume of smoke trailing from the barrel. All the cars take off as fast as they can. The Saturn, however, gets out in front leading the pack. It now outdistances all the others leaving them in a huge trail of gritty dust.

As the camera pans out, further and further away, what you thought was a minor dirt backwater racing track now becomes obviously the rings of the planet Saturn. Another resonant and authoritative voice is now heard saying, "**Saturn runs rings around the**

competition." Some form of appropriate racing music plays in the background throughout.

Unfortunately, because of the worldwide recession in the first decade of the new millennium and new century, Saturn's fortunes as a car company on the automobile horizon has turned out to be a setting sun rather than a rising one. Along with Saturn's fortunes my commercials are more likely to remain in my mind than on the small screen. However, this failure didn't daunt my imagination and I continued to have commercial fantasies.

I'm really into the commercial mode and my OCD mind is in overdrive. Now I envisioned a professional photographer in his well appointed studio photographing a beautiful model for one of those make-up or hair coloring product commercials. As he moves around snapping poses at different angles he coaxes her to smile more. "Come on give me a big smile. Smile. Say cheese."

The scene now changes to the United Nations and all the heads of state are standing on bleachers to have the traditional yearly group photo taken of these collected leaders of the world. While standing very dignified and stately the photographer attempts to get them to relax more and change their mausoleum countenances to a more friendly pose. "Everyone listen, I need you to smile like you're running for office. Smile everyone, say cheese."

The scene changes for a third time and you now see a dad at home for his four-year-old son's birthday party. His wife holds the uncooperative little tyke on her lap as he attempts to take a snapshot with his point and shoot camera purchased form a discount department store. "Come on son, hold still for daddy and smile. Give daddy a big smile and hold still. Say cheese," as he snaps away furiously and frustrated.

A narrative voice now says, "What do all these people have in common? (slight pause) They all know what the best dairy product in America is. The next time you go to the supermarket, say CHEESE."

The commercial theme is now occupying all my thoughts and another commercial popped into my head.

A middle class man in his white shirt and tie along with his 2.5 kids and wife are at the breakfast table on an average weekday morning eating Kellogg's Smart Start cereal to get ready for the day.

Off to work he goes. At a brainstorming session at work he comes up with a plan to increase efficiency that no one else had thought of. It's creative and unique. His boss says, "Smith, that'll fly. It's really original and I'm going to give you a bonus for thinking of approaching the problem in a fresh non-traditional way."

The narrator now comes on and says. "If you want to become more creative and think out of the box, be Smart and Start your morning meal by having breakfast from within our box."

God forbid that I should turn on the TV some evening and see any of these commercials flash across the screen. So far He has forbid it.

While watching television recently and paying more attention to commercials I was struck by the Enterprise Car Rental advertisement with the ending catchy phrase, "We pick you up." Every time I hear it I keep waiting for the second punch line which never happened. Why didn't those slick Madison Ave. types add, we pick you up and don't let you down.

While we're on the topic of automobiles, another commercial for car tires occurred to me. Picture a series of different models and makes of cars and trucks appearing momentarily while focusing on the tires they all ride on. The camera is ground level and emphasizes the tires instead of the vehicles. The stop on a dime, turn with incredible precision and handle in an emergency situation with great maneuverability. The narrator then resonates with, "Whatever vehicle or type of car or truck you drive, let U.S. American Tire Company be your **Roll model**.

My only imaginary commercial adventure that actually matured into reality happened when a friend of mine was starting her own full medical service company in Lexington. Anxious to have a clever and catchy name for her new business enterprise she enlisted me to help develop one. After a week's obsession of thinking of different possibilities I finally conjured up *Achilles Heal* with the logo of *"Providing for all your medical needs from Head to Heal"*.

Making the Left Turn in Life

I believe in taking a left turn out of the physician's parking lot. Turning to the left means negotiating two stop signs and driving twenty times the distance than I would if I were to turn right against the flow of traffic and the faded white arrow urging me left from the black asphalt.

Turning left instead of the more convenient and "illegal" right means going the extra distance for the common good rather than engaging my narcissistic self- interest. Even in the late hours of the evening when the parking lot is empty and I am tired and anxious to reach my final destination, home, I still exit to the left. That's the most critical time to make that decision. No one is around and no one will know except the most important person - me.

I believe that the morality that governs our lives does not appear out of a one time inspirational epiphany but rather evolves from the very small consequential and deliberate moral decisions we make daily. Whenever I decide to take time to answer the questions that a patient's relative poses about their mole even though they're not in the office for an appointment or when in the supermarket check-out line and the woman behind me is holding a crying child in one hand and groceries in the other and I let her go ahead of me, I'm practicing that belief.

All this practice is for the more challenging decisions that I will eventually face in the more dramatic moments of my life. Making the correct decision in a crisis is driven by our moral compass. I believe my true north is easier to find if I practice it in all the small ethical dilemmas I face daily.

The next time late at night when I'm leaving the physician's parking lot I will make that left turn. Hopefully I will be prepared to make another left turn at the next flashing yellow light of my life's personal crossroads when no one else is around.

WARTHOUSE WIT

Rash Decisions and Growth Experiences
from the Best Little Warthouse in Kentucky

'My sense of humor is the only sense that hasn't deserted me' finds its way as a theme into many, if not most, interactions with my patients. The smile or occasional chuckle or even the rare event of laughter from my patients always seems to diffuse the anxiety of being in a medical office and adds to the connection between physician and patient. While many of my one liners are pre-rehearsed and used over and over again, they invariably have the desired effect with a patient hearing it for the first time.

****

Mrs. Jones had been my patient for many years and we had developed a very comfortable and familiar friend/professional relationship. "How's my favorite patient?" I asked nonchalantly. "I'm doing just fine, doctor." She answered friendly and swiftly with a smile on her face. I immediately interjected with, "No, no. Have you seen her? When you do, say hello for me."

Just as quickly her repartee was "Oh, she's visiting with my favorite doctor at the moment." We both laughed.

Preparing to do a minor surgical procedure on one of my long established patients of many years and who was well aware of my sense of humor I asked in a serious tone, "Do you have insurance?" He responded with, "Oh yes, Doctor, I have excellent health insurance." "No, not health insurance, life insurance. I'm your doctor."

No matter how much you explain to a patient pre- surgically what you plan to do or how many diagrams you draw, they frequently marvel at how large the surgical scar is that results from removal of their skin cancer. They will frequently ask why the incision is so long. Before giving the rational technical explanation I preface it with, "It wouldn't have been nearly as long if I hadn't sneezed in the middle of the surgery."

Often they come back jokingly with maybe I'll sue you, Doc? I'll suggest that they get a lawyer and they probably wouldn't need a very good one. However, if they want an excellent one my nephew just opened up his practice and could use the business.

Stuart Tobin M.D.

Sometimes I'll add "If you really want to sue me, however, take a number and get in line."

Many times after immediately performing a large excision of a skin cancer I'll ask the patient if he would like to see what it looks like. Since patients have an understandable emotional barrier looking directly at the area in a mirror postoperatively I show them a digital photo of the excision.

Regardless again of how much you warn them about what to expect it is not unusual for them to utter a groan of complaint about the surgical scar's appearance. "Doc, you say it looks beautiful but I think it looks terrible." I'll often counter with, "Give it a few months and I'll think you'll be quite surprised at how well it will heal.

"By the way," I'll add as I turn to the family in the room, "to keep all this in proper perspective about my surgical abilities, this is the same person who upon visiting the Louvre in Paris and gazing on Da Vinci's Mona Lisa commented 'dark water color' and when he saw Ansel Adam's iconic historic photographs of Yosemite sneered, 'Oh, black and white snapshots.'"

I had a very dear and loyal patient who unfortunately lost one of his legs to an amputation because of his diabetes which resulted in him having to walk with a crutch. However, it didn't diminish his spirits and energy nor did it affect his sense of humor.

One day while operating on his face for a skin cancer he questioned, "Doc, what could I do if you slip and give me a much bigger scar on my face and ruin my beautiful looks?" I answered with, "You could get a lawyer and sue me, but you wouldn't have a leg to stand on." He started to laugh which crescendoed into a howl and I momentarily thought if he keeps moving from the laughter I just might slip.

To further relax my patients while performing surgery on the face or the upper part of the body I always after infiltrating the area with a local anesthetic ask them, "I want to be sure that you are numb before we start the procedure. Do you feel anything in your

263

left big toe?" followed by the expectant pause. Half the time they ask, "My big toe?" And I repeat slightly exasperated, "Yes, your left big toe!" invoking the authority of the surgeon in charge. Invariably they wiggle the toe and say, "Yes, I can feel my toe." "Good, then we can cancel the call to the 'toe' truck." While terrible inane vaudeville, in the operating room theatre it is a wonderful anxiety diffuser invariably producing a laugh.

As I continued to operate and remove the skin cancer the patient inquired, "How's it going doc?" I answered with, "Hold on a second and I'll open my eyes and take a look." When I've extracted the growth and about to place it in a specimen container, I added to my patient's amusement with the non-spontaneous observation, "Well, I've gotten the specimen out and it's a boy." I proudly announce. "You know how we tell the difference between a boy growth and a girl growth? The boy growths come out easily and cooperatively, while the girl growths are not."

Frequently when operating on a female patient I respond to their unintended sexist comments with a spot of humor as well. Many of my women patients will come in asking for the removal of this mole or wart or blemish that they find cosmetically unattractive. They most often phrase their request with, "I don't like him on my skin and want it off." "HIM???" I counter. "Why is it every time a female patient has something on their skin that they don't like they always refer to it as a 'him'" I continue with a false sense of injured pride in my voice, "My gender takes great offence at that sexist characterization of your unwanted growth. However, I will be most happy to accommodate you and remove 'her' from your skin." with a sheepish and triumphant smile.

Then there's the patient who presented with a benign or harmless growth on his scalp and with his wife accompanying him he asked me what I thought about it. I stroked my chin and thoughtfully responded after examining it with an overlarge Sherlock Holmes magnifying lens with, "Well, it's too big to be your brain." My patient didn't find my remark nearly as amusing as his wife did.

Stuart Tobin M.D.

Then there was the young man in his thirties who wanted a benign growth removed from his scalp and after anesthetizing the area remarked, "You know, Doc, my whole life people have called me a numbskull but this is the first time I actually am one." That left my usually quick tongue as numb as his scalp.

Many of my patients I have seen for close to thirty years. While they may only return for yearly check-ups we have developed a significant bond not only professionally but personally as well. Because they recognize that much of my life is in service of humor they often bring their own style of levity to the office. Frequently it takes the form of good hearted jabs about "the rich doctor syndrome."

As one of my dear patients quipped, "Doc, you must have made a million dollars off me over the years that I've been your patient." "No, I've only made about $500,000 but if I had you come back twice as often I could get there.

"Also, if you think I've done a particularly good job we have a tip jar out front and you could put something in it. The last tip I got was, 'Doc, Leave town'."

Another patient remarked, "Doc, I've probably paid for your big old expensive car over the years." I shot back, "Yup, It's great to drive a luxury vehicle. Three more visits and you'll have earned a ride in my car that you paid for." They all enjoy that kind of banter and so do I.

Another patient remarked once, "Doc, I've sent you all my family and referred a bunch of my friends to see you over the years. You should give some kind of rebate or kickback."

"Sure." I answered. "Do you have change for a quarter?"

I had one old farmer with a modest education in his seventies say to me once, "Doc, with as many patients that you see and as long as you've been in practice, you must be the richest person in the county." He then sat back with a satisfied smirk on his face having expressed and confronted me with his keen financial farmer's almanac insight.

Rash Decisions and Growth Experiences
from the Best Little Warthouse in Kentucky

I didn't look up and continued to write in his chart and answered in a matter of fact, monotone way, "No, Mr. Smith, my ex wife is the richest person in the county. That's why I'm still working."

Another elderly farmer in his Bibb overalls and with his weathered complexion and severely sun damaged skin remarked while his wife sat in the treatment room with him, "Doc, you're so busy and working so much, I bet you can't even spend all the money you make." He too leaned back with that air of satisfaction and smirk which quickly slipped into a sly grin.

I answered without even thinking, "Of course not. That's why I have a wife. Isn't that what you have a wife for? If she's not spending all your money then she's not doing her job." He sat there dumbfounded but the sly grin that had been fixed on his face was successfully transplanted to her lips.

Whether you are a native Kentuckian or not plays importantly or at least semi- importantly in many of my rural country and mountain patients' perceptions. Since my mannerisms and humor speak of a culture not native to Kentucky or Appalachia and since many of my patients through networking with their families come to the office armed with the knowledge that I'm a transplant from New York, I'm often bombarded with the question "So Doc, how did you end up in Richmond, Kentucky from New York City?"

"Closest place to mid town Manhattan that I could find a parking spot," I answered.

"Well, doc. Looks like you are going to have to move again. It took me a half hour to find a parking spot today," answered one of my more savvy patients.

I had a wonderful and dear patient who used to love to harass me about being a New Yorker. At the time a popular television commercial was airing about a group of cowboys on the range and how the cook had the nerve to serve up a salsa sauce that was made in New York City followed by the punch line of, "New York City? Get a rope!"

266

Stuart Tobin M.D.

To add to the drama of this ongoing humor, one day on a routine follow-up visit he brought a noose to the office. On that day's visit I didn't want to stick my neck out any further on rendering a questionable diagnosis.

Over the years my practice has grown significantly and consequently I'm unable to accommodate many of my patients with appointments as quickly as they or I would like. To help remedy the delayed waiting time dilemma, I added a physician extender, a Nurse Practitioner, to my practice. However, the waiting time can still be longer than some patients want. Finally, when my patients do get an appointment, they understandably express their frustration about the delay.

These complaints are usually articulated as, "It took forever to get in to see you, Doc." "Yes, I know," and I apologize followed by, "Frankly, Mr. Smith, honestly I don't think I'm worth the wait."

When performing the most minor to larger skin cancer surgeries the unstated or often non-verbalized question most on my patients' minds is, "Is it going to hurt?" Some patients are reluctant to ask while many others do so freely. Regardless whether articulated or not it remains in the forefront of their minds.

With my medical assistant as well as a family member present in the procedure room when asked about the amount of expected pain they will experience during the procedure, I often quip before giving them the factual answer, "It's not going to hurt three out of the four people in the room. Those are pretty good odds. If that's not good enough odds for you we can invite more people into the room." Invariably they laugh and when they do the pain is always less.

The lion's share of my patients is retired senior citizens. Along with the fact they have extremely fair skin coupled with excessive sunlight exposure, many of them have severe photo aging or wrinkles.

267

Rash Decisions and Growth Experiences
from the Best Little Warthouse in Kentucky

Living in a tobacco state where the unstated logo for Kentucky is "tobacco is a vegetable," often brings up the discussion of exposure of nicotine and other toxins contributing significantly to the photo aging and wrinkling process.

Consequently, most of my surgical cancer patients have advanced wrinkling. When they usually return a week after their surgery to have the sutures removed, I usually comment, "The surgical scar is healing quite well and because it lies in a skin fold it will look like a wrinkle if you ever get one." This is invariably followed by a laugh or "If I ever get a wrinkle?"

As an amateur photographer and since I've exhibited a number of my prints on my walls to relieve the monotony of bare painted drywall, many of my patients often comment on them in a complimentary way. My handwriting is barely decipherable to pharmacists so it's not surprising that many patients were unable to read my signature on my landscape photo prints as well. They ask if they are my work. I answer, "Yes, they are. The only person I could convince to hang my photographs up was me and that took a lot of convincing."

Occasionally they will continue and tell me how much they enjoy the prints and how beautiful they are. I have always found it difficult to accept flattering comments and will respond with, "You really need to develop higher standards," or "I used to believe that I couldn't give my photos away but to my surprise I can to charitable causes."

Then there was the patient who presented with a rash and few other complaints and then added sheepishly with, "Doctor, I also have a growth on my back. Would you look at it, too?" I quickly answered with, "Did you bring your back with you today?" "Yes, I don't go anywhere without it" was his inevitable response. "Well, since you bothered to bring it along with you, I'll be happy to look at it for you as well."

Since most of my patients are self referred rather than physician consults they have arrived at my office for the first time very knowledgeable about me as a practitioner. One would normally assume that patients referred by a fellow physician would engender more confidence in me than one referred by a lay person. However, time and experience has proved the opposite to be true.

These "new patients" have already discussed with their spouse, relative, or friend everything that is on their mind about a new physician about to participate in their care. What am I like? Do I know what I'm talking about? Did they get better with my care? Do I spend much time with them? How much do I charge? Am I competent? How long do you have to wait to be seen? All the questions they couldn't or wouldn't ask their referring physician they have garnered from the referring lay and friend source. Consequently, I always feel more comfortable with a patient referral than a physician one. Frequently, I hear a variation of the same comment. "Doctor, I have heard a lot of good things about you from my wife or friend, etc."

I frequently meet this compliment with the wry reply, "Well, I wouldn't believe everything you hear." This often breaks the formal mood and helps the patient to feel more comfortable in recognizing the sense of humor of this particular practitioner.

The fear of skin cancer, especially melanoma, is a driving force that compels many of my patients to seek out my services. I'm frequently bombarded with the request to check a patient's moles. These patients understandably present with a high level of anxiety, especially if someone they knew had a recent bout or encounter with melanoma. Anxiously they ask, "Would you look at my moles?"

To break the initial ice I often ask, "Are the moles on your skin or in your yard? I hope they're on your skin because I'm very expensive if I have to make a house call." This touch of humor invariably reduces the patient's anxiety and I'm able to perform a complete exam of their growths more easily, which translates into the patient being more attentive in discussing their lesions.

Because a complete examination requires that the patient undress, I often after completing the exam will say, "I'm done with my examination and I will step out of the room so you can get dressed, which will have the added benefit of improving your hearing."

Many children come to my office with pre adolescent acne, moles that are changing, ringworm, or eczema. They are always shy and anxious about their visit to any physician's office. So I usually banter with them to relax them. First, I open the chart to review their history and comment. "I see, Jaden (who is nine), that you are single and still looking. Haven't found the right one yet?" This is followed by giggling from the child and a smile from the parent. I know I'm on the way to winning their confidence, trust, and attention. Then I'll ask them what grade of school they are in. Whatever they answer, I respond with, "You know that was my favorite grade of all time. I liked it so much that I took it three times. Do you think you will like to take that year three times like I did?" I asked. Invariably the answer comes back, "No." "Well, I guess you just don't like it as much as I did."

"I see, Jaden, in your chart that you are nine years old. Do you have a driver's license to prove how old you are? It's been my experience that women and even some men don't always tell the truth about their age."

Many adolescents come to the office for attention and treatment of their acne conditions. Teenagers have that flat affect coupled with a sense of disinterest and ongoing opposition with their parents and other authority figures. When they present for the first time I ask them why are they here. Frequently they will point to their mom across the room added with some form of the impersonal third person reply as if they have no idea who that person is that gave birth to them. "She made me come."

I continue with, "The chart says you're here for treatment for your acne. I would love to help you with your complexion problems and there is a lot I can do for you. But, if you're not here for yourself and only because your mother made you come you're wasting your time and your parents' money. However, if you want treatment for yourself I'll do everything I can to help you. So what do YOU want?" Followed by the long expectant pause and continued eye contact. I've never had a teenager leave the office and grudgingly or non-grudgingly they agree that they want treatment for themselves.

To continue on this theme of personal responsibility I add. "Part of growing up and becoming an adult means taking responsibility for yourself and taking care of yourself. Acne is a good place for you to start. After all it's not your mother's or father's acne but yours. So, I'm going to put you in charge of your own care. So the first thing I'm going to do is relieve your mom from checking on you. I then turn to the parent and add, "You're fired as the acne policewoman. It's not your job to check on your child whether they have washed their face or taken their medications. You have enough other things to do. If he does what needs to be done then he decided to do it for himself, if he doesn't then he decided he didn't want to do it. Then there won't be the need to bring him back." All the parents readily agree and are relieved by defaulting on having to have one more unnecessary confrontation with the oppositional teenager. On return visit the vast majority of youngsters have been very compliant with their treatment.

It often represents a challenge to capture the attention of an adolescent in the office for their acne or other skin issue. To wake them from their semi stupor denial and skeptical posture I'll often use a one liner. Pulling my eyeglasses down to the bulb of my nose and peering over them with a serious and imposing demeanor I'll make direct unrelenting eye contact and utter, "You know young man, when I was your age..... I was thirteen. Now remember that." Even the most stoic adolescents are amused and now let their guard down.

Frequently when performing surgery for excision of a skin cancer or other growths, the patients will occasionally comment on my suturing ability. "Doctor, your stitching is so even and neat." I spout back with, "Thank you. I come from a long line of tailors." Although not original I extracted that quip from a line from Billy Crystal in which he played a surgeon in one of his cowboy movies with Jack Palance. When repeating that tailor reference I often

Rash Decisions and Growth Experiences
from the Best Little Warthouse in Kentucky

experience the minor frustration of the missed pun opportunity of my name being Tobin instead of Taylor in which case I would have come from a long line of Taylors.

Fridays has traditionally been my surgical morning when I perform larger excisions for skin cancers, mostly on the face. Needless to say, patients in the waiting room have some degree of anxiety about their upcoming impending surgery. I frequently enter the waiting room to escort them back to the operating room with the following remark, "Is there a John Smith in the studio audience? Come on down, John, the price is right."

After completing the surgical procedure and instructing the patient and family member in post surgical care I will add a few humorous observations. I often find myself operating on patients' noses, which is not an unusual location for skin cancers, and I'll add to the post operative orders, "Oh, one other suggestion. Keep your nose out of other people's business just for the next week."

When prescribing a pain medication for the patient I'll turn to their spouse who has accompanied him to the office and suggest as I hand them the prescription, "You know, Mrs. Smith, if he gets to be a pain you take the pain medication instead." One wife responded with, "Doc, you don't know him like I do. I'll probably need to take two."

As the patient is about to exit the operating room and head home for recovery, I'll frequently add, "Oh, one other thing, I don't know if I can say this or not," followed by a thoughtful pause and stoking my chin. "Oh, I guess I can. I couldn't have done the procedure without you."

Another remark I have often made to patients after completing their surgical procedure, whether a small one or more complicated, is "I hope I didn't hurt you too much today and if I did I hope you're blessed with a short memory."

Stuart Tobin M.D.

Another frequent follow-up question by many patients, also after performing surgery is "Doc, how long will the numbing last." I answer, "Hopefully till you're out of earshot in the parking lot," followed by a more factual answer of "two to three hours."

Rarely some patients express a disproportionate concern about the pain of the needle in anesthetizing the area before surgery. "Doc, I'm tough. Do you have to give me a shot?" "No, I don't have to. However, do you see the indentations in the ceiling tiles above your head? They were made by patients' fingernails that had refused anesthesia. We can rub some numbing medication on your skin prior to the shot to make it less painful if you like." They become much more receptive to having the area adequately numbed.

Since I service an elderly geriatric population it is not unusual to have patients who have been married for a very long time. Many of my patients have been wed to their spouse in excess of fifty years. Every day a patient with their spouse will present who have been married thirty or forty plus or even sixty years. I frequently inquire how long they have been married. After they respond with say forty-six years I quickly interject with, "You know the medical literature says that the first forty-six years of marriage are the hardest and the second forty-six are much easier, mostly due to hearing and memory loss."

Continuing on that theme of age, I'll frequently comment to them after I treat them, "Mr. Smith, we are treating you so the next eighty-five years will be as good as the last eighty five."

A cure is rarely accomplished in our specialty and mostly control of the disease process is what we have to offer. The old mantra of dermatology has been that we never kill them and we never cure them. In many ways that is often true. Frequently patients ask can their skin condition be cured and just as frequently I have to respond that I cannot. This is often followed by the question, "You mean, doc, I'll have to put up with this condition for the rest of my life?" "Yes, but no longer than that."

The underlying question that most patients have, whether articulated or not, is do they have skin cancer. While I have found it is very important to address that issue with almost all my patients it can be done with a sense of humor. After determining that the growth is benign I'll address the issue with, "Those bumps on your skin are harmless or just barnacles on the ship of life that have attached to your skin hull. Since you find yourself in Dermatology dry dock, I could perform a hull of a scraping." Most of my patients just need a prescription of reassurance, and most opt for no intervention but feel markedly relieved that they don't have skin cancer.

A young man in his thirties presented with the early stages of male pattern hair loss. Very concerned about his premature balding he petitioned me with the following request. "Doctor, I'm single and anxious to meet women and want to look my best and I'm losing my hair on the top of my head and my father is bald. It bothers me. What should I do?"

I stroked my chin and gave a thoughtful pause followed by an even more thoughtful gaze and then answered, "Date short women. Don't date any women who are centers on female basketball teams."

I quickly followed this with a detailed explanation of the state-of-the-art therapies for male pattern hair loss. He elected to take Propecia orally which halted his hair loss and at the same time allowed his dating life to reach new heights.

A number of years ago I was invited to a medical function at the University of Kentucky Department of Medicine which was undergoing a transition in leadership. A young energetic and articulate internist introduced himself to me. "Hello, I'm 'Dr. Jones', the Acting Chairman of the Department of Medicine." I smiled the expectant smile and reached out my hand in the traditional greeting and responded with, "So how is your acting career going?"

Stuart Tobin M.D.

Having practiced for 33 years in the growing town of Richmond, Kentucky, I'm occasionally asked by a new patient to my practice, "Doctor, are you the only dermatologist in Richmond?" "I prefer to think of myself as the best dermatologist in Richmond, but the only would be equally as accurate."

Occasionally I'll mention to an established patient after entering the examination room. "Do you mind if I sit down to talk to you. I usually think a lot better when I put pressure on my brains."

Finding myself a patient for a routine colonoscopy I asked the gastroenterologist who had just completed the examination if he would mind doing me a favor. He asked, "What?" I answered, "Would you mind telling my wife that you didn't find my head stuck up there." Before undergoing the procedure the nurse asked me if I had taken all the cathartics to empty out my lower bowel. I responded with, "Nurse, I'm so clean that when I whistle I sound like a duet in stereo."

Frequently to document a skin cancer or other lesions as to their appearance and location I photograph them. While my cameras over the past 31 years have changed, my humor has not. When taking a close-up of a toe or a lesion on the back I'll frequently ask the patient to smile or say cheese while snapping the shutter.

With the advent of digital photography has come the instant visual photo. After performing a surgical procedure for removal of cancers or other lesions the patients stare at the surgical results. I'll ask them if they would like to order the six wallets and an 8" X 10" at a special discounted rate. No one has ever taken advantage of this once in a lifetime offer which I remind them will not be seen on TV and cannot be extended beyond midnight tonight because of circumstances beyond my control. However, if they place their order within the next 60 minutes they can receive a genuine diamondelle in a zirconium setting for just $19.99. Still no takers.

It's not unusual for a patient to ask my opinion on how their surgery looks after completing the procedure. "How's it looking, doc?" "It looks great but you'll never be handsome," I answered. Many patients preempt me on this by asking in a humorous and sarcastic manner, "Doc, can you make me look beautiful?" I answered, "Hey, I'm a physician not a magician."

Sometimes while engaged in performing a surgical procedure I'll ask the open question, "Does anybody know where the instruction manual is for this procedure so I can figure out what the next step is?"

Even after over 30 years in practice I occasionally encounter a patient who wants to know if I have ever done the procedure before. I have two stock answers. "I've got good news and bad news for you. The bad news is I've never done this procedure before. The good news is that I only charge half-price for anything I've never done before." The other retort is "Once, in 1982."

A patient once asked me, "What is the indication for the particular skin surgical procedure?" I quipped, "Car payment."

Frequently during a surgical procedure the anxious patient understandably wants it over as quickly as possible. They often will inquire how much longer it will take to complete the operation. I answer with, "It takes longer to put something back together than it requires taking it apart. That goes for carburetors in cars, kitchen appliance blenders, and the left side of the face. But don't worry. I'm much more adept working on the face than things mechanical."

Also in an attempt to reduce anxiety of a patient whom I would be operating on around the mouth, I'll comment. "You know, Jane, we got the oddest phone call this morning just before you arrived. It was from a male whose last name was the same as yours who asked if we had enough time could we sew your mouth shut as well."

As with most geriatric patients, some loss of memory occurs. Many of my patients when questioned about their medical history just cannot remember. I'll often relate that my memory doesn't serve me as well as it did in the past either and that I've invented a new TV game show. "It's called *Jeopardy for Seniors*. They ask you the question today and you give the answer tomorrow provided you remembered the question from yesterday."

I often find myself operating on the noses of my patients for skin cancers. I always reassure them that I am going to give them a cute little nose just like mine, which in reality is neither cute nor little. The hardest part of this surgical procedure is getting the mask over my nose. While my answer is not overly reassuring it does provide a lead into my nasal humor, some of which is original and some of which has been extracted from the movies:

"My greatest fear is that I will fall and break my nose which is 70% of my body weight."

"I know that you are a very polite person and haven't had the courage to ask me about my nose, but the answer is yes, it does affect the tides."

"No, it's not a bus parked on my face."

"I went to a plastic surgeon and asked him if he could augment my nose and make it a little longer and wider. He wouldn't. He said it would throw off my balance."

"If anyone needs nasal augmentation in Kentucky I'm the first person they call as a donor."

"When looking for things around the house I'll often ask my wife where is it? She'll shout back that it's right under your nose. I'll shout back, but honey, that could be anywhere."

"My mother had extreme difficulty delivering me since I was a nasal presentation."

It is often not enough to provide a diagnosis and treatment plan for my patients many skin maladies. Understandably, most patients want an explanation as to why they have this condition or growth on their skin. So the frequently asked question, "Why did I get this rash or growth?" migrates from my patient's mind to their mouth a number of times a day. I thoughtfully paused and stroke my chin and answer, "I can't remember if it's from sinning too much or not enough," followed by a slightly more accurate explanation about the inheritance of disease patterns or the idiosyncratic explanation of we haven't figured that one out just yet.

When I first started practice and was presented with "Why did I get this skin disease?" I would tell the patient that it was God's will. As people became more medically astute and educated I would answer with a biological explanation, "You've inherited this genetically from your family and it's part of your DNA pattern." With the advent of computer technology I would then explain, "Your genetic software has been preprogrammed to have this condition and your skin printer has decided to print it out onto your personal hardware. Since we can't find the delete button on your genetic software I can't erase it from your system." With the resurgence of religious conservatism in the Bible Pants, formerly the Bible Belt, I find myself now answering "It's God's will."

Another tangentially related issue often arises when considering the inherited nature of my patient's skin condition. "You mean I inherited this from my parents?" Well aware of family dynamics, the underlying judgmental question relates to another negative entity they've inherited from their mother or father. So I often add the caveat. "Yes, it's inherited and most likely your parents inherited it from you." This touch of humor has never failed to defuse at least one item from the list of inherited injustices children like to visit on their parent or parents.

Despite my patients' confidence in my opinions on their skin conditions, the lingering thought of an error in judgment can raise itself during any office visit. Occasionally a patient will then ask "Doc, are you sure that is what is wrong with me?" I will often retrieve a quarter from my pocket and flip it into the air, catch it on my sleeve, and look at the resulting head or tail and answer, "Yes, quite sure."

This is always followed by a more realistic answer that I could be wrong and have been in the past and if the first plan I've made to getting you better fails to work, let's have a backup plan to look into your problem more completely with a set of indicated tests.

Many of my medical assistants have been in my employment for years and patients who have also been visiting me for a long time will often ask, "How long has Jane or Mary Lou been working for you?" "She has worked FOR me for about a year and has been working AGAINST me the last fifteen."

Many medical students in their fourth year, as well as residents in the Family Practice Program at the University of Kentucky Medical Center, elect to spend a month in my office learning dermatology. It has been a very rewarding experience to help guide these young, bright, and energetic medical professionals in their education. As they acquire new skills and perform well, which is usually the case, I'll quip, "I don't care what all your peers and professors say about you, I think you're very smart."

Kentucky is one of the states that is divided culturally over the question of selling alcohol legally. Consequently, there are counties that allow alcohol to be sold and others which prohibit its distribution. Counties that permit the sale are referred to as "wet" areas while those with a prohibition are considered "dry." My own community has precincts that allow the sale of alcohol while other areas are dry. So our county is considered "moist".

This concept, while well known and accepted by residents of our fair Commonwealth, is a bit confusing to people from other states that don't have these types of local regional restrictions. To help some of my friends from outside of Kentucky to understand this concept I find it helpful to explain by example. Christian County is wet and Bourbon County is dry. Or it used to be.

Since I perform a number of surgical procedures on skin cancers, e.g. basal cell, squamous cell, or melanoma, I find myself frequently operating on patients' scalps and faces. I perform these procedures under a local anesthetic in my office, often engaging the patients in conversation to reduce their anxiety and to make time go by more quickly. Because of the increased vascularity (blood vessels) of these areas it frequently becomes necessary to fulgurate or desiccate (burn) bleeding vessels to assure hemostasis (stop the bleeding). I'll often remark to my patients much to their amusement while desiccating these small but annoying bleeding vessels, "Since you come from a dry county we'll send you home nice and dry."

Many patients will comment on how busy my office practice has become. I often respond with, "I don't know if the reason why I'm so busy is that I'm the world's best dermatologist or that I'm the world's worst dermatologist and I can't get anybody better and they have to come back to the office."

Sometimes I'll respond with, "Yes, I've become so busy that I no longer have to plant poison ivy in town or spray the air with fluorocarbons to reduce the ozone layer to drum up business."

As I conclude my office visits with my patients I will often hand them their chart to take to the check-out window. Frequently, they will ask me, "Doc, what do you want me to do with the chart?" "You can take it home as a souvenir or take it to the exit window."

An elderly geriatric patient at least 25 to 30 years my senior returned for a routine yearly skin check. After thanking me for screening him and undertaking care of his pre cancers as well as his skin cancers over the years, he remarked wryly, "Doc, I hope you live to be one hundred years old, and I'm a pallbearer at your funeral."

An avid and eclectic reader I will frequently purchase books to add to my personal library at home. One particular title that I enjoyed so much I found serendipitously at the dollar store for one dollar. Wanting to share a copy with a friend I purchased an additional copy as a gift. Returning from lunch I laid them on my desk at the office. My office manager asked, "Why did you buy two copies of the same book?" I quipped, "It looked like such an interesting book, I might want to read it twice."

Stuart Tobin M.D.

After performing surgery on my patients I'll often cover the wound site with a dressing and an antibiotic ointment underneath to enhance the healing. Before doing so patients will often ask if I am going to cover the area. Frequently, I'll answer with "Since you didn't have the foresight to wear a red shirt, I guess we'll put a band aid over the site for you."

Sometimes I think I really am making a difference in my patients' cultural attitudes towards sun protection and the use of sunscreens and sometimes I don't think that I am.

One of my elderly patients returned for his yearly skin check up with an interesting anecdote. "Doc, I thought I had the whitest legs of anyone in the county. Last summer I was walking down the street and I actually saw someone whose legs were even whiter than mine. I looked up and it was you, doc."

My generation of physicians was a bit more formally attired than the more casual contemporary ones of today. Consequently I always wear a tie to the office. One of my patients commented on my neckwear one day with the wry remark, "Doc, that's quite a handsome tie you have on. I have one just like it at home. Got it at a yard sale."

Because I try to maintain and ebullient and upbeat presence throughout the day, many of my patients often ask, "Doc, are you always so happy?" "Yes," I answer and add, "I'm heavily medicated."

Because many skin cancers occur on the scalp or close to it I have to shave the hair in many of my patients to expose the surgical area. Needless to say many are concerned about the haircut they're about to experience. To reduce this anticipated anxiety, I frequently remark, "Mr. Smith, I have good news and bad news for you. The bad news is I'm going to give you the worst haircut of your life. The good news is I wouldn't have the nerve to charge you for it."

Rash Decisions and Growth Experiences
from the Best Little Warthouse in Kentucky

One year at a holiday party an acquaintance cornered me and asked me about a new growth that had recently appeared on his buttocks. I told him that it should be checked.

Before I could even suggest that he contact my office for an appointment he had bent over and dropped his pants to reveal all before me and the other couples.

"Well, doc, what do you think?" he asked unembarrassed. "I'd say all your problems are behind you and I think everyone here should offer up a toast in your honor. Bottoms up," I quipped.

Many years ago as a college student my father through the assistance of a good family friend managed to arrange a summer job for me in the mail room of the home offices of the General Cigar Co. in New York City. Dressed in a workman's gray jacket I spent the summer sorting mail to be delivered or sent. The plush executive offices of the vice presidents, etc. were located on the floor above in a skyscraper office building complex in mid Manhattan.

One day while on my pedestrian mail rounds, the need to evacuate my bladder found me searching for the nearest restroom, which in this case turned out to be the executive bathroom. I quickly entered hoping to empty a part of my anatomy without leaving a trace. As I was about to leave a young executive impeccably dressed in an expensive blue tailored suit entered. Seeing me in my gray work coat he angrily demanded to know what I was doing there. Without even thinking as if leaping from my brain to my mouth I shot back. "You look like a bright fellow, one of two things. Guess," as I smiled and left with the sound of the flushing urinal in the background as a harmonic hint.

Continuing on the theme of bathroom humor, one of my patients related this humorous story about a young Kentuckian who had just matriculated to Harvard as a freshman undergraduate. Not accustomed or oriented to the Boston campus he stopped an upperclassman and asked. "Where's the library at?" The upperclassman petulantly answered, "You know young man you are attending the finest institution of learning on this continent and probably in the world. And if we knew of intelligent life anywhere else in the

282

unknown universe it would undoubtedly be the best there as well. So if you want an answer to your question you must phrase it properly and you never end a sentence with a preposition." The young Kentuckian replied, "Oh, where's the library at, asshole."

As the story continues the Kentucky freshman student finally located the library and immediately searched out the bathroom since his bladder was full from having consumed a Kentucky breakfast of a Moon Pie and an Ale-8 soft drink. As he is about to leave the bathroom he encountered another upper class man who approached him with, "Hmmm, young man, where I was brought up we were instructed to wash our hands after emptying our bladders." The Kentuckian turned to him and retorted, "Where I was brought up we were taught not to pee on our hands."

I've told this anecdotal fictional story to my cousin who is a graduate of Harvard College, and Medical School, and post graduate training at that fine Cambridge institution. Much to my delight he had heard it. And even more to my delight he in turn related a story that had happened to him.

While in high school in Massachusetts during the Depression, he visited my dad who at the time was attending medical school at George Washington University in our nation's capital. My father, anxious to impress his bright young nephew, had saved enough money to take them both out for a special dinner.

Since the country was still in the grips of the Great Depression, my brilliant cousin had never traveled anywhere. So while intellectually rich he was culturally and socially poor. My father turned to him at the restaurant and asked. "Les, to start the evening off right how would you like to have a shrimp cocktail?" Les answered, "Lou, I don't drink."

Since my practice has spanned over thirty-three years in Richmond, Kentucky, frequently a patient will appear whom I haven't seen for fifteen, twenty, or even thirty years. So many of them, however, recall having seen me before and will often attempt to trigger my shrinking memory with a prompt like, "Doc, I don't know if you remember but I came to see you about twenty years ago." I equally often will respond with, "Oh, you remember seeing me when I was young and handsome. Oh, change that to just young." As they get ready to leave I will add, "Come back every twenty-five years whether you need to or not."

Many patients are accustomed to having procedures scheduled at a later date rather than at the time that they first present to a practitioner's office. Since so many of my patients travel great distances from Appalachian counties in rural Kentucky to see me, I make an attempt to perform the desired or needed surgery that day. This often takes the request of "Can you take that mole off today?" "Sure." I'll answer, "It's hard to remove it when you're not here."

Since my office is well equipped with two surgical suites I perform all my surgeries in-house which spares the patient additional expenses for hospital operating suites as well as the emotional trauma of being in a hospital. Some are surprised that I'm able to remove their skin cancers in my office setting and will ask, "Doc, are you going to do the surgery here?" "Yes," I answer, "unless you want me to do it in the parking lot."

Very common findings on my patients are those small 1 to 3 millimeter cherry red or occasionally purple growths scattered over the body. Usually patients will grow a multitude of them. After explaining that they are harmless and are of cosmetic concern only, my patients will sometimes ask what they should do about them. I'll answer, "You can just ignore them as I do on myself, or if your spouse ever gets bored with you she can connect the dots and see what the picture is."

The nature of my patient population often lends itself to long lapses between office visits. Frequently, a patient whom I haven't seen for five, ten, and even twenty or thirty years will reappear in my office. Since I avoid sunlight exposure, and obsess about my weight and haven't changed my hairstyle in over forty years, many of my patients will comment, "Doc, you haven't changed since I last saw you." I answered, "I have a great dermatologist. As a matter of fact it is the same one you have, come to think about it."

Stuart Tobin M.D.

No one likes to have a surgical procedure performed on them. It's not unusual for a patient to articulate their anxiety just prior to operating on their face, etc. for a skin cancer. It usually comes out in the form of, "I really dread having this done today." To which I respond, "That's very normal. If you were looking forward to having it done, I would send you to a psychiatrist. So try to relax. Anything I'm going to do to you today in the office pales next to the risk you took by getting into your car and driving over here to see me."

One of the more frequent skin rashes I evaluate is hives or what is referred to as urticaria. Patients often call this waxing and waning eruption "welts". A clinical finding of hives is that upon scratching the skin one can reproduce the wheal. This clinical finding is called dermatographism, which as it name implies, 'derm' meaning skin and 'graph' the ability to write on the skin. A pamphlet that I give the patient on hives has a photo of a person with the name "Terry" written across his chest.

After going through an extensive history in an attempt to deduce the trigger for the hives and then explaining to the patient what goals we have to make them comfortable with treatment of antihistamines to counteract the effects of the histamine induced hives. I go on to add that the only upside to the condition is that if they forget their grocery list at home they can write on their skin the needed items.

To demonstrate this finding to the patient and their family I'll often take a ball point pen and scratch the skin in a grid like pattern and add. "We could play tic tack toe on your skin. How about I'll be X and you can be O." This invariably has the tension relieving comic effect and never fails to be received positively by patient and family alike.

Acne is to the skin what urinary tract infections are to the urologist and what colds and flu are to the primary care physician. They represent the high fiber bread and unsaturated butter of our profession. All acnes are not the same. Some patients present with deforming cystic and scarring acne while most have a much milder form of pimples (papules), pustules, and whiteheads, as well as the blackhead or more properly referred to in medical nomenclature and jargon as the comedeo. Since all acne lesions begin as blackheads or comedeos they represent the origin of all acne lesions. Consequently, I often refer to myself as a "comedeoian".

While visiting and attending to the care of one of my long-term patients, he felt comfortable enough to ask whether I would refill a prescription for his wife, who also had been a patient of mine for her rosacea medication. He produced a piece of scrap paper from his front pocket with the name of the medication and handed it to me. Since metronidazole cream has a very low incidence of side effects I felt that was a very legitimate and reasonable request.

His wife also had listed beneath the medication the word "cream cheese" as a reminder to him to pick up at the supermarket. I said, "Sure, I'll be happy to refill her medication. It'll save her an unnecessary trip to my office." So I leaned over the laptop computer and printed out the prescription for the metronidazole cream.

"Let me also write out a prescription for the cream cheese as well." He laughed. "Would you like the generic or the trade brand Philadelphia Cream Cheese? I'll have it labeled take daily as needed. Let me also give you half a dozen refills as well."

We both now laughed, as I wondered how his wife reacted when she saw the cheesy prescription or was I spreading myself too thin. I would guess more favorably if he had filled it.

That wasn't the only unusual prescription I have written in my practice. Many of my female patients have severe hand eczema which is exacerbated by soap and water exposure. Consequently I frequently ask if they have a dishwasher at home. Many do not and answer with sarcasm and resignation, "I'm the dishwasher at home." I will then write them a prescription to take to their spouse to buy an electric dishwasher of any brand and will check off the area that says substitutions allowed. They find it more amusing than their husbands do.

Stuart Tobin M.D.

The summer before I entered medical school my proud father took my brothers and me to Los Angeles for the American Medical Association convention. I was so proud of my newly earned status. I wandered to the convention booth that had all the textbooks I might need. The woman behind the counter directed me to fill out a form with my mailing address which I did. She then said, "Doctor, we'll be sending you in the mail a month supply of tampons." Startled I looked up and realized I had wandered over to the booth next to the book one. I blurted out, "Lady, a month supply? For me, that'll be a lifetime supply."

The eloquence of many dermatological topical skin products have improved dramatically over the years. Often when prescribing one of these improved salves in an attempt to prevent the patient from wasting the product and applying too much I'll often instruct them. "This is a white vanishing cream so rub it on till you disappear. If you have someone at home that you want to disappear you can rub it on them as well."

My wife and I had been invited to a black tie charitable event in Lexington which was held at the Keeneland Racetrack Barn, which is anything but a barn. One of the events featured that evening was a fashion parade performed by a bevy of attractive young female sorority coeds from the University of Kentucky. Many of the dresses were quite revealing of their youthful figures.

Afterwards they had an auction of assorted U.K. sports memorabilia as well as a 5 day stay at a chalet on Lake Cumberland called "Peace of Mind". The tuxedo dressed man seated next to me whom I didn't know leaned over and asked, "Are you going to bid on Peace of Mind?" "No," I whispered. "I'm waiting for Piece of Ass to come up for auction." He laughed but my wife kicked me under the table.

Often when operating on my patients' faces for skin cancer, I outline the area with gentian violet to guide me in my excisions. Anxious to inform them on what I'm doing, and why, I explain, "I'm outlining the area I'm going to cut on with a marker. I'll be cutting along the dotted line. I learned that principle in kindergarten and didn't realize at the time that I would eventually become a surgeon. You never know what you learn in life that you can use later on."

One of my patients wryly observed, "Doc, I hope you learned a few other things after kindergarten."

After completing skin cancer surgeries on patients and we have spent anywhere from an hour to two plus, I will apply a bandage covering the treated area. Often I will explain, "I'm going to put a dressing over your wound site. What is your favorite dressing? They often join in with Honey Mustard, or French or Ranch. "Sorry, we only have the house dressing."

A family recently moved from Las Vegas to Richmond as a result of a job opportunity. The mother brought her young eight-year-old son to my office with a common skin condition which had become quite itchy. After acquiring a complete history of the treatments tried and examining the boy she turned to me and said, "I've taken him to two different physicians in Las Vegas and they didn't help him. What do you think, Doctor?" I responded, "I guess what happens in Vegas doesn't stay in Vegas."

Many medical students and residents from the University of Kentucky Medical Center rotate through my office for their dermatology experience. In 2007, with the economy plummeting into the depths of severe recession bordering on depression, many observed that the medical field while not immune is better insulated from the vagaries of the mainstream spiraling down economy. They will often ask me what I thought. "Yes," I'll remark, "death and dying is one of the last growth industries in America."

It's not unusual for many patients to present to my office with a mole or wart or some other growth on the bottom of their foot for me to examine. After rendering an opinion and discussing a treatment plan I remarked, "I hope it wasn't too difficult for you to bare your sole to me today? Don't worry; you're going to be a sole survivor."

James had been a patient of mine for over thirty years and now in his eighties he would appear yearly for skin cancer checks. Always well kempt and with a keen sense of humor as well as a keen appreciation for the opposite gender and always with a quick retort he often amused me with his anecdotes.

I had a twenty dollar gold piece that my mother had given me before her death. I told James that it had originally belonged to my father, the dermatologist, and it had been given to him by a grateful patient. Injecting an overdose of hyperbole, I added, "You know James, when a patient has had the same physician for over thirty years it's not unusual for him to show his appreciation by giving a lovely gift such as the twenty dollar gold piece like the one that my father had received from one of his very grateful patients."

James retorted without a moment's hesitation, "Doc, I would lay down my life for you. I would sacrifice my right arm for you. I would gladly give up any of my appendages with the exception of perhaps one. But to give you money would seem so crass and would debase my gratitude for you that it would certainly be perceived as more of an insult than a reward for your wonderful years of service," as he smirked and chuckled.

Another common set of harmless growths patients often ask about are the small flesh colored skin tags that have a tendency to cluster around the neck, underarms, beneath the breasts and even the groin. Because of their unsightly as well as nuisance value becoming irritated when shaving or from jewelry as well as clothing rubbing them, my patients often request to have them removed.

Unfortunately all insurance companies when they see the diagnosis of skin tags will reject them as a cosmetic procedure and refuse to pay. After explaining this to my patients their frustration always becomes apparent with a comment like. "You mean they won't pay for these growths no matter what?" I often respond with, "Yes, that's correct. Your insurance company doesn't care if you trip on them. They still won't pay for it."

Rash Decisions and Growth Experiences
from the Best Little Warthouse in Kentucky

My grandson's thirteenth birthday was rapidly approaching and my wife suggested, "Let's take all the grandchildren to the Cincinnati Zoo." I said, "Well, if the zoo wants them that badly let them come and get them."

Shortly after entering the zoo the following week an attendant was walking thru the park with a Quetzal perched on his thickly gloved hand. He explained to the crowd that had gathered around him about the habitat and nature of this small falcon like bird of prey. He went on to explain how the zoo acquired him. All the while the obedient Quetzal remained firmly nestled on the attendant's well protected hand.

After his discourse he turned to his attentive audience and asked if there were any questions. I raised my hand and inquired. "Yes, I have one question."

"What is it?"

"Is a bird in the hand worth two in the bush?" I not so sheepishly asked. He never laughed and I guess my bird brain humor just flew over his head.

Many of my patients require periodic follow up for skin cancers, pre cancers, or for chronic skin conditions. Usually, I'll have them return three or six month or at yearly intervals. It's challenging to remember the exact date to return so many months in advance. Like many other medical offices we call them a few days prior as a reminder.

If their return appointment however, coincides close to the Thanksgiving Holiday season I'll add the additional key reminder. "We'll see you again around Thanksgiving time. So when you think of turkey, think of Tobin, a necessary and important correlation to make."

An established patient of mine of many years had wandered out of the waiting room into the treatment area of my new medical office with a searching quizzical look as I was coming down the hallway. "Can I help you, Jewel?" I asked. "Yes, Doctor, I'm looking for the restroom." "Oh, no problem. Just go out the front door and turn your car onto the by-pass till you come to the BP service station......... or if you prefer it's the first door on your right."

As a newly minted dermatologist I had been in solo practice in Richmond, Ky. for a short time when a new patient presented to my office. I gave him the customary greeting and warm handshake and asked him what was on his mind. He said, "I want to talk to you about Jesus." I said incredulously, "What?" Again he answered very seriously as well as determinedly, "I want to talk to you about Jesus."

I countered with, "I've set aside fifteen minutes for your appointment. We can talk about the uncomfortable itchy rash that you made the appointment for or if you like we can talk about Jesus. We're down to twelve minutes so which is it going to be?"

After pausing to think for a moment he relented, "Let's talk about the rash."

"Sure, now let's look you over and see what I can do to help you." The rest of the time proceeded as a normal visit would.

Very involved in teaching residents from the Community and Family Practice program at the University of Kentucky Medical Center as well as fourth year medical students, I am seldom without an aspiring junior peer at my side while undertaking care of my private patients. Most of my patients are very accustomed to this teaching environment in my private practice.

When a new patient presents at my office, however, I'll first introduce myself then the other physician in training at my side. I'll quickly add, "Who says medicine is getting more expensive? You're getting two doctors for the price of one."

Many of the drug companies to promote their products will leave samples as well as discount-like credit cards which make the patients co-pay considerably less. Although I most frequently prescribe generics, sometimes the trade name meds are actually less expensive for some patients.

When I decide to prescribe that particular medication, I'll turn to the patient and ask, "Pick a number between 1 and 100."

Rash Decisions and Growth Experiences
from the Best Little Warthouse in Kentucky

Whatever number they choose I'll add, "That's the lucky number. You have won dermatology lotto and will receive free samples of your medication as well as a discount card worth..... so many dollars."

While operating on a patient with a skin cancer on his face and since the patient had been on blood thinners, he asked in the middle of the procedure. "Am I bleeding much?"

"No, but don't worry. If you do I'll put a tourniquet around your neck."

Much to my dismay, I recently read in the newspaper about a young man in an attempt to stem the bleeding of his girlfriend's traumatic gash to her head that occurred while they were hiking in the woods had done exactly that. I doubt that I will say that again.

As with most physicians' offices, keeping on time task becomes more difficult as the morning and afternoon wears on. I, like most physicians, get behind on our scheduled patient's visits and patients end up waiting longer to see me than they or I want.

Often I will pop my head into the wrong exam room as I scurry from room to room. Realizing I was seeing the wrong patient I will excuse myself with, "You're the next patient to be seen and I'm sorry to keep you waiting so long. I should be freed up to visit with you in just a few moments. If I'm not back shortly, however, send out a search party to find me."

I perform many surgical procedures. Some are quite involved requiring multiple sutures, skin grafts, and flap repairs. I am well equipped in my office surgical suites to perform these under a local anesthetic.

Patients who haven't had these procedures before will often ask anxiously, "Doctor, are you going to put me to sleep to do the operation?" "No, I can't find my hammer so I'm going to do it under a local."

So many new patients in reality aren't new to my office. Since many have accompanied their parents or other relatives to the office their faces are quite familiar although I have difficulties remembering exactly where I may have seen them.

Occasionally, I miscalculate with "Your face looks so familiar. Have you been here before with a relative?" When they answer, "No, I haven't," I'll redirect with, "You do look so familiar. Were we in the witness protection program together?"

Since so many of my patients often require only yearly checkups for their skin cancer screenings, I'll often end our visit with, "You're doing so well. How about coming back just once a year? You probably have better things to do with your time than sit in my office. Unfortunately, I don't have anything better to do."

An elderly patient developed a rapidly growing skin cancer on his face which required a rather involved and large surgical excision. Unfortunately he developed a post surgical complication of bleeding which required taking the whole excision apart to clean out the blood clots and tying off the bleeders followed by re-suturing the wound.

His recovery afterwards, however, proceeded smoothly. To be sure he didn't develop any additional complications I had him return frequently over the next week to assure continued good healing.

He acknowledged all the post operative care with, "Doc, I really appreciate you coming in to take care of me to be sure that things went well."

"Well, I just wanted to be sure that things went well after that complication of unexpected bleeding. I believe in taking care of my patient come Hell or high water. Hmmm, let me change that to just high water."

Rarely as a dermatologist do I affect a patient's lifespan. However, the early intervention and removal of a melanoma can truly prolong a patient's life. Occasionally, I find myself with a patient who will thank me profusely for my care. Always embarrassed with this type of compliment, and if I know the patient well

Rash Decisions and Growth Experiences
from the Best Little Warthouse in Kentucky

enough I'll deflect their remark with a humorous one, "You know, Mr. Smith, it's really odd. I've received a lot of phone calls from your relatives complaining that I did that procedure." Fortunately, my patients will see the humor.

I've been fortunate that my surgical scars usually heal well and the patients seem pleased with the cosmetic outcome of their skin cancer surgery. On follow-up visits many will comment, "Doc, you can hardly see the scar on my face." I'll retrieve my magnifying glass and scrutinize the area carefully, followed by stroking my chin, and add in a surprising tone, "Hmmm, that's the first time that ever worked out right."

As the banner hanging in my waiting room pronounces, "The Best Little Warthouse in Kentucky" I actually see some patients suffering from common warts. Many are adolescents. The hands are our most exposed part of our body. That skin comes into contact with others and the environment more than any other area of the body. Consequently the hands present as a favorite location for the wart virus.

Frequently, I'm asked by these adolescents, "What causes warts?" I respond with, "Have you been holding hands with toads looking for Prince Charming? If you have you really need to be more selective in the future."

After completing surgical procedures on a patient I often invite the family into the operating room to listen to the post operative care instructions. On seeing their loved one with a rather large dressing covering the surgical wound they will often ask their loved one in a concerned tone, "Are you all right?" Before the patient has a chance to respond, I pipe in with, "Yes, I'm doing fine. Thank you for asking."

Many medical students and residents rotate through my office to learn the art of the specialty. Very competent and also eager to learn, they prove to be quite apt at acquiring suturing skills and performing minor surgical procedures. Carefully, supervising them in each step I grant them more autonomy as their technical abilities as well as their confidence improve.

As with most talented young student/doctors they require feedback as to their performance. While suturing an awake patient they will often ask, "How's it looking, Dr. Tobin?" I'll quickly answer with, "I would only make one minor suggestion. Open up your eyes."

When I first opened practice in the late '70s, I was anxious to start a local dermatology society that could meet monthly to discuss interesting and problematic cases. It wasn't long until I was drafted to become the president of the Central Kentucky Dermatology Society which was mostly comprised of dermatology private practitioners in Lexington.

President meant doing all the work for each meeting - arranging for patients to show, arranging for an office to present them, notifying all the members, finding a different restaurant each month to dine, and of course managing all the finances, which became my monthly charge and medical migraine headache.

After 10 years I felt it was time to relinquish the mantle and for someone else to step up to take over the responsibilities. No one volunteered. I suggested that I was amenable to recall, resignation, impeachment, coup de-tat anything short of assassination. Still no takers. Finally, I authored a short letter of resignation to the membership:

"Dear fellow member,

I am tendering my resignation as leader of our dermatology society. After 10 years as President, I received a letter from our parent organization, the American Academy of Dermatology, addressed to me as Emperor. Consequently, I feel it's time for me to abdicate and allow someone else to sit on the throne of leadership.

Sincerely,

Stuart Tobin, President, aka Emperor

Central Kentucky Dermatology Society"

In any event it worked. I wonder if in keeping with the Emperor theme, maybe I should have addressed the letter to my subjects, instead of a peer "fellow member" greeting.

Rash Decisions and Growth Experiences
from the Best Little Warthouse in Kentucky

Many times it is necessary to touch a skin lesion for its texture and to feel the skin to detect subtle early pre-cancer changes. Since my hands remain perpetually cold patients often comment on how cold they feel.

"Yes, my hands died two weeks ago and I hope the rest of me doesn't follow soon," I quipped.

My good friend Ben, as our attorney consultant who volunteered for years with me on our ten year quest to establish a public library came by my house one Friday afternoon and asked, "Stu, are you going to use your MGB? I'd like to borrow it."

"Sure Ben you can use it," I glibly replied as I handed him the keys assuming he would be driving it for the weekend.

He must have really enjoyed it for he kept it for a year. People would stop me months later and ask if I had sold the little sports car to Ben since they saw him driving it around town. "No, I had loaned it to him and I guess he still has it," would be my reply.

After a year he showed back at my house with the MGB and said, "Stu, I really like that little machine and would like to buy it. However, I can't give you much for it because it has high mileage." Talk about going for a test drive.

Many adult females develop acne and many of those didn't have it in their adolescent years. Frustrated they frequently vent their feelings. To empathize I respond with, "Yes, it must be very frustrating to have all the side effects of a teenager without any of the benefits. Or as George Bernard Shaw said, 'Tis a pity that youth is wasted on the young'. They don't appreciate it and they don't know how to use it."

Since my operating room often doubles for an examination room as well, I will frequently have to move a patient out to the operating room which is occupied by someone who doesn't needs a small surgical procedure. This requires the patients exchanging rooms. As they pass each other in the hallway I'll remark. "When the music stops everyone grab a chair."

296

Stuart Tobin M.D.

Most of my patients are very accustomed to seeing medical students or residents rotating through my office. However, some aren't and will inquire how they ended up in my practice. Before the student has a chance to explain I interject with, "They draw straws to see who will come down from the medical center and he drew the short one."

Many of my male patients develop skin cancers on their ears because of their long history of sunlight exposure coupled with their outdoor occupational exposures and their fair complexion heritage. This occurs much less often in women because of their hair covering their ears.

A patient once asked me while I was operating on their ear for a skin cancer what the procedure was called. I answered, "The Mike Tyson procedure. Good thing you didn't have it on your forearm or we would have to do the Venus de Milo procedure."

Since so many of my patients are referred by someone they know they will often introduce themselves with, "My friend told me about you."

"I'll quickly add with a surprised look, "You have a friend?"

In 2010 I retired from private practice to accept a teaching professorship at the University of Kentucky Medical School in Lexington. Part of the vetting process included attending learning sessions as a new faculty member.

One of the symposiums emphasized the importance of acquiring tenure. The speaker announced, "If you expect to earn tenure after five years you have to as new faculty build a convincing record of accomplishments. You have to document all the teaching that you do, list all the research you engaged in and all activities performed off campus that enhances the reputation of the Medical Center. Consequently, you must have a five year plan and you need to start right now with that five year plan."

Rash Decisions and Growth Experiences
from the Best Little Warthouse in Kentucky

I raised my hand. "Yes, Dr. Tobin?" She courteously responded. "My five year plan is to be alive in five years. I may even want to extend that to a ten year plan. " I dryly answered. Everyone laughed.

Sam is a friend and patient of mine who is physically active as an octogenarian of 84 years. I often see him at the YMCA performing his daily workout routine. One day he came up to me and confided.

"Did you see that guy who was struggling to work out? He looks like he is 90 years old. So I asked him how old he was and to my utter surprise he said he was only 80. He looks older than me!"

I guess age, like beauty, is in the eye of the beholder and often a perspective of your own reference group.

Jim, a retired farmer, who had multiple skin cancers and severely sun damaged skin found himself more often in my office for screenings and treatment than he wanted. He turned to me one morning and said, "Doc, I only have six friends and they're all doctors. I don't have time for anyone else."

Then there was the patient who was also elderly and retired. I greeted him in my usual manner with a smile and "Glad to see you here today."

"Doc, I'm happy to be anywhere at my age," as he slyly smirked.

Then there was the octogenarian in his mid-eighties who when asked, " How are you doing today?" answered in a slow and feeble voice, "Well, I'm still on this side of the sod."

The American Academy of Dermatology has their annual meeting in different cities every year. Washington D.C. is one of those sites. One year while attending the professional gathering I decided to dine at the Willard Hotel, which is one of the great American icon hotels in an iconic city.

Stuart Tobin M.D.

I took a taxi from my more modest accommodations to this residence of Presidents and walked into the opulent and historically magnificent dining room for dinner. The well tailored tuxedo clad maitre d' inquired with an aura of condescension and class, "Sir, do you have reservations?" I answered with equanimity, "Yes, I have reservations about eating here but I'm gonna eat here anyway." I was ushered non-ceremoniously back to my taxi to search out another dining facility.

Having transitioned from private practice to a teaching professorship at the University of Kentucky Medical School in Lexington, Kentucky, I found myself lecturing medical students on the fundamentals of dermatology. While giving an introductory lecture to a group of third year medical students I kept noticing one young woman who was texting throughout my presentation.

I had just finished showing the group a power point slide of syphilis. I stopped the lecture and went over to the young woman and grabbed her cell phone out of her hand and announced to the class as I pretended to be reading her text message.

"Honey, I have good news and bad news for you. The bad news is I'm listening to some old fart give a boring lecture on skin diseases. The good news is that stubborn rash of ours that we have had for weeks will go away with an injection of penicillin."

At my next scheduled lecture to that group she sat in the back of the classroom and nobody texted during my presentation.

A patient came to the office with many of those little nuisances, redundant pieces of skin hanging by a tiny thread of skin commonly found around the neck and under the arms. We refer to them appropriately as skin tags. Like many of my patients, she found them a solvable bother and wanted them off. They are removed easily, quickly and relatively painlessly with a special surgical scissors which I keep for just such requests.

After removing a large number of thirty or forty of her tags, she turned to me and remarked, "Doctor, thank you for taking all those growths off for me. You know we make a pretty good 'TAG Team'."

Rash Decisions and Growth Experiences
from the Best Little Warthouse in Kentucky

In our occupational capitalistic defined society, I often find myself asked at parties and other social functions on meeting some-one new as to my occupation. I find myself answering, "A physi-cian." In our sophisticated society that response is inadequate and the follow up question is always, "What kind of physician are you?" I responded with, "Occasionally a good one." Sometimes I'll answer, "I'm the only person in the county that gets paid for making rash decisions." If they still give me a quizzical look, I'll add, "I own the best little warthouse in Kentucky."

Having seen and attended to countless patients over a life-time of practice, it has become impossible to recall everyone's names especially when encountering them out of the office at a restaurant or local department store. I'm often greeted with, "Hello, Dr. Tobin." To extract myself from this name disassociation situa-tion and unable to retrieve their name as they did mine, I'll respond, "I almost didn't recognize you with your clothes on." Although I'm not quite sure their spouse appreciates my humor as much as they do.

A friend of mine invited me one weekend to his home to see his very extensive and proud collection of antiques. He took me on the grand tour saving his most prized possession for the last and pro-nounced, "This bed goes back to Louis the fifteenth. What do you think?" "That's nothing. I have a bed at home that goes back to Sears on the eighteenth, mostly for nonpayment," I responded.

CPSIA information can be obtained at www.ICGtesting.com
Printed in the USA
LVOW080605210313

325069LV00001B/1/P

9 781937 508135